# Nonideal Social Ontology

# Nonideal Social Ontology

*The Power View*

ÅSA BURMAN

Oxford University Press is a department of the University of Oxford. It furthers
the University's objective of excellence in research, scholarship, and education
by publishing worldwide. Oxford is a registered trade mark of Oxford University
Press in the UK and certain other countries.

Published in the United States of America by Oxford University Press
198 Madison Avenue, New York, NY 10016, United States of America.

© Oxford University Press 2023

All rights reserved. No part of this publication may be reproduced, stored in
a retrieval system, or transmitted, in any form or by any means, without the
prior permission in writing of Oxford University Press, or as expressly permitted
by law, by license, or under terms agreed with the appropriate reproduction
rights organization. Inquiries concerning reproduction outside the scope of the
above should be sent to the Rights Department, Oxford University Press, at the
address above.

You must not circulate this work in any other form
and you must impose this same condition on any acquirer.

Library of Congress Cataloging-in-Publication Data
Names: Burman, Åsa, author.
Title: Nonideal social ontology : the power view / Åsa Burman.
Description: New York, NY : Oxford University Press, [2023] |
Includes bibliographical references and index.
Identifiers: LCCN 2022030878 (print) | LCCN 2022030879 (ebook) |
ISBN 9780197509579 (hardback) | ISBN 9780197509593 (epub)
Subjects: LCSH: Social sciences—Philosophy. | Ontology. | Critical theory.
Classification: LCC H61.15 .B87 2023 (print) | LCC H61.15 (ebook) |
DDC 300.1—dc23/eng/20220715
LC record available at https://lccn.loc.gov/2022030878
LC ebook record available at https://lccn.loc.gov/2022030879

DOI: 10.1093/oso/9780197509579.001.0001

1 3 5 7 9 8 6 4 2

Printed by Integrated Books International, United States of America

# Contents

| | |
|---|---|
| *Acknowledgments* | vii |
| *Permissions* | ix |
| Introduction: Ideal and Nonideal Social Ontology | 1 |

## PART I.  CRITIQUE
### *Ideal Social Ontology*

| | |
|---|---|
| 1.  The Standard Model of Ideal Social Ontology | 19 |
| 2.  Critique of the Standard Model of Ideal Social Ontology | 83 |

## PART II.  RECONSTRUCTION
### *Nonideal Social Ontology*

| | |
|---|---|
| 3.  Nonideal Social Ontology | 121 |
| 4.  Critique of Nonideal Social Ontology | 157 |
| 5.  Telic Power | 176 |
| 6.  A Taxonomy of Social Facts | 199 |
| *References* | 229 |
| *Index* | 235 |

# Acknowledgments

I have been working on the ideas in this book over a number of years and have benefited from helpful discussions and support from many philosophers and friends during that time.

The initial idea for this book came to me over the course of three workshops on *Nonideal Social Ontology* between 2016 and 2018. I was able to arrange these workshops due to generous support from the Department of Philosophy, Stockholm University. I wish to thank the participants in these workshops for fruitful discussions on social ontology in general and for their comments on some of the material in this book: Ásta, Eyja Brynjarsdóttir, Johan Brännmark, Staffan Carlshamre, Robin Dembroff, Esa Díaz-León, Katharine Jenkins, Beatrice Kobow, Alex Madva, Rebecca Mason, Mari Mikkola, Katharina Berndt Rasmussen, Dan Lópes de Sa, Amie Thomasson, and Robin Zheng. I offer special thanks to my co-organizers, Staffan Carlshamre and Katharine Jenkins, and my long-time discussion partner, Johan Brännmark.

Substantial parts of this book have been presented in research seminars at Stockholm University's Department of Philosophy. I wish to thank the participants, including organizers Erik Angner and Jonas Olson and commentators Stina Björkholm, Mats Ingelström, and Niklas Möller, for their detailed and helpful comments. Special thanks to my friends and colleagues Krister Bykvist and Anandi Hattiangadi for inspiring philosophical discussions and other support along the way. Furthermore, my friends and colleagues at the Institute for Futures Studies provided not only the best kind of research atmosphere but also, through Emma Engström, the artwork for the cover.

viii ACKNOWLEDGMENTS

I have also benefited from feedback from engaged and insightful audiences at the University of Nottingham; Stetson University; the Conceptual Engineering Workshop at Uppsala University, which was arranged by Matti Eklund; the Nordic Network of Metaphysics Conference at Lund University, which was arranged by Tobias Hansson Wahlberg and Robin Stenwall; and the Social Ontology conferences at Tufts University and Tampere University, which was arranged by Brian Epstein and Arto Laitinen. Finally, my social ontology students always manage to provide me with new energy and new perspectives.

In looking back at the process of writing this book, I owe a special and profound debt to my friends and fellow philosophers Katharine Jenkins, Martin Jönsson, Joshua Rust, and Peter Sahlén, who provided extensive comments on all the chapters. Your philosophical insights and support meant more to this book and to me than you might have realized at the time. Thank you so much. Any remaining errors are my own.

Looking back even further, this book began quite some time ago with the Berkeley Social Ontology Group and continued with an invitation to a workshop on Feminist Ontology at MIT, arranged by Sally Haslanger. These two different philosophical contexts convinced me that there are two different paradigms, or research frames, in social ontology. Editor Peter Ohlin offered kind support and flexibility for me to develop this and other ideas into a book. Thanks also to Sally Haslanger for much philosophical inspiration.

Last, but not least, I thank my parents, Ann-Marie and Per-Åke, and my brother, Markus, and his family for always encouraging me and my projects. During the writing of this book, I was lucky to meet Amelie. Thank you for your stoic presence and kind heart and for the experience of true collective intentionality.

# Permissions

I am grateful for the permission to use previously published material from the following sources:

Some sections in Chapter 1 and Chapter 6 draw partly on material published in Åsa Andersson [now Burman], *Power and Social Ontology*, Lund: BokBox Publications, 2007.

Some sections in Chapter 3 and Chapter 4 draw partly on material published in Åsa Burman, "Categories We Do Not Know We Live By," *Journal of Social Ontology* 5, no. 2 (2020): 235–243, De Gruyter, and

Burman, Åsa, "Review of Categories We Live By," *Notre Dame Philosophical Review*, 2019.

# Introduction

## Ideal and Nonideal Social Ontology

### 0.1 The Two Worlds of Contemporary Social Ontology: Consensus or Conflict?

Consider this scenario: you work as a coder in San Francisco. You go into your office where you are one of the guys. After work, you tag along with some friends at work to a bar. It is a very heteronormative space, and you are neither a guy nor a gal. You are an other. You walk up the street to another bar where you are a butch and expected to buy drinks for the femmes.

> —Ásta, *Categories We Live By: The Construction of Sex, Gender, Race, and Other Social Categories*, 73.

Consider a simple scene like the following. I go into a café in Paris and sit in a chair at a table. The waiter comes and I utter a fragment of a French sentence. . . . The waiter brings the beer and I drink it. I leave some money on the table and leave.

> —John Searle, *The Construction of Social Reality*, 3.

Social ontologists live in two different worlds. The first is a harmonious social order where small groups of people go for walks and have picnics together. It is an equal society organized around formal positions (being a professor or being a citizen), certain informal

*Nonideal Social Ontology*. Åsa Burman, Oxford University Press. © Oxford University Press 2023.
DOI: 10.1093/oso/9780197509579.003.0001

## 2 INTRODUCTION

social positions (being a friend), and the transparent or discernible powers that come with these roles. In general, there is consensus around the formal roles, and conflict is neither frequent nor severe. The inhabitants of this social world are blind to gender and race in the sense that differences of gender, race, sexuality, and the like are not considered relevant. The philosophers of this world aim to uncover the fundamental principles of society and offer a general theory of social phenomena. Their method is to start from simple cases and abstract away from the messiness of everyday life, such as material circumstances and most differences between individuals. Let us call this first world "Ideal Social Ontology."

The second world is characterized by inequality and overt and covert conflicts that play out in everyday interactions between people, such as someone who insists on deciding their own gender pronoun or someone who decides who counts as a woman at a feminist activist meeting. It also plays out among large and hierarchical groups, where some groups oppress or dominate other groups, sometimes without the awareness of the people involved. This society is not organized around only contested formal roles. In addition, a person's various and intersecting informal social roles—gender, race, sexuality, level of functioning, and so on—are of utmost importance for the organization of society and a person's life chances.[1] A few philosophers of this world aim to offer a general theory of social phenomena, but most aim to offer theories of specific social phenomena, like gender and race. Their theories should not only describe these phenomena correctly but also provide useful tools for social change. Their method is to start from the messy and material circumstances of everyday life by using difficult and complex cases, refusing to abstract away from this messiness by

---

[1] It is an anomaly that the inhabitants of this social world are class-blind in the sense that a person's class is not considered relevant. Other categories have been discussed at great length, but class is still missing. I thus include the intersection of gender and class as one of my central examples.

INTRODUCTION 3

using simplistic examples. Let us call this second world "Nonideal Social Ontology."

So, do we live in a world where a bunch of people are having a picnic together or a world of constant conflicts in need of a revolution? The question is, of course, rhetorical and the contrast above is somewhat exaggerated for effect, but the contrast between ideal and nonideal social ontology is certainly very pronounced and it can be seen both in the research questions posed and in what are taken to be paradigmatic social phenomena. If we examine both, it becomes clear that they either assume a consensus-oriented view of social phenomena or a view of conflict and contestation.[2]

Taking some things and not others to be examples of paradigmatic social phenomena is a central theoretical choice that highlights some aspects of social reality while hiding others. The problem is that both worlds offer only a partial view of our social world while presenting that view as comprehensive. We actually live in both worlds, and our theories of the social world thus need to capture all aspects of social reality. The challenge in contemporary social ontology is the great divide between the two worlds and the few narrow bridges that span them. And the philosophers of these two worlds move only in one direction and not the other—some nonideal social ontologists have engaged with the main works in ideal social ontology, but the converse is not true.

My objective is to build a new bridge between these two worlds. I use social power as the central building block because I argue that nearly all the relevant social phenomena are about different types of social power. Power remains an underdeveloped concept that is

---

[2] The consensus-oriented view of society is also clearly visible on the front covers of the main works in ideal social ontology. On the first edition of Searle's *The Construction of Social Reality*, people are literally holding hands while dancing. On Margaret Gilbert's recent book, *Rights and Demands*, a peaceful picture of a few people crossing a courtyard is displayed on the front cover. Given the title, one might have expected less peaceful and more violent historical images, perhaps of suffragettes or civil rights activists. Finally, Raimo Tuomela's *The Philosophy of Sociality* depicts small groups of white people eating together at a café.

## 4 INTRODUCTION

nevertheless central in both worlds and it can thus help to bridge the divide. More specifically, I offer an account of social power and the various forms it takes, an account I call the "Power View." In addition, I suggest that the different forms of social power can be used as a basis for a taxonomy of social facts. The key idea is that social power is the central social concept and nearly all the social facts in which we are interested contain one form of social power or another. Hence, I offer a taxonomy of social facts in virtue of social power. Although the taxonomy might not be exhaustive, it expands on existing accounts of social power in contemporary social ontology in significant ways.[3]

## 0.2 Purpose and Main Claims

This book argues for the use of nonideal theory in social ontology. It has three main aims. The first is to show that the key questions and central dividing lines within contemporary social ontology can be fruitfully reconstructed as a clash between the two worlds I refer to as ideal and nonideal social ontology. The second is to show that, when taken together, the objections to the "standard model" (the dominant version of ideal social ontology) imply that this model needs to be given up in favor of nonideal social ontology.[4] In other words, we should look to nonideal, rather than ideal, social ontology for core concepts. Third, I offer my own positive account, called the power view, of nonideal social ontology. This account places the concept of social power at the core and replaces the flat and narrow conception of power in ideal social ontology with

---

[3] I hope to return to the refinement of the power view in light of insights from related fields. For instance, theories of power, domination, and oppression developed outside contemporary social ontology, narrowly understood, could give us a more refined view of what I refer to as "structural power," among other things.

[4] Francesco Guala coined the term "the standard model of social ontology" and listed three of its elements: collective intentionality, reflexivity, and performativity. I agree that these features are accurately identified, but I identify more features, such as the sole emphasis on the deontic, and I argue that the standard model also entails a consensus-oriented view of social phenomena.

INTRODUCTION 5

a richer and more extensive conception. In addition, it rectifies a shortcoming in nonideal social ontology by attending to class, which has been notably and oddly overlooked in that literature.[5] I use real-world examples of the intersection of class and gender because class also significantly impacts people's life chances, and I discuss the type of power involved here.

The central claim is that a paradigm shift is underway from ideal to nonideal social ontology and that this shift should be fully followed through. This claim should be understood in relation to the two main aims of the standard model of ideal social ontology, aims that I certainly share: to offer general theories of the ontology of social and institutional reality and to offer theories that are the foundation of the social sciences. Given these aims, the paradigm shift should be fully followed through. So, I am not claiming that there needs to be a paradigm shift for specific domains and that theories in ideal social ontology about these specific domains cannot be, or are not, correct. For example, work on collective intentionality and collective responsibility has greatly expanded our knowledge of these important phenomena.

To develop and defend this central claim, I first need to characterize ideal social ontology. I do this by developing the standard model of ideal social ontology, which synthesizes the main aims, central assumptions, and methodological concerns that shaped this tradition. I then turn to criticizing ideal social ontology. I show that one of its basic building blocks—collective intentionality—is not a necessary condition for the existence of institutions, despite the claims of ideal social ontology to the contrary. I also show that the standard model has the effect of making central social phenomena,

---

[5] It is interesting to note that the anomaly I have pointed out—that class is almost entirely missing from view in nonideal social ontology—is also a concern in related fields. For example, Sherry B. Ortner writes: "I question the basically classless notion of identities operating in contemporary politics, both out in the world and within contemporary social and cultural analysis. Instead, I try to bring to light several aspects of what I call 'the hidden life of class' in the United States" (1998, 1).

## 6 INTRODUCTION

like opaque kinds of social facts, drop out of sight. Consequently, to fulfill the main aims of the standard model—to offer general theories of the ontology of social and institutional reality and to offer theories that are the foundation of the social sciences—we need to shift away from this model. Finally, I turn to what the paradigm shift is, and should be, a shift to. I do this by characterizing nonideal social ontology and showing how it has certain advantages over the standard model of ideal social ontology. However, there are still two shortcomings with nonideal social ontology: other forms of social power besides deontic power are underdeveloped, and certain crucial social phenomena, such as economic class, are still excluded. I develop my own version of nonideal social ontology—the power view—to overcome these limitations.

The background and relevance of my contribution is that social ontology is a rapidly growing but highly fragmented field. It would thus be of enormous help to provide it with a systematic overview and synthesis, a project to which I contribute to through this volume. I demonstrate how the fragmentation shows in the following disagreements, which are disagreements regarding the very foundations of the research field. The first disagreement concerns the question, "Which are the social phenomena?"[6] There is not only disagreement about what the paradigmatic social phenomena are but also regarding what phenomena count as social in the first place. Furthermore, different theories use different ontological categories, such as social objects, social facts, social kinds, and social properties of individuals.[7] The second disagreement concerns

---

[6] For an illuminating overview with respect to the question, "Which are the social phenomena?" see Ásta's "Social Kinds" in which she shows that one of the main disagreements about social kinds is "What makes a social kind *social*?" (2017, 290, emphasis in original).

[7] Brian Epstein notes this disagreement and argues for choosing social facts as the ontological category: "Among the various candidates, *social facts* turn out to be a practical category for inquiry, because they are fine-grained enough to make the distinctions we want and general purpose enough to accommodate the other categories as special cases" (2016, 150, emphasis in original). I follow Epstein in using social facts as the ontological category in my power view.

the very purpose and aims of theorizing, translated into the question, "What conditions of adequacy should a theory in social ontology fulfill?" In a related concern, "Is the role of the social ontologist primarily to describe the fundamental structure and nature of social reality (or at least some of its parts) or primarily to change it?" The third disagreement involves the philosophical method to be used in answering the research questions, especially the use or non-use of empirical case studies against which to test the theories in social ontology. These fundamental disagreements need to be resolved, or at least explicitly addressed, to make further progress and, continuing with the paradigm analogy, to move to a state of what Thomas Kuhn (1962) called "normal science."

Let me briefly return to the first disagreement that concerns the question, "Which are the social phenomena?" There is disagreement about what the paradigmatic social phenomena are with respect to both content (gender, race, or money) and form, or kind. Regarding the latter, consider Muhammad Ali Khalidi's (2015) classification of social kinds. He starts from the familiar idea that social properties depend on our propositional attitudes in different ways and then he asks us to consider two questions to clarify those differences (Khalidi 2015, 103, emphasis in original):

(i) Does the existence of the *kind* depend upon our having certain propositional attitudes towards it?
(ii) Does the existence of *instances of the kind* depend on our having propositional attitudes towards them, namely that they are instances of that kind?

The answers to these questions result in a three-fold classification (Khalidi 2015, 104):

|  | (i) | (ii) |  |
| --- | --- | --- | --- |
| First kind of social kind | NO | NO | racism, recession |
| Second kind of social kind | YES | NO | war, money |
| Third kind of social kind | YES | YES | permanent resident, prime minister |

The shift from top to bottom in the classification is a shift from weaker to increasingly stronger mind-dependence. The first kind of social kind is mind-dependent in the sense that some mental states about other social phenomena need to exist for the kind to exist, but these mental states need not be about the kind itself. The second kind of social kind is mind-dependent in the sense that there must be mental states about the kind itself for it to exist, but there need not be mental states about each individual token for the token to exist. The third kind of social kind is mind-dependent in the sense that there must be mental states about both the type and the token for each to exist. I show that the first kind of social kind has dropped out of sight in ideal social ontology. Furthermore, I show that one reason behind the anomaly that class is still missing in nonideal social ontology is that it belongs to the first kind of social kind. Consequently, I start from a variety of examples with respect to both content and form and I pay special attention to examples of the first kind of social kind, such as economic class, in developing the power view.

This section has relied on a distinction between ideal and nonideal social ontology, a distinction to which I now turn.

INTRODUCTION 9

## 0.3 Ideal Theory and Nonideal Theory

### 0.3.1 Charles Mills on Ideal and Nonideal Theory

> What distinguishes ideal theory is the reliance on idealization to the exclusion, or at least marginalization, of the actual. . . . But ideal theory either tacitly represents the actual as a simple deviation from the ideal, not worth theorizing in its own right, or claims that starting from the ideal is at least the best way of realizing it.
>
> (Mills 2005, 168)

In this section, I clarify how one influential characterization of "ideal theory" and "nonideal theory" can be applied to social ontology. Consequently, I begin the crucial task of clarifying how I use "ideal social ontology" and "nonideal social ontology" in the coming chapters.

Both "ideal" and "nonideal" carry multiple senses in the philosophical literature, so there are different ways of drawing the distinction between ideal and nonideal theory.[8] One common understanding, from John Rawls' *A Theory of Justice*, is ideal theory as strict compliance theory and nonideal theory as partial compliance theory. I will, however, not use "ideal theory" in line with Rawls' understanding of it as "strict compliance theory" that seeks to provide a theory for a well-ordered "society in which (1) everyone accepts and knows that the others accept the same principles of justice, and (2) the basic social institutions generally satisfy and are known to satisfy these principles" (Rawls 1971, 4–5).

Another common way of distinguishing between ideal and nonideal theory is to view the former as about normative issues

---

[8] For a clear overview of the different debates about ideal and nonideal theory in political philosophy, see Laura Valentini (2012). For illumination discussions in social ontology, see, for example, Johan Brännmark (2019b), Sally Haslanger (2018), and Mari Mikkola (2018).

10    INTRODUCTION

and the latter as about descriptive issues. Charles Mills refers to this sense of ideal theory as "ideal-as-normative" (2005, 166). In this sense, all works in normative and applied ethics, along with political philosophy, are examples of ideal theory, while works in traditional social ontology are examples of nonideal theory, but this is also not the distinction I have in mind. Rather, in contemporary social ontology, the relation is the opposite of this way of drawing the distinction: ideal social ontologists aim to *describe* the fundamental nature of social reality *without* starting from any normative ideals or commitments. By contrast, nonideal social ontologists also aim to describe (some parts of) the fundamental nature of social reality, but their investigations are clearly guided by normative ideals and commitments.

Rather, I have in mind Mills' characterization of ideal theory as idealized theory: "What distinguishes ideal theory is the reliance on idealization to the exclusion, or at least marginalization, of the actual" (2005, 168). An "idealized social ontology" involves abstracting away from historical injustices, domination, and oppression and from differences between individuals. Furthermore, it assumes "ideal social institutions" in the sense that little or no attention is paid to how institutions such as the family systematically disadvantage some of their members (Mills 2005, 168). I draw on Mills' work in distinguishing between ideal and nonideal social ontology since it captures the theoretical and methodological disagreements in contemporary social ontology in an illuminating way.

Mills' highly influential—and controversial—article "Ideal Theory as Ideology" is rich in content. His main claim is that nonideal theory (in ethics and political philosophy) is superior to ideal theory and that there thus ought to be a shift from ideal to nonideal theory. Furthermore, philosophers should stop using ideal theory in ethics and political philosophy because it is not at all helpful. Actually, ideal theory serves the interests of privileged groups and is, in this sense, ideology. There are a number of interesting and controversial claims to engage with here. For my purposes, Mills' characterization of ideal and nonideal theory, and some of the disadvantages of the former and advantages of the latter, are of importance for understanding the debate in social ontology. Thus, I focus on these aspects of Mills' work, leaving aside the questions of whether ideal theory is really ideology and whether nonideal theory is superior to ideal theory.

Mills characterizes ideal theory in normative ethics and political philosophy as a way of theorizing that involves idealization, not merely abstraction. There is thus a necessary *link* between ideal theory and idealization in the sense that ideal theory employs idealization. It is also characteristic of ideal theory that one must start with the ideal to understand the nonideal and to realize the ideal. So, ideal theory is *prior* to nonideal theory in these two ways. Furthermore, ideal theory downplays the importance of how our societies actually work in certain respects in its theorizing; for instance, it often excludes historic and current injustices such as racial and gender inequities. And the difference between the ideal and the nonideal is viewed as "a simple deviation from the ideal," in Mills' words (2005, 168), or as small enough in the sense that one can understand the nonideal once one has understood the ideal. More specifically, the conceptual resources developed in ideal theory are helpful for understanding the nonideal, or actual. Due to these characteristics, ideal theory is silent on oppression, domination, and coercion, according to Mills. In other words, ideal theory is silent on illegitimate power relations.

In stark contrast, proponents of nonideal theory are deeply skeptical of all the above claims, especially the silence on illegitimate power relations. Nonideal theorists worry that attributing idealizing capacities to people and the circumstances they find themselves in hides important aspects of social and moral reality, such as systemic injustices and oppression. So, there is no necessary link between theorizing and idealizing, although one cannot do without abstraction in nonideal theory. Nonideal theorists also question the priority of ideal to nonideal theory in two ways: first,

12 INTRODUCTION

they argue that the nonideal deserves to be theorized in its own right; second, they insist that one should start with the nonideal or actual workings of our society, paying special attention to systemic injustices such as gender, racial, and class injustices in one's theorizing. Furthermore, nonideal theorists believe that there is a significant difference between the ideal and the nonideal. This means that concepts developed to understand the ideal will often not be helpful, or simply cannot be helpful, in understanding the nonideal, so nonideal theorists view the difference between ideal and nonideal theory as a difference in kind rather than in degree. Most importantly, in contrast to being silent on oppression, domination, and coercion, nonideal theory takes these phenomena as absolutely central. Real-world experiences and examples of these phenomena are starting points in nonideal theorizing and they are also often the objects of its analysis. So, the central dividing point between ideal and nonideal theory is whether one is silent or vocal on illegitimate power relations.

More specifically, Mills characterizes ideal theory as involving some, or all, of the following concepts and assumptions:

(i) An idealized social ontology that "will typically assume the abstract and undifferentiated equal atomic individuals of classical liberalism. Thus it will abstract *away* from relations of structural domination, exploitation, coercion, and oppression, which in reality, of course, will profoundly shape the ontology of those same individuals, locating them in superior and inferior positions in social hierarchies of various kinds" (Mills 2005, 168).

(ii) Idealized capacities that amount to individuals having "completely unrealistic capacities attributed to them" (Mills 2005, 168). Mills makes the further point that the privileged are closer to having these capacities than those who are subordinated due to differences in opportunity to develop these capacities.

(iii) Silence on oppression, which means that "little or nothing will be said on actual historic oppression and its legacy in the present, or current ongoing oppression" (Mills 2005, 168–169). This silence applies to how systemic oppression both influences individuals and our basic social institutions. Consequently, according to Mills, ideal theory cannot provide the conceptual resources to understand oppression.

(iv) Ideal social institutions, a process by which basic social institutions like the family and legal system will be theorized in terms of the ideal-as-idealized model rather than the ideal-as-descriptive model. This means that ideal theory fails to understand how these institutions "actual workings may systematically disadvantage women, the poor, and racial minorities" (Mills 2005, 169).

(v) An idealized cognitive sphere that leads to the failure of ideal theory to theorize or acknowledge the consequences of oppression on our thinking. In Mills' words, "little or no attention [is] paid to the distinctive role of hegemonic ideologies and group-specific experience in distorting our perceptions and conceptions of the social order" (2005, 169).

(vi) Strict compliance, by which Mills refers to two related features of Rawls' work: first, to investigate the principles of justice that would regulate a well-ordered society in the sense that everyone acts justly and does her part in upholding just institutions; second, that one needs to start with ideal theory before one can address nonideal theory or problems of partial compliance (Mills 2005, 169).

## 0.3.2 Ideal Social Ontology and Nonideal Social Ontology

Drawing on Mills' characterization above, I understand ideal theory in social ontology, or "ideal social ontology" for short, in

## 14 INTRODUCTION

terms of the following features: An idealized social ontology, silence on oppression, ideal social institutions, and an idealized cognitive sphere.[9] The silence on oppression is especially important because the most significant difference between ideal and nonideal social ontology is being silent on or vocal about oppression or illegitimate power relations.[10] In Chapter 1, I show that the most prominent theories in traditional social ontology (those by Searle, Gilbert, and Tuomela) share these features. Any theory that displays these four features will be referred to as "ideal social ontology." By contrast, "nonideal social ontology" will be used for any theory that rejects or lacks at least one of these features. Importing this distinction into social ontology and showing its usefulness means that it has wider scope or is even more applicable than previously assumed.

There is a relationship between Mills' characterization of ideal theory and the standard model of ideal social ontology, a model I develop to characterize an influential research paradigm in social ontology. The standard model of ideal social ontology is more basic, or fundamental, than Mills' distinction in the sense that most of Mills' features—an idealized social ontology, the silence on oppression, and an idealized cognitive sphere—follow from the central elements of the standard model, while another feature in Mills' characterization, ideal social institutions, is the same as in the standard model. On my account, ideal and nonideal social

---

[9] I downplay or exclude two features—idealized capacities and strict compliance—from the characterization of ideal social ontology. There are tendencies toward these two features in ideal social ontology, but these features do not figure as prominently as the other features. Some accounts of collective intentionality show the tendency of idealized capacities to result in agents having an infinite hierarchy of beliefs. Ideal social ontology still has interesting similarities with strict compliance by painting a rosy picture of institutions and the collective (or "we") making up institutions, and there is seldom discussion of noncompliance with the institution.

[10] I use "illegitimate power relations" to also include the ill treatment of other animals than humans, in contrast to prominent accounts of oppression that view oppression as a relation between persons or groups of persons (cf., Ann E. Cudd [2006] and Marilyn Frye [1983]).

ontology should be understood as positions along a continuum in terms of how many of the features of the standard model of ideal social ontology they exhibit.

In Chapter 1, I turn to developing the standard model of ideal social ontology.

# PART I
# CRITIQUE
*Ideal Social Ontology*

# 1
# The Standard Model of Ideal Social Ontology

## 1.1 Introduction

The aim of this chapter is to characterize what I refer to as the standard model of ideal social ontology by drawing out its explicit and implicit assumptions about social reality. The standard model is exemplified by the works of Margaret Gilbert, John Searle, and Raimo Tuomela.

The relevance of characterizing the standard model is three-fold. First, it is part of presenting a more general and systematic critique of ideal social ontology than has hitherto been offered. To this point, objections have been discussed in a piecemeal fashion against one theory at a time. By showing that some objections apply to all the main theories in ideal social ontology and examining the central objections at once calls ideal social ontology itself into question. Second, by showing that most fundamental assumptions of the standard model merit interrogation, the paradigm shift from ideal to nonideal social ontology becomes discernible. Questioning the fundamental assumptions of the standard model is also part of my argument that the shift from ideal to nonideal social ontology should be fully followed through. Third, I design my own account—the power view—with the benefits and limitations of the standard model in mind. That is, I build on the important insights and benefits of the standard model, such as the centrality of deontic notions for understanding society, but overcoming its limitations is among the conditions of adequacy for my own account. Thus,

*Nonideal Social Ontology.* Åsa Burman, Oxford University Press. © Oxford University Press 2023.
DOI: 10.1093/oso/9780197509579.003.0002

20  CRITIQUE: IDEAL SOCIAL ONTOLOGY

the power view draws on standard model elements that I take to be correct (e.g., the centrality of deontic notions) while modifying other elements (e.g., developing the conception of social power), and discarding some altogether (e.g., collective intentionality as a constitutive element).

## 1.2 The Standard Model of Social Ontology

> SMOSO [the standard model of social ontology] is a framework precisely in the sense that it 'frames' the debate. A bit like a Kuhnian paradigm, it defines the problems to be tackled, provides a unified language and some tools to be used in tackling such problems.
>
> (Guala 2007, 961)

Francesco Guala coined the term "standard model of social ontology" to criticize two influential research frameworks in the philosophy of social science—evolutionary game theory and social ontology—for "tackling what are essentially empirical questions from an a priori viewpoint" (2007, 957). Instead, he calls for an "empirical social ontology" that takes the results of social scientists into account to a much larger extent. Social ontology is exemplified through the works of Margaret Gilbert, John Searle, Raimo Tuomela, Barry Barnes, Michael Bratman, and Ian Hacking. Guala shows that these theorists share certain assumptions that he unites in the standard model of social ontology (hereafter SMOSO). This model consists of three features: reflexivity, performativity, and collective intentionality.

Reflexivity amounts to "the idea that social entities are constituted by *beliefs about beliefs*" (Guala 2007, 961, emphasis in original). Robert K. Merton's "self-fulfilling prophecies" (1948), like runs on a bank, are offered as an illustration of this idea. Consider a solvent, but unlucky, bank. A rumor that the bank is insolvent starts

THE STANDARD MODEL OF IDEAL SOCIAL ONTOLOGY 21

to spread. People quickly withdraw their deposits, and after a short while, the bank really is insolvent, and it ceases to operate. Daya Krishna (1971), in a critical review of Merton's work, had already generalized this idea in the early 1970s, arguing that self-fulfilling prophecies are partly constitutive of social reality[1]:

> The phenomenon of the self-fulfilling prophecy . . . is a clue to the nature of social reality and to its essential difference from the one studied in the natural sciences. Consciousness, beliefs, ideals, imaginings, prejudices, values—whatever term one chooses to use—enter essentially and constitutively into the being of the reality studied in the social sciences. *What is conceived to be real also tends to become real.* (1971, 1107, my emphasis)

Reflexivity has been viewed as an essential mark of the social by a number of theorists. However, emphasizing reflexivity means that the first kind of social kind in Muhammad Ali Khalidi's classification of social kinds drops out of sight. A recession or a class-system can exist without being conceived to exist. It is noteworthy that, in describing the first feature of the SMOSO, Guala omits a quantifier before "social entities." Whether reflexivity holds for *all* or *some* social entities is important for the objection that this reflexivity means that the SMOSO cannot handle opaque kinds of social facts. If we choose the weaker interpretation—that reflexivity holds for some social entities—then this objection does not apply. If we choose the stronger interpretation—that reflexivity holds for all social entities—then the objection does apply. I consider this objection in the next chapter.

---

[1] It is interesting to note that Barry Barnes also identifies the first feature of the SMOSO, reflexivity, citing Krishna. Barnes writes that, "the operation of the array can at best celebrate a tautology: 'what we take to be money is money'" (1983, 533). Barnes then generalizes this idea to social life: "We have here a picture of social life as a gigantic inductive bootstrap operation: and so it is" (1983, 537).

## 22 CRITIQUE: IDEAL SOCIAL ONTOLOGY

Performativity, the second feature of the SMOSO is the idea that a certain group can create and re-create social entities using speech acts. Language does not merely describe the world (as in assertives) but can also create a new social reality (as in performatives). Guala writes, "if social entities are somehow made of beliefs, they (unlike natural entities) must be constantly re-created (or 'performed') by the individuals who belong to a given social group" (Guala 2007, 962). As an illustration, consider two people getting married. The new institutional fact—that these two people are married— depends on other institutional facts, such as the fact that the person uttering the statement is in fact an official with the appropriate institutional power to make the two persons into a married couple. This feature of the SMOSO goes back to the works of J. L. Austin (1955) and Barry Barnes (1983):

> Consider first the simple case of a society wherein a specific form of cognitive authority is allocated entirely to a single individual, acting in a recognized role. Such an individual may instantiate a term by fiat. He may be entitled to *pronounce* any entity an S, or any entity of kind A an S, and thereby *make* it an S. Such a pronouncement is what Austin would have called a purely *performative* utterance, one that does something to a particular rather than describing it. (Barnes 1983, 526, emphasis in original)

This formulation shapes much of the subsequent discussion of the relevance of performatives for the social world. Note that Barnes refers to both a type and a token above; that is, there is a distinction between instances of a kind, "any entity an S," and the kind itself, "any entity of kind A an S." This distinction remains central to the discussion in contemporary social ontology, including the debate between ideal and nonideal social ontology. For example, Khalidi builds on this distinction in his classification of three kinds of social kinds, in which the third kind relates to token cases and the second to type cases. Similarly, Ásta—a major proponent of nonideal

# THE STANDARD MODEL OF IDEAL SOCIAL ONTOLOGY 23

theory—uses this distinction in characterizing conferralism and clarifying a central difference between conferralism and its key rivals, such as Searle's account of social reality. Ásta clarifies that conferralism is committed to the idea that all social kinds are of the third kind in Khalidi's classification, while constitution accounts such as Searle's also admit to the second kind of social kind.[2]

The third feature of the SMOSO—collective intentionality—is the idea that collective belief partly constitutes social reality. Collective belief is understood in a strong sense: these collective beliefs cannot be reduced to an aggregate of individual beliefs and common knowledge. Guala captures the centrality of this third feature in a nice slogan: "*No social reality without collective intentionality*" (2007, 963, emphasis in original). In other words, collective intentionality is a necessary condition for the existence of institutions and other social phenomena, according to the SMOSO.

I think that Guala has correctly identified certain central features in the early debate in traditional social ontology, which I call "ideal social ontology." Consequently, I include these features in my standard model. However, my discussion departs from Guala's in three important respects. First, I show that Guala has identified three features of a standard model of *ideal* social ontology rather than social ontology per se. Second, I create a more *extensive* standard model than Guala by listing more central features, thus offering a *more detailed* characterization of the standard model of ideal social ontology. Third, my standard model differs from Guala's in the sense that I include only features that *all* the theories share rather than including features that only *most* theories share. This is partly done by restricting the number of theorists I draw on to Gilbert, Searle, and Tuomela, and thus excluding Barnes, Hacking, and Bratman. Including only features that all theories

---

[2] It is worth noting that the neglect of this distinction has been part of the cause of central objections to Searle's theory of the social world (Thomasson 2003) and his theory of human rights (Burman 2018).

## 24  CRITIQUE: IDEAL SOCIAL ONTOLOGY

share is relevant in relation to the critique of the standard model of ideal social ontology because I want to show that the objections are to this standard model rather than only one particular theory. It is worth considering this difference between Guala's standard model and mine in greater detail:

> Notice that not all philosophers who work within the framework of SMOSO necessarily subscribe to all three theses. SMOSO is a framework precisely in the sense that it 'frames' the debate. A bit like a Kuhnian paradigm, it defines the problems to be tackled, provides a unified language and some tools to be used in tackling such problems. Even the identification of the basic elements of SMOSO should be taken loosely, because different versions are endorsed by different authors. (Guala 2007, 961)

By the standard model of ideal social ontology, I refer to the central aims and key assumptions shared by Gilbert, Searle, and Tuomela. The reason for this selection is that these philosophers started the field of ideal social ontology as a separate branch of philosophy and shaped its subsequent direction. Guala bases his standard model on these three theories as well, along with the works of, for example, Bratman, Barnes, and Hacking. The reason for my selection is that the former three philosophers offer general theories of social and institutional facts rather than focusing specifically on joint intention, as Bratman does, or focusing specifically on social power and reflexivity, as is true of Barnes, or adhering more readily to the nonideal camp, as is true of Hacking. This means that I attempt to show that Gilbert, Searle, and Tuomela do share all the features of my standard model. In addition, and in contrast to Guala, I want to clarify the basic elements of my standard model to show the *particular theses* to which these three philosophers subscribe. I motivate the standard model of ideal social ontology through a description of these theories and by quoting crucial passages from their work.

THE STANDARD MODEL OF IDEAL SOCIAL ONTOLOGY   25

I turn now to motivating the standard model of ideal social ontology by discussing the works of Gilbert, Searle, and Tuomela. This requires discussing their theories at some length. Readers already familiar with these theories and to whom my standard model of ideal social ontology already looks right (Section 1.6.) can move directly to Chapter 2, where I criticize some of its elements. Other readers might find it helpful to read the section "The Standard Model of Ideal Social Ontology" first to get the big picture and then return to Section 1.3.

## 1.3  Margaret Gilbert's Plural Subject Theory

Gilbert's overall project is to *explain sociality* by developing plural subject theory. For her, analytic philosophers like David Lewis have investigated certain paradigmatic social phenomena, such as social conventions, but not *sociality as such*. Rather, it was the "founding fathers" of sociology, Max Weber, Georg Simmel, and Émile Durkheim, who made the greatest contributions to the issue of sociality. Gilbert's work is particularly interesting, I think, because she seeks to develop an entire theory around the notion of joint commitment rather than focusing only on analyzing this notion. Another of her aims is to argue against the Weberian (i.e., individualistic) stance that is so prevalent in the philosophy of social science. Instead, she takes the side of Simmel and Durkheim, arguing for a holistic account of social phenomena: "Collective ways of acting, thinking, and feeling . . . have at their foundation not a set of detached individuals but individuals associated or unified through a joint commitment" (2000, 10). In *On Social Facts* ([1989] 1992), Gilbert begins to develop plural subject theory with the aim of explicating our everyday concepts of the social and of answering the question: Which are the social phenomena?

The main claim is that many of our everyday collectivity concepts, such as a social group, a group's beliefs, a group's language,

## 26 CRITIQUE: IDEAL SOCIAL ONTOLOGY

along with any social convention, have the notion of a plural subject at their core. In short, many central social phenomena are plural subject phenomena, and analyzing the concepts that refer to these central social phenomena allows us to generalize the analysis to concepts that refer to social phenomena per se. Gilbert writes, "the main thesis of the book will be that our collectivity concepts incorporate the concept of a *plural subject*. The nature of plural subject phenomena will be carefully explained. They are so special, and so apt for the label 'social' that one can argue it should be reserved for them" (1992, 2). She concludes as follows: "There is, then, an argument for seeing our general concept of a social phenomenon as equivalent to that of a phenomenon of plural subject-hood" (442). So, one of the main aims is to offer a general theory of sociality. This exemplifies what I call *the scope claim*—that the main aim is to offer general theories of the ontology of social and institutional reality.

Gilbert is also clear that her theory is meant to be the foundation of the social sciences, and the quote below nicely illustrates this idea. She writes of the concepts she discusses in *On Social Facts*:

> These concepts are thus freed to be candidates for the role of foundational concepts of social science. I shall argue that from an intuitive point of view this is indeed their proper role. That is, the vernacular concept of a collectivity and its relatives initially locate the concerns of the disciplines most aptly referred to as social sciences. In that sense they will be foundational concepts of social science. This is by no means an unimportant sense. For the concepts which are accepted as foundational in this sense give direction to subsequent enquiry in a given discipline. (1992, 8)

This exemplifies what I call *the foundation claim*—that theories in social ontology are the foundation of the social sciences either by providing and clarifying fundamental concepts or by giving an account of the nature and existence of social phenomena. In addition to providing the foundational concepts of social sciences, Gilbert argues that social ontology is the foundation of political philosophy.[3] Consequently, these foundational concepts are also important for questions of value or moral normativity. Gilbert makes it clear that questions of ontology and of value should not be mixed up: "If the original issues are ontological, they are separable in principle from questions of value. Moreover, if things are to proceed in their proper order, a clear understanding of what there is must precede evaluations" (1992, 429). As will become clear, this separation of ontology and value is a matter of substantial disagreement between ideal and nonideal social ontology: ontology precedes and is independent of questions of value for ideal social ontology. By contrast, nonideal social ontology emphasizes that what one understands the central social phenomena to be, and thus what phenomena to analyze, does depend on questions of value. And emancipatory social ontology—a particular instance of nonideal social ontology—takes it one step further by including the value dimension in the very concepts that are developed.

### 1.3.1 Basic Building Blocks: Plural Subjects and Joint Commitments

It is worth examining the basic building blocks of Gilbert's theory: plural subject and joint commitment:

> People often speak of what we intend when they mean to refer to something other than what we both or all intend. They seem to imply that there is what we might call a "collective" or "shared" intention. But what might reasonably be so-called? More to the point, what is it we mean to refer to when we say that we intend in this collective sense? (2000, 8)

---

[3] For example, Gilbert writes, "In order meaningfully to engage in political philosophy one needs an accurate social ontology" (1992, 436).

## 28 CRITIQUE: IDEAL SOCIAL ONTOLOGY

Her answer is that "we" refers to a plural subject, so joint intention is understood in terms of plural subjects. The plural subject theory can be stated as follows: "Generalizing: for any set of people, $P1, \ldots Pn$, and any psychological attribute $A$, $P1, \ldots Pn$ form the plural subject of $A$-ing if and only if they are jointly committed to $A$-ing as a body" (1996, 8). Hence, we need to understand both what a *joint commitment* is and what it means to be jointly committed *as a body*.

The closest we come to a statement of the components of a joint commitment is when Gilbert explains its genesis. In forming joint commitments, "each party must express to every other party his or her personal readiness to be jointly committed in the relevant way" (2000, 5). A joint commitment to overthrow the king, for example, is formed when *each of the relevant parties is willing to share* in overthrowing the king, this willingness is *mutually expressed*, and there is *common knowledge* among the parties about this goal. That is, the *formation* of a joint commitment has these three components, but Gilbert denies that this constitutes an *analysis* of joint commitment.

Still, one might think that a joint commitment could be reduced to these three components and indeed view that fact as an analysis of joint commitment. However, if this were intended as an analysis, it would be circular because Gilbert is relying on the notion of joint commitment for her account of what a joint commitment consists of. Recall that the agents must express their willingness to share in a joint commitment to form one. Gilbert claims that the relation only obtains in one direction; each individual's willingness, mutual expression of willingness and common knowledge are required for a joint commitment, but that relation does not obtain in the other direction. A joint commitment cannot be reduced to these three components.

Gilbert does provide us with three special features of joint commitment: ontological holism, conceptual holism, and inherent normativity. She is an ontological holist in the sense that plural subjects

THE STANDARD MODEL OF IDEAL SOCIAL ONTOLOGY   29

or groups do exist in their own right: "A joint commitment is the commitment *of two or more individuals considered as a unit or a whole*" (1996, 2, emphasis in original). There are such things as plural subjects that are something more than merely the sum of individual agents related in a particular way. How Gilbert intends the expression "to be jointly committed as a body" to be interpreted is in line with her ontological holism, because "as a body" is used interchangeably with the expression "to be jointly committed as a single person."

Joint commitment is a holistic concept: "Not only does the concept of the plural subject of a goal, for instance, not break down into the concept of a set of personal goals. The concept of a joint commitment that lies at its core does not break down into the concept of a set of personal commitments" (1996, 2). This is an expression of Gilbert's conceptual holism.

Joint commitments are also inherently normative. Whenever there is a joint commitment, the members of the plural subject have certain rights or entitlements and certain obligations or responsibilities they would not otherwise have had. These rights and obligations follow from the very structure of joint commitments:

> The deep basis for the rights and responsibilities that accrue to one who enters a group is to be found precisely in the concept of a plural subject, the core conception here. . . . My articulation of the concept of a plural subject enables us to explain how membership in a group can entail a set of *sui generis* responsibilities and rights, and to become clearer about their nature. (1992, 413)

This illustrates the use and importance of deontic notions in plural subject theory.

In an illuminating discussion of different kinds of "oughts," Gilbert also makes clear that the "ought" following from plural subjects is neither the "ought" of individual rational agency in the sense that one who wills the end wills the means, nor the "ought"

## 30   CRITIQUE: IDEAL SOCIAL ONTOLOGY

of intrinsic value. There is thus a clear dividing line between a "social ought" and a "moral ought" in plural subject theory, and it is a social, or associational, "ought" that is entailed by the concept of a plural subject. These rights and obligations generate reasons for action and thus affect our behavior. In fact, Gilbert claims that the glue holding the social world together consists of people's perceptions of themselves as members of plural subjects. So, reasons for action derived from the goals of a plural subject can outweigh reasons for action derived from one's personal goals, a claim Gilbert illustrates with "the Father-example":

> Father says 'So, we're agreed that an afternoon at the beach is best?' He then goes into the garden and settles into a deckchair with *The Golden Bowl*. Fathers may do this sort of thing sometimes, but such action is surely bizarre. According to the view of the matter presented here, this is because, in accepting going to the beach as 'our' preference, Father implicitly dedicated his own will to that project. But if he really has done this, then he understands that his will is not available for the pursuit of contrary projects. (1992, 425)

This shows that deontic notions such as commitment, right, and obligation are key notions that comprise the very fabric of society. Gilbert's claim that the glue of the social world is people's perceptions of themselves as members of plural subjects, in combination with the claim that social rights and obligations follow from plural subjects, is an example of what I call *the deonticity claim*. More generally, the deonticity claim amounts to the idea that deontic notions, such as commitment, right, and obligation, are key notions, and, indeed, the very glue of society.

There is another important claim emanating from this discussion of joint commitment. Recall Guala's slogan: "No social reality without collective intentionality." The role of joint commitment in Gilbert's theory illustrates this slogan: social phenomena are

THE STANDARD MODEL OF IDEAL SOCIAL ONTOLOGY    31

analyzed in terms of plural subjects that are in turn partly analyzed in terms of joint commitments, which is Gilbert's preferred conception of collective intentionality. This exemplifies what I call *the collective intentionality claim*—that collective intentionality is the basic building block of social reality (and a necessary condition for the existence of either all or standard institutions).

To sum up the discussion so far, the two main aims of *On Social Facts* consist of the scope claim and the foundation claim, while the discussion of the basic building blocks of social reality shows that Gilbert adheres to the collective intentionality claim and the deonticity claim.

## 1.3.2  Ontological Holism and "the Restaurant Case"

We return to the ontological holism of plural subject theory. This is indeed a strong position that Gilbert advocates: there are plural subjects in addition to individual subjects.[4] Gilbert offers explanatory reasons for assuming the existence of plural subjects. She argues that the three features of joint commitment—ontological holism, conceptual holism, and inherent normativity—can explain how statements about groups who act can be literally true *and* explain the normative aspect of social phenomena.

According to Gilbert, a joint commitment unifies the participants in a way that makes it intelligible to talk about *our* acts; that is, groups really can act. The statement, "this group is dedicated to overthrowing the king," is literally true and is not to be translated into statements about either an aggregate of like-minded individuals acting or as representatives of a group acting. One possible benefit of plural subject theory is that it can

---

[4] This position is stronger than Searle's; he posits an extra kind of intention but no extra kinds of subjects. It is also stronger than the positions of Bratman, Kutz, and Tuomela, who hold that we do not need to posit an extra kind of intention to explain collective actions, only individual intentions with irreducibly collective content.

## 32 CRITIQUE: IDEAL SOCIAL ONTOLOGY

explain how statements about groups as agents can be *literally* true. Furthermore, joint commitments are inherently normative, and rights and obligations thus follow from the structure of joint commitment. This means that the *normative* dimension of social phenomena can be explained without invoking any external moral principle or similar notion.

Gilbert also provides an example that she calls "the restaurant case" to demonstrate the existence of plural subjects. She claims that a central narrow sense of "we" in our everyday talk can plausibly be taken to refer to a plural subject. I take it that it would mean that individuals with a collective intention would not be sufficient to explain this stronger sense of "we." Gilbert writes:

> A group of people are eating together in a restaurant at the conclusion of an academic conference. Two of their number, Tony and Celia, are engaged to be married. The restaurant is famous for its sweet pastries, and at one point Tony asks Celia 'Shall we share a pastry?' Celia nods agreement. Then one of the other men, Bernard, turns to Sylvia, who is sitting on his right, and whom he hardly knows, and asks 'Shall *we* share a pastry?' She finds his use of 'we' inappropriate. (In fact one could say that she resents it; she finds it presumptuous.) She tries to show this by replying: 'I'm willing to share something with you, yes.' (1992, 175)

Gilbert argues that the inappropriateness Sylvia feels is due to the semantics of "we." Bernard is using "we" inappropriately, in the stronger sense that refers to a plural subject, even though Bernard and Sylvia have not formed anything close to a plural subject. By contrast, there is no sensed inappropriateness of using "we" in this strong sense when it comes to the engaged couple, because they are a plural subject.

But it is problematic to rely too much on this case because our linguistic intuitions seem to differ a great deal; while Gilbert takes this case to show that there is a strong sense of "we"—a plural

THE STANDARD MODEL OF IDEAL SOCIAL ONTOLOGY     33

subject sense—by arguing that this felt inappropriateness is *semantic*, others might simply explain Sylvia's feeling of inappropriateness in different ways, most obviously, by saying that Bernard is making a move on her and she is not interested.

Gilbert's method is traditional conceptual analysis relying on our linguistic intuitions, and her aim is to explicate our everyday concepts, often through the use of everyday examples, like walking together or eating together. The restaurant case has an interesting gender and power dimension, and Gilbert picks up on it and further develops themes of gender and social power at times in *On Social Facts*. For instance, there are examples of how social conventions about appropriate clothing and behavior differ with respect to gender and how this imposes restrictions upon agents, but gender is not taken to be a paradigmatic social phenomenon.

In addition to the restricting aspects of power, Gilbert's examples often involve the enabling aspects of being a member of a plural subject, or the existence of a particular social convention. Recall that rights and obligations, which are crucial forms of the enabling and restricting nature of social power, are entailed by the concept of a plural subject. In this way, a form of social power is necessarily a part of social phenomena, according to plural subject theory. However, the concept of social power is only explicitly discussed in relation to how one is to understand Durkheim's conception of a "social fact." Gilbert argues against an interpretation in which coercive power is an essential feature and in favor of an interpretation in which acting as a social group is an essential feature of social facts (1992, 244–250). In short, the enabling and restricting aspects of social and institutional power are emphasized, while the productive aspects of power (say looping effects and adaptive preferences) are absent. This illustrates what I refer to as *the power claim*—that the enabling and restricting aspects of social and institutional power, such as rights and obligations, are emphasized as key phenomena.

We can now address the reflexivity claim in relation to plural subject theory. Recall that joint commitment is a core notion and

## 34  CRITIQUE: IDEAL SOCIAL ONTOLOGY

that in forming joint commitments, "each party must express to every other party his or her personal readiness to be jointly committed in the relevant way" (Gilbert 2000, 5). A joint commitment to overthrow the king, for example, is formed when each relevant party is willing to share in overthrowing the king, this willingness is mutually expressed, and there is common knowledge among the parties about this goal. Note that the genesis of joint commitments involves common knowledge, which is a phenomenon that entails reflexivity. Gilbert makes clear that common knowledge is a necessary, but not sufficient, condition of plural subjects: "Common knowledge does not automatically give rise to plural subjecthood, though it is a requirement of plural subjecthood" (1992, 203). And social phenomena are understood as plural subject phenomena. This is, then, an example of what I call *the reflexivity claim*—primary social phenomena are constituted by "self-fulfilling prophecies."[5]

In fact, this also exemplifies what I call *the performativity claim*— social phenomena are created and maintained by individuals who belong to a given social group through explicit performatives or acts that have the same logical structure as performatives. In expressing one's personal readiness to be jointly committed, the parties either use an explicit speech act, or an act that has the same logical structure as a speech act.[6] An exchange from Gilbert's "Walking Together: A Paradigmatic Social Phenomenon" (1990) illustrates this point:

> Suppose Jack Smith coughs to attract Sue's attention, and then asks if she is Sue Jones and would she mind if he joins her? "No,"

---

[5] "What I have said so far, then, does not give us a definition of what it is to be a plural subject of something. Rather, it gives us a logically necessary condition for the existence of such a subject. The statement of this condition itself *uses* the notion of a plural subject. It is a notion the members of a plural subject must have in order to become members of a plural subject. For they must experience and manifest willingness to be members of such a subject" (1992, 18).

[6] Another example Gilbert (1992) offers is when a small group of people make an agreement (a performative speech act) to travel to London together.

THE STANDARD MODEL OF IDEAL SOCIAL ONTOLOGY    35

Sue says, "that would be nice. I should like some company." This is probably enough to produce a case of going for a walk together. Once the exchange has taken place, both parties will be entitled to assume that the attitudes and actions appropriate to their going for a walk together are in place. (1990, 6–7)

Furthermore, the central role of performatives is clear in Gilbert's rich discussion of social conventions. Examples of social conventions include having tea at 4 pm or having a steak for Sunday dinner. The plural subject account of a social convention is an important contribution to social ontology, not least for its contribution to clarifying central disagreements between the plural subject account and game theoretical accounts like David Lewis' classic contribution ([1969] 2002).[7] I cannot do justice here to either Gilbert's full account or her critique of Lewis' account of conventions. Rather, I consider her account purely in light of the performativity claim.

According to plural subject theory, the everyday concept of a social convention is the joint acceptance of a principle of action: "PPL [a principle of action] has the following form: whenever a member of P is in circumstance C, he/she is to perform action A. It is understood to be a *simple fiat*. . . . Thus PPL is a self-imposed decree, a *fiat* issued by the population itself" (1992, 373). Gilbert develops the example of "the peaceable mushroom-pickers" to illustrate the idea of a group fiat and how a social convention might evolve. The peaceable mushroom-pickers have a coordination problem to solve: to avoid bumping one another's heads when picking mushrooms. To solve this coordination problem, one person comes up with an idea. She blows a horn to get everyone's attention and then presents her idea of implementing the following rule: each of the mushroom-pickers must look up once having picked a dozen mushrooms.

---

[7] One such disagreement is whether or not social conventions are inherently normative; Gilbert answers in the affirmative.

36  CRITIQUE: IDEAL SOCIAL ONTOLOGY

They all agree on this rule and start to act in accordance with it, and there are social sanctions against non-compliers (376). This again illustrates the performativity claim: social conventions are created and maintained by explicit performatives (as in the mushroom-pickers case above) or by actions that have the same logical structure as a performative, as when the mushroom-pickers have forgotten about the original agreement but still act in accordance with the rule.

### 1.3.3  Paradigmatic Features in Gilbert's Examples

> To this extent, then, going for a walk together may be considered a paradigm of social phenomena in general.
>
> (Gilbert 1990, 2).

A central question in social ontology is: Which are the social phenomena? As we have seen, Gilbert's answer is that they are plural subject phenomena. It is fruitful to dig deeper into this issue of the central social phenomena by investigating what Gilbert takes to be the paradigmatic social phenomena and discern some common features among them.

One such feature is the so-called "string quartet paradigm of social groups." This phrase was coined by Christopher Kutz (2000) in criticizing contemporary accounts of collective action for failing to take large and hierarchical groups into account. Kutz writes that:

> Philosophers studying collective action have tended to focus only on the fully cooperative form, the string quartet paradigm. Such examples inevitably generate a conception of collective action thick with mutual obligations and egalitarian dispositions: an account unsuited to the depersonalized, hierarchic, bureaucratic, but nonetheless collective institutions that characterize modern life. (2000, 11)

THE STANDARD MODEL OF IDEAL SOCIAL ONTOLOGY   37

This feature is clearly present in most of Gilbert's examples. Recall, for instance, the restaurant case, the example of Sue and Jack going for a walk together, and the example of the father as examples of plural subjects. Using small groups as the paradigmatic example of collective action is not an accidental feature; rather, it is an explicit methodological choice and substantive claim about social reality. Gilbert takes small informal and ephemeral groups to be the "bedrock" of society, making up larger social groups like nations:

> My own sense is that the ephemeral, two-person group is far from being an unimportant curiosity, an 'end-of-the-spectrum-case' one just might mention for completeness, but might just as well ignore. It is, rather, a fundamentally important case, which it would be more than arbitrary to ignore . . . these are the cases that spawn all the others; the little groups are causally crucial for the beginning and life and change of larger groups and societies. (1992, 232)

Another feature in Gilbert's paradigmatic examples is that "the bright side of institutions" is emphasized to a significantly larger extent than the "dark side of institutions." Consider both the examples of the father and the Sunday steak dinner as a case of a social convention as illustrations of this feature. In relation to this, recall Charles Mills' claims that ideal theory understands institutions like the family in a romanticized, or idealized, sense, meaning that this type of theorizing will inevitably fail to understand how "their actual workings may systematically disadvantage women, the poor, and racial minorities" (Mills 2005, 169) and that ideal theory is silent on oppression. In contrast, emphasizing the dark side of institutions to the same extent as the bright side might mean that emphasizing things like the division of labor within the heterosexual family (which is generally skewed to women's disadvantage) might distort children's sense of justice (Okin 1987). The Sunday steak dinner example fails to mention the dark side of this

## 38 CRITIQUE: IDEAL SOCIAL ONTOLOGY

convention altogether: there is immense animal suffering involved for us to have steaks for dinner. In contrast, a major proponent of nonideal social ontology, Sally Haslanger, offers the following statement as an example of a deeply problematic generic: "Cows are food" (2011, 191–193).[8]

Still another significant feature of Gilbert's paradigmatic examples is that direct social phenomena are emphasized almost to the exclusion of indirect or derived social phenomena. There are a few mentions or discussions of the latter, such as economic classes and unintended consequences, but the most frequent examples, as well as those used in developing the theory and against which the theory and its rivals are tested, are examples like the departmental meeting, whether or not there is a convention to have tea at 4:00 pm, and a small group of people agreeing to travel to London together. These are all social phenomena whose existence depends directly on the joint commitments of the participants.

Similarly, the visible aspects of social reality are at center stage. The examples most frequently used are about social phenomena that the people in question know about; they are transparent to those participants in question. There are a few illuminating discussions of phenomena that might be opaque to the people in question at both the macro and micro levels. One such discussion of opaque social phenomena at the macro level is whether economic classes who are not aware of themselves as a group really are social groups. One might also interpret the so-called "hyper-responsible woman" as an example of an opaque social phenomenon at the micro level. A new heterosexual romantic couple are influenced by and uphold the social convention that women are more responsible than men for keeping the conversation pleasant. Still, the couple might not be aware of how this convention impacts their everyday interactions.

---

[8] Haslanger notes that people usually say "beef is food" but that this hides what is really going on, that people are accepting the assumption that cows are for eating (2011, 192).

THE STANDARD MODEL OF IDEAL SOCIAL ONTOLOGY    39

Again, the focus on transparent, rather than opaque, social phenomena is not accidental. Intentionalism more naturally lends itself to explaining the social world through the first-person intentionalist perspective rather than a third-person external point of view, so it uses concepts that the participants themselves have readily available—the visible aspects of social reality. This does not necessarily exclude opaque kinds of social phenomena. For example, an opaque gender system might be an unintended consequence of how the participants have chosen to organize family life, as could conventions like the hyper-responsible woman. Hence, plural subject theory might be consistent with including opaque kinds of phenomena, but there is a risk that it will not take us to an analysis of these phenomena (cf., Mills' claim that ideal theory in political philosophy will deal with nonideal phenomena later, once the ideal theory has been completed, but still has not gotten around to it).

### 1.3.4  Cooperation, Consensus, and Equality

It is time now to return to the two-worlds metaphor from the introductory chapter. The first world of ideal social ontology is characterized by cooperation, consensus, and equality. The discussion thus far shows an emerging picture of the social world in which cooperation and consensus are the default approaches. Furthermore, it suggests that equality is the default and inequality an aberration. For example, in showing how a perceived initial baseline of equal responsibility for members of a plural subject to bring about a joint goal is in fact consistent with an unequal division of responsibility, Gilbert asks us to consider a society-wide social convention that women are more responsible for keeping a relationship with men pleasant than the other way around:

# 40 CRITIQUE: IDEAL SOCIAL ONTOLOGY

> Quite generally, then, even if everyone understands that in doing something together they share the ultimate responsibility for achieving the desired outcome, conventions may develop which ensure that, in effect, responsibility devolves more on one party than the other. It may now be up to one person to do more, in order that things go right. Meanwhile, were the relevant convention to be abolished, everyone would presumably re-emerge as equally responsible. The idea of an acknowledged initial basic equality of responsibility in relation to a plural subject's 'cause' is consistent, then, with the fact that *in particular cases one or more participants may come to be granted more responsibility than the rest.* (1992, 412, my emphasis)

Note that the default is initial basic equality, with the convention pointing to a gender imbalance viewed as the exception. Once the convention is gone, the social world arches back to equality. It is illustrative to quote the continuation of this passage because it also exemplifies an ideal of equality between the members of a plural subject:

> Precisely how things progress in a given case evidently depends on the personalities, needs, capacities, ideals, and expectations of the parties. Given an initial egalitarianism in both parties individually, equality of responsibility may emerge as a joint ideal. If we are following a trail in the woods, there will be no master and no slave, no one trying to keep up with or slow down for a regal pacemaker. Each of us will work to accommodate us both. We may happily feel that in our small community we have achieved true democracy and perpetual peace. (1992, 412)

Note also that the explanation for how things progress is given an individualist explanation that refers to individual beliefs and desires, in contrast to common sociological explanations that invoke structural explanations like gender and class systems. Of course, these beliefs and desires are likely to be affected by structures, but structures are clearly out of sight in plural subject theory.

### 1.3.5 Summing Up: Gilbert's Plural Subject Theory and the Standard Model

In sum, in describing Gilbert's project, I have discerned elements in the standard model of ideal social ontology. These elements consist of the scope claim and the foundation claim in describing the main aims of plural subject theory. The three features picked out by Guala—reflexivity, performativity, and collective intentionality—are clearly discernible as basic building blocks along with the deonticity claim and the power claim. In addition, there are four central features in the paradigmatic examples used by Gilbert: the string quartet paradigm of social groups, emphasis on the bright side of institutions, and emphasis on direct and transparent social phenomena. In the next section, I show that Searle's project shares all these elements.

### 1.4 John Searle's Construction of Social Reality

We now consider the second theory that shaped the research field of ideal social ontology. Searle's aim is to develop a theory of the ontology of social reality, of how social institutions, social facts, and institutional facts exist. He attempts to explain the general structure of social reality by using tools developed in *Speech Acts* (1969) and *Intentionality* (1983). In fact, his focus is on institutional reality, a specific subclass of social reality. His first key question is, "How do we construct an objective social reality?" This entails several related questions: How are institutional facts possible and what is the nature of such facts? What is the mode of existence of

## 42  CRITIQUE: IDEAL SOCIAL ONTOLOGY

institutional reality? The second key question is, "How does social reality fit into the physical world?" These questions and his answers resemble one of Gilbert's main aims, to explain sociality as such. So, Searle also adheres to the scope claim—to offer a general theory of the ontology of social and institutional reality.

In fact, Searle shares the foundation claim—theories in social ontology are the foundation of the social sciences—with Gilbert. In the introduction to *The Construction of Social Reality*, Searle provides a clear expression of the foundation claim: "Because these questions concern what might be thought of as problems in the foundations of the social sciences, one might suppose that they would have been addressed and solved already in the various social sciences, and in particular by the great founders of the social sciences" (1995, xii).

Searle (1995) is particularly interesting for many reasons. First, from just a few building blocks and a clear statement of the relation between them, it promises to explain a large and important part of social reality: institutions and institutional facts. Along with this, Searle argues that what appear to be vastly different institutional facts—the fact that two people are married, that Magdalena Andersson is the Prime Minister of Sweden, and that the Euro is a valid currency—in fact have a simple underlying structure that can be represented by the formula "X counts as Y in context C." If Searle is right, this would be the core principle of any society:

> Human societies have a *logical structure*, because human attitudes are constitutive of the social reality in question and those attitudes have propositional contents with logical relations. Our problem is to expose those relations. Now it might seem that this is too daunting a task. Human societies are immensely complex and immensely various. If there is one thing we know from the cultural anthropology of the past century, it is that there is an enormous variety of different modes of social existence. The assumption I will be making, and will try to justify,

is that even though there is an enormous variety, the principles that underlie the constitution of social reality are rather few in number. What you discover when you go behind the surface phenomena of social reality is a relatively simple underlying logical structure even though the manifestations in actual social reality in political parties, social events, and economic transactions are immensely complicated. The analogy with the natural sciences is obvious. There is an enormous difference in the physical appearance of a bonfire and a rusty shovel, but the underlying principle in each case is exactly the same: oxidization. Similarly, there are enormous differences between baseball games, $20 bills, and national elections, but the underlying logical structure is the same. (2006, 15–16)

Critics have questioned the basic formula of "X counts as Y in context C" in several ways. To bring some order to these concerns, it is helpful to view the debate between Searle and his critics in terms of scope and simplicity: ideally, we would find a theory that manages to explain a great portion of social reality with the smallest possible number of elements. Initially, Searle's theory seems to fulfill this ideal; it has a wide scope and makes use of only three building blocks—collective intentionality, imposition of function, and constitutive rules—in analyzing institutions and institutional facts. But a number of critics argue that, despite what Searle claims, the theory is actually of limited scope and these tools are thus not sufficient to account for a large part of social reality; if we want to account for these phenomena, we must assume additional building blocks and make the theory increasingly complex. For instance, critics object that Searle's theory accounts for neither "free-standing Y-terms" (abstract social objects like corporations and the U.S. Constitution), nor opaque kinds of social facts like economic cycles and power structures (Smith 2003; Thomasson 2003). Given that these kinds of phenomena cannot be explained by "X counts as Y in

## 44 CRITIQUE: IDEAL SOCIAL ONTOLOGY

context C," we are left to wonder whether this really is the principle of society. I turn to some of these objections in the next chapter.

To anticipate a bit, the answer to the first question of how we construct an objective social reality is that we create an objective social reality by collectively imposing functions on objects or phenomena according to the structure of constitutive rules, where the functions imposed exceed the purely physical features of those phenomena. The answer to the second question is that there is a continuous line instead of a radical break between the physical world of nature and the social reality of culture. The move from nature to social reality is made by collective intentionality, while the move from social reality to institutional reality is made by our capacity to symbolize or represent. To understand these claims, the three notions of collective intentionality, imposition of function, and constitutive rules must be explained.

Searle makes the strong claim that these notions are jointly necessary and sufficient to account for the ontology of social reality. Here, we have an example of the collective intentionality claim— that collective intentionality is the basic building block of society.

It is essential to distinguish between brute facts, social facts, and institutional facts. Brute facts require no institutions or collective intentionality for their existence, social facts are any facts that involve the collective intentionality of two or more agents, and institutional facts require institutions for their existence (in a way to be explained). For instance, the existence of a mountain is a brute fact, two people going for a walk together is a social fact, and the existence of money is an institutional fact.

### 1.4.1 The Three Building Blocks of Social Reality

Collective intentionality is the first building block. Intentionality is directedness or "aboutness"; more precisely, it is the capacity of the mind and brain to relate to the world, to be directed at something

THE STANDARD MODEL OF IDEAL SOCIAL ONTOLOGY    45

beyond itself: objects or states of affairs in the world. The mind relates to the world by way of intentional states, which are states that are directed at something beyond themselves, such as beliefs, hopes, fears, and desires. Collective intentionality means engaging in cooperative behavior and sharing intentional states. This is the fundamental building block of social reality: "Whenever you have people cooperating, you have collective intentionality. Whenever you have people sharing their thoughts, feelings, and so on, you have collective intentionality; and indeed, I want to say, this is the foundation of all social activities" (Searle 1999, 120). This, again, is a clear example of the collective intentionality claim.

Searle writes of collective intentionality as follows: "Obvious examples are cases where *I* am doing something only as part of *our* doing something.... If I am a violinist in an orchestra I play *my* part in *our* performance of the symphony" (1995, 23). This is engaging in the cooperative behavior of performing together and sharing the belief (an intentional state) that you are performing a symphony together. Searle claims that collective intentionality is a primitive notion; it cannot simply be reduced to individual intentionality plus mutual beliefs. For Searle, in cases of collective intentionality, the I-intention is derived from the we-intention. For example, in the above case, the singular intention of the violinist—I intend to play my part—is derived from the collective intention: we intend to perform a symphony. Searle argues that in addition to singular intentionality of the form "I believe" or "I intend," there is collective intentionality of the form "we believe" or "we intend." A collective intention is a separate kind of intention.

The second building block is the imposition of function. Human beings have the capacity to assign, or impose, functions on objects. This is a feature of our intentionality, and this is used when we create institutional facts. There are two categories of the assignment of function: nonagentive and agentive functions. Nonagentive functions are "assigned to naturally occurring objects and processes as part of a theoretical account of the phenomena in question"

46 CRITIQUE: IDEAL SOCIAL ONTOLOGY

(Searle 1995, 20). For example, the heart functions to pump blood. Agentive functions are dependent on the practical intentions and activities of human agents, on our use of objects in different ways. There is a subcategory of agentive functions called status functions. Searle writes, "within the category of agentive functions is a special category of those entities whose agentive function is to *symbolize, represent, stand for,* or—in general—to *mean* something or other" (1995, 23, emphasis in original). It will turn out that "the class of existing status functions is identical with the class of institutional facts" (1995, 124).

The third building block is constitutive rules. The contrast between regulative rules and constitutive rules is helpful to explain a constitutive rule: "Regulative rules regulate a pre-existing activity, an activity whose existence is logically independent of the rules. Constitutive rules constitute (and also regulate) an activity the existence of which is logically dependent on the rules" (Searle 1969, 34). Constitutive rules create the possibility of certain activities, and the activity in question partly consists of acting in accordance with these rules. Consider chess: "the rules of chess create the very possibility of playing chess. The rules are *constitutive* of chess in the sense that playing chess is constituted in part by acting in accord with the rules" (Searle 1995, 28). The form of constitutive rules is "X counts as Y in context C." For instance, this move (X) counts as checkmate (Y) in the context of playing chess (C). The form of constitutive rules, "X counts as Y in context C," is taken to be the underlying structure of social reality.

## 1.4.2 Institutional Facts

Applying Searle's three notions—collective intentionality, imposition of function, constitutive rules—to a famous example from the history of philosophy demonstrates their roles in creating institutional facts. The three notions are also used to explain what

THE STANDARD MODEL OF IDEAL SOCIAL ONTOLOGY   47

an institutional fact is. In the *Discourse on Inequality*, Jean-Jacques Rousseau writes that:

> the first man who, having enclosed a piece of ground, bethought himself of saying "this is mine," and found people simple enough to believe him, was the real founder of civil society. From how many crimes, wars and murders, from how many horrors and misfortunes might not any one have saved mankind, by pulling up the stakes, or filling up the ditch, and crying to his fellows: "Beware of listening to this impostor; you are undone if you once forget that the fruits of the earth belong to us all, and the earth itself to nobody." ([1754] 1997, 397)

The existence of the piece of ground is a brute fact, and the existence of private property ("this is mine") is an institutional fact. The move from brute facts (nature) to institutional facts (culture) is explained in the following way: the man saying "this is mine" found people simple enough to believe him, meaning that people accepted private property. They collectively agreed that the piece of ground had the status of private property, and with the status of being private property came certain functions, including who was allowed inside the stakes. In short, people imposed a status and with it a function on the piece of ground by collective agreement, thereby creating the institutional fact of private property. After their acceptance of the "this is mine" claim, the piece of ground began to represent something beyond itself, something more than its purely physical features: private property.

In sum, an institutional fact is identical with the status function that is imposed on an object by collective agreement according to the structure of constitutive rules. Collective agreement presupposes collective intentionality. People must share the belief (an intentional state) that the piece of ground is private property for the piece of ground to become private property. This means that the collective belief is constitutive of the piece of ground's being

48    CRITIQUE: IDEAL SOCIAL ONTOLOGY

private property. In general, collective acceptance is partly constitutive of institutional facts. It follows that institutional facts exist relative to the intentionality of observers. Because observer-relative features are ontologically subjective, institutional facts are also ontologically subjective. Furthermore, seeming to be private property comes prior to being private property. Consequently, the logical relation when it comes to institutional facts is: seeming to be X comes prior to being X. Searle writes, "for any observer-relative feature F, *seeming to be F* is logically prior to *being F*, because—appropriately understood—seeming to be F is a necessary condition of being F" (1995, 13, emphasis in original). This is an example of the reflexivity claim.

This relation leads to the first substantial problem concerning the scope of Searle's theory; it appears to exclude the possibility of types of social facts that the members of a society have no beliefs about or do not know exist, such as economic cycles and power structures. If this is correct, then the scope of the theory is limited. Amie Thomasson (2003) objects that opaque kinds of social facts cannot be accounted for by Searle's theory because these types of facts can exist without anyone having any beliefs about them. Hence, they do not meet Searle's interpretation of the condition "seeming to be F is logically prior to being F." I regard this objection as central and discuss it in detail in the next chapter.

There is a logical structure underlying the imposition of status functions that can be spelled out in the form of constitutive rules: "X counts as Y in context C." For example, the piece of ground X becomes private property Y by collective agreement in context C. It is important to understand the role of constitutive rules in the theory. The creation of institutional facts can be represented by the form of constitutive rules. When we represent a physical object as a status function—when we make the move from X to Y— an institutional fact is created. The nature of institutional facts is also explained through the form of constitutive rules because an institutional fact is represented by the Y term in the formula when

THE STANDARD MODEL OF IDEAL SOCIAL ONTOLOGY    49

interpreted in a specific way. The constitutive rule also explains what an institution is: an institution is a system of constitutive rules. It is important to make clear that people must collectively accept the constitutive rule that defines an institution. Only when the constitutive rules are accepted can we create individual institutional facts within the institution. The people in Rousseau's example accept the institution of private property; that is, they accept that all pieces of land that are relevantly similar to the "impostor's piece of land" are private property, and that is a constitutive rule. Thomasson puts this point well: "In order to impose status functions, we must collectively accept constitutive rules, rules that stipulate that a certain x 'counts' as y in the relevant context C" (2003, 276). So, an institutional fact, such as the fact that I own my apartment, can only exist given that we have accepted the constitutive rules of private property. Recall the performativity claim of which this is an example.

The thesis of constitutive rules helps to explain the role of language in this theory. Language understood as a system of symbolization is constitutive of institutional facts because these kinds of facts cannot exist without being represented as existing. The important thing is that the physical features of the X term are insufficient for the existence of institutional facts, so some way of representing the move from the X term to the Y term is needed. This move can only be made by symbolization. Institutional facts are essentially linguistic because they contain this element of symbolization or representation. This implies the view that language is the fundamental institution in the sense that you can have language without other institutions such as property, but you cannot have other institutions without language. Searle argues that other social theorists fail to see this constitutive role of language; they take language for granted and then try to explain how society is possible. By contrast, if you have language, you already have society and an institution, according to this view.

To make this underlying logical structure more powerful, the idea of iteration is employed: status functions can be piled on top

50 CRITIQUE: IDEAL SOCIAL ONTOLOGY

of one another. Iterations of this basic structure can be made in different ways, and these iterations help to explain how such a simple basic structure can account for the great variety of institutional facts. The Y term from one level can be the X term at a higher level. In other words, we can impose status functions on entities that have already had status functions imposed on them. "For example, only a citizen of the United States as X can become President as Y, but to be a citizen is to have a Y status-function from an earlier level" (Searle 1995, 80). And the Y term from an earlier level can be the C term at a higher level. For instance, a marriage ceremony requires the presence of a registrar as part of the context C, but being a registrar means precisely to have previously acquired that status function. Searle concludes that, "It is no exaggeration to say that these iterations provide the logical structure of complex societies" (1995, 80). The idea of iteration both illustrates the centrality of performatives in Searle's theory and the performativity claim.

### 1.4.3 The Background and the Performativity Claim

Recall that the performativity claim consists of a disjunction: social phenomena are either created by explicit performatives or by actions that have the same logical structure as performatives. I now want to clarify this latter part of the disjunction.

The notion of the Background is important in understanding the thesis of constitutive rules. People do not need to be aware of the structure of constitutive rules; nor do they need to explicitly accept these rules for institutional facts to exist. Rather, the Background is employed to explain how people's behavior can be causally sensitive to rules without awareness of the structure of those rules. The three building blocks can only function against the Background because the Background enables all representing to take place.

What, then, is the Background? "The Background is a set of non-representational mental capacities that enable all representing to

THE STANDARD MODEL OF IDEAL SOCIAL ONTOLOGY    51

take place. Intentional states only have the conditions of satisfaction that they do, and thus only are the states they are, against a Background of abilities that are not themselves Intentional states" (Searle 1983, 143). The Background consists of various mental capacities, so it is located in the human brain and mind. The Background is nonrepresentational, which means that it does not consist of mental states, representations, or even in unconscious mental states (unconscious in the sense of us not being aware of having these mental states). The Background has no intentionality. Roughly, the idea is that some apparent beliefs are actually too fundamental to qualify as beliefs, such as "Objects are solid." These presuppositions are part of the Background. To make this clearer, consider Searle's example of the man who forms an intention to run for the presidency. This intention is located in a network of other intentional states such as beliefs and desires; for example, the man believes that United States is a republic, and he wants people to vote for him. The example is used to illustrate the idea that each intentional state only has its content and determines its conditions of satisfaction in relation to other intentional states—the network. If we continued to ask what this man must believe to run for the presidency, we would eventually reach the Background. If we tried to state all the presuppositions of the beliefs in the network, we could eventually list things like elections are held near the surface of the earth and that people can only vote when conscious. These presuppositions are part of the Background.

Besides a stance toward what the world is like, or presuppositions of intentional states, the Background includes the capacities to do certain things, such as walking, or—for tennis professionals—playing tennis. There is a distinction between the *deep Background* and the *local Background*. The former is common to all humans due to our biological makeup, while the local Background is culture-specific because it consists of local cultural practices. For example, appropriate ideas of personal space differ from culture to culture.

## 52  CRITIQUE: IDEAL SOCIAL ONTOLOGY

The Background consists of both biological capacities and cultural practices and habits.

The Background becomes visible once it breaks down, or when there are ruptures in it. It can either be a break against the stance one has toward what the world is like or a failure in one's normal capacities. For example, people who did not grow up in California would find their first earthquake a clear break from their Background presupposition that the ground does not move, while for Serena Williams suddenly to become unable to play tennis is a break against her individual Background capacities. Normally however, Serena Williams is far beyond thinking about the constitutive rules of tennis or how to make a specific stroke. The rules and technique of tennis are in her Background, but her behavior is causally sensitive to those rules. In general, the Background is sensitive to the constitutive rules of institutions, even though it does not contain any representations of those rules. This helps to explain how our actions within institutions can be causally sensitive to the structure of constitutive rules even when we are unaware of them. It also explains how social phenomena can be created and maintained by actions that have the same logical structure as performatives, even if we are unaware of this structure and thus not explicitly using performatives to create or to maintain the social phenomenon in question.

In sum, the answer to the initial questions of what an institutional fact is and how it is created is, "the class of existing status functions is identical with the class of institutional facts" (1995, 124). In other words, an institutional fact is represented by the Y term in the formula "X counts as Y in context C." An institutional fact is created by the imposition of a status and with it a function on an object by collective agreement, according to the form of constitutive rules.

THE STANDARD MODEL OF IDEAL SOCIAL ONTOLOGY    53

## 1.4.4  Institutional Facts Are Conventional Powers

It is time to turn to an examination of institutional facts themselves, the Y terms, to give an answer to the question of what kind they are. Another way to put this question is, "What is the content of Y?" We have seen that an institutional fact is identical with the status function that is imposed on an object by collective intentionality and that this imposition follows the form of constitutive rules: "X counts as Y in context C." Therefore, the question, "What kind of statuses are these?" is actually a question about the intentional content of the Y term:

> Because the Y content is imposed on the X element by collective acceptance, there must be some content to these collective acceptances (recognitions, beliefs, etc.); and I am suggesting that for a large class of cases the content involves some conventional power mode in which the subject is related to some type of action or course of actions. (Searle 1995, 104)

The answer is that status functions can be analyzed in terms of conventional powers. Consequently, institutional reality is a system of conventional power. To explain this claim, the distinction between two types of power is relevant: brute power, such as bodily strength, and conventional power, such as rights and obligations. The main difference between the two is that the former works through a person's intrinsic features and remains unaffected by collective acceptance, while collective acceptance is constitutive of the latter because conventional power exists only because people believe it exists. Note that conventional power has the following structure in common with institutional facts; just as seeming to be X is prior to being X, seeming to have power is prior to having power. However, this may be too narrow a view because not all forms of power constituted by collective intentionality need to depend directly on collective beliefs in this way.

## 54  CRITIQUE: IDEAL SOCIAL ONTOLOGY

Searle ends up with two main categories of conventional power: positive and negative deontic powers. Positive deontic powers are rights in different forms, privileges, entitlements, and authorizations. In these cases, the agent is endowed with some new power that grants the agent the ability to do something she could not otherwise have done, such as veto legislation. Negative deontic powers are obligations in different forms, such as requirements, duties, and penalties. In these cases, the agent is compelled to do something she otherwise would not have done or prevented from doing something she otherwise would have done (1995, 100).

In sum, we have seen that institutional facts are conventional powers and that collective intentionality is constitutive of institutional facts and conventional powers. In other words, collective intentionality is a mechanism for creating power. If collective acceptance is removed—if people stop treating X as Y—our institutions collapse.

The background of the claim that status functions are conventional powers is that status functions serve the purpose of regulating behavior and expectations, by which they make society possible. To do this, status functions must be associated with deontic powers. Society functions by our recognizing these deontic powers and thereby creating desire-independent reasons for action. This is the connection between *The Construction of Social Reality* and *Rationality in Action* (2001), in which Searle develops an account of practical reason. The connection is that the mere recognition of a status function as binding on you gives rise to a desire-independent reason for action.

If this is correct, it makes the theory more general and powerful because it provides a link between the ontology of the social world and human action. The notion of a desire-independent reason for action is therefore nothing less than crucial to the theory. Still, most commentators and critics have focused on the ontology, leaving aside the connection to motivation and action. The emphasis on deontic powers and their relation to desire-independent reasons

# THE STANDARD MODEL OF IDEAL SOCIAL ONTOLOGY    55

for action is related to deontic powers' role as the glue of society. Recall the deonticity claim: Deontic notions such as commitment, right, and obligation, are key notions and, indeed, the very glue of society. As seen above, Searle shares this idea with Gilbert.

The discussion of the two categories of conventional power—positive and negative deontic powers—also provides a clear example of the power claim. The power claim is the view that the enabling and restricting aspects of social and institutional power, such as rights and obligations, are emphasized as key phenomena. Recall that the explanation of negative deontic powers is about regulating *pre-existing* desires: the agent is compelled to do something she otherwise would not have done or prevented from doing something she otherwise would have done. This exemplifies the restricting aspects of power. Furthermore, the following text passage shows the centrality of the enabling aspects of power:

> In our intellectual tradition since the Enlightenment the whole idea of power makes a certain type of liberal sensibility very nervous. A certain class of intellectuals would rather that power did not exist at all (or if it has to exist they would rather that their favorite oppressed minority had lots more of it and everyone else had lots less). One lesson to be derived from the study of institutional facts is this: everything we value in civilization requires the creation and maintenance of institutional power relations through collectively imposed status-functions. These require constant monitoring and adjusting to create and preserve fairness, efficiency, flexibility, and creativity, not to mention such traditional values as justice, liberty, and dignity. But institutional power relations are ubiquitous and essential. Institutional power—massive, pervasive, and typically invisible—permeates every nook and cranny of our social lives, and as such it is not a threat to liberal values but rather the precondition of their existence. (Searle 1995, 94)

## 56 CRITIQUE: IDEAL SOCIAL ONTOLOGY

In sum, we have seen that Searle's theory shares central features with Gilbert's theory. First, the main aims are to offer a general theory of the ontology of social phenomena and this theory is the foundation of the social sciences. Collective intentionality, reflexivity, and performativity are essential features in this theory, too. Furthermore, and similarly to Gilbert, Searle adheres to both the deonticity claim and the power claim. It is time to return to the question—which are the social phenomena?—by discerning paradigmatic features in Searle's examples.

### 1.4.5 Paradigmatic Features in Searle's Examples

Similar to Gilbert, the examples used in analyzing collective intentionality display the string quartet paradigm of social groups. In developing his account of collective intentionality, the example used is the act of making a hollandaise sauce together (Searle 1990, 410). And many examples in *The Construction of Social Reality* are about a few persons pushing a car together, performing a symphony together, or dancing together.

Recall the second feature in Gilbert's paradigmatic examples— the bright side of institutions. The quote above has bearing on the bright side of institutions: institutions are the precondition of most things we value in civilization. Furthermore, the power relations between different groups, and especially its dark sides, such as one group oppressing another group, is not central to the ontological investigation.

The third feature was the direct social phenomena. This work clearly displays this feature. The examples used to develop and illustrate the theory are exclusively phenomena that are directly dependent on the collective intentionality of the participants, such as money, marriages, presidents, kings, and professors. There are a few mentions of phenomena that are indirectly dependent on collective intentionality, such as the discussion of latent functions, but

THE STANDARD MODEL OF IDEAL SOCIAL ONTOLOGY    57

this is not further developed. In fact, the reason seems to be the same as in Gilbert's work: Searle makes an explicit methodological choice in choosing the first-person intentionalist perspective over a third-person view: "In this book we are interested primarily in the internal point of view, because it is only from the internal point of view of the participants that the institution can exist at all" (1995, 98).

This methodological choice is likely related as well to the fourth feature that Searle's paradigmatic examples shares with Gilbert's: the focus is on transparent social phenomena; that is, phenomena that the participants know exist. Recall the above examples of being a professor or the president or whether a certain paper bill is money. Searle writes: "The important point is that the internal microlevel is ontologically primary. There is no way that the bishop, the head of the Federal Reserve Board, and the anthropologist can have their points of view without the lowest-level participants in the very trenches of money and marriage having the basic form of intentionality that constitutes the structure of institutional facts" (1995, 98–99). In connection to this, there are some interesting observations about the participants being able to be mistaken about the nature of the phenomena, such as thinking that the king's power is ordained by God. So, the phenomena under discussion are transparent in the sense that the participants know they exist, but this is consistent with them being mistaken about the true nature of the phenomena in question.

### 1.4.6  Summing Up: Searle's Construction of Social Reality and the Standard Model

To sum up, an institutional fact is identical with the status function that is imposed on an object by collective intentionality according to the form of constitutive rules: X counts as Y in context C. Institutional facts are observer-relative, ontologically subjective

## 58 CRITIQUE: IDEAL SOCIAL ONTOLOGY

but epistemically objective. Collective acceptance is constitutive of institutional facts, and this has the consequence that what seems to be the case comes prior to what is the case and that seeming to be F is necessary for being F. Institutional facts are deontic powers, and society functions by rational agents' recognition of these deontic powers, creating desire-independent reasons for action. The system of status functions is essentially a system of deontic power; consequently, institutional reality is a matter of deontic power. This insight is represented by the formula "We accept (S has power (S does A))," which we can refer to as the deontic power account. According to Searle, the two formulae "X counts as Y in context C" and "We accept (S has power (S does A))" are two aspects of the same thing. When we impose a status function on someone, we impose deontic powers on that person, and this imposition can be described by both formulae.

In describing Searle's project, I have shown that his theory shares central elements with Gilbert's. These elements consist of the scope claim and the foundation claim in describing the main aims of *The Construction of Social Reality*. The three features picked out by Guala—reflexivity, performativity, and collective intentionality—are clearly discernible as basic building blocks, along with the deonticity claim and the power claim. In addition, the four central features in the paradigmatic examples used by Gilbert are also present in Searle: the string quartet paradigm of social groups, emphasis on the bright side of institutions, and emphasis on direct and transparent social phenomena. In relation to the last two features—direct and transparent social phenomena—recall that the following two formulae "X counts as Y in context C" and "We accept (S has power (S does A))" are central in this theory. When we impose a status function on someone, we impose deontic powers on that person, and this imposition can be described by both formulae. This means that the emphasis is on transparent and direct social phenomena rather than derived and opaque types of social phenomena. This illustrates both the features of the paradigmatic examples: direct and visible social phenomena. In the next section, I show that Tuomela's account shares all these central elements too.

## 1.5  Raimo Tuomela's Collective Acceptance Account of Sociality

> The most central—and novel—claim of this book is that collective intentionality in the form of shared we-attitudes is constitutive of standard social practices and social institutions.
>
> (Tuomela 2002, 2)

We turn now to the third theory that shaped the research field of ideal social ontology. The epigraph above tells us some important things about Tuomela's *The Philosophy of Social Practices: A Collective Acceptance View*. The objects of study are shared we-attitudes, social practices, and social institutions. The basic building block of social practices and social institutions is collective intentionality, which is explicated as shared we-attitudes.

Tuomela sets out to clarify the concepts of social practice and social institution by using the collective acceptance account of sociality. His answer to the question, "In what sense is the social world an artifact?" is that a central part of the social world is collectively constructed by collective acceptance, which is understood in terms of we-attitudes. Here we have an expression of the scope claim—to offer a general theory of the ontology of social and institutional reality.

Tuomela's aim is to provide a new theory of social practices and social institutions, referred to as the collective acceptance account of sociality, based on the notion of a shared we-attitude. In doing so, he attempts to provide a new conceptual system for theory building in the social sciences, by giving shared we-attitudes a *central role* in the analysis of the social world, and clarifying some important

## 60 CRITIQUE: IDEAL SOCIAL ONTOLOGY

issues in the social sciences, and by giving a more *precise* account of social practices and social institutions. This exemplifies the foundation claim—theories in social ontology are the foundation of the social sciences either by providing and clarifying fundamental concepts or by giving an account of the nature and existence of social phenomena.

Most works in ideal social ontology focus on collective intentionality, social groups, institutions, and institutional facts. Tuomela gives social practices a central role in the analysis of the social world. According to Tuomela, there has not been any detailed philosophical analysis of social practices prior to his own work. This is similar to one of his earlier claims: he notes the previous lack of philosophical discussion of social action (actions performed together by several agents). He goes on to argue that social action, understood in terms of shared we-attitudes, plays a crucial role in understanding social reality. Still, it has not received enough attention in the social sciences. In this way, he wants to draw our attention both to shared we-attitudes and social practices.

### 1.5.1 Basic Building Block: Shared We-attitudes in the We-mode

This basic notion—shared we-attitudes in the we-mode—is not, contrary to what many commentators think, conceptually reductive, or conceptually individualistic: "my analysis of joint intentions and we-intentions is conceptually non-reductive, although it is ontically individualistic or, better, interrelational. These notions presuppose at least a pre-analytic notion of joint intention—viz. one involved in the participants' minds when engaged in joint intention (and joint plan) formation" (2005, 342–343). Tuomela's analysis of a we-intention presupposes an individual intention with irreducible collective content:

THE STANDARD MODEL OF IDEAL SOCIAL ONTOLOGY    61

A member $A_i$ of a collective g *we-intends* to do X if and only if (i) $A_i$ intends to do his part of X (as his part of X); (ii) $A_i$ has a belief to the effect that the joint action opportunities for an intentional performance of X will obtain (or at least probably will obtain), especially that a right number of the full-fledged and adequately informed members of g, as required for the performance of X, will (or at least probably will) do their parts of X, which will under normal conditions result in an intentional joint performance of X by the participants; (iii) $A_i$ believes that there is (or will be) a mutual belief among the participating members of g (or at least among those participants who do their parts of X intentionally as their parts of X there is or will be a mutual belief) to the effect that the joint action opportunities for an intentional performance of X will obtain (or at least probably will obtain); (iv) (i) in part because of (ii) and (iii). (2005, 340–341)

Tuomela emphasizes that the action X should be understood as an irreducible joint action, which makes the analysis conceptually non-reductive. If this particular we-intention happens to be shared by other agents, we have a joint intention which consists of each participant's we-intention to perform the joint action, together with mutual belief; that is, the participants must know of one another's intentions to perform the action. An irreducible we-attitude is the basic notion in this conceptual framework and is used in analyzing more complex social notions, such as social practices and social institutions. Recall the slogan: "*No social reality without collective intentionality*" (Guala 2007, 963, emphasis in original). The role of shared we-attitudes in Tuomela's theory exemplifies the collective intentionality claim—collective intentionality is the basic building block of social reality and a necessary condition for the existence of either all institutions or standard institutions. In fact, this analysis also shows that Tuomela has the reflexivity claim in common with Gilbert and Searle because mutual belief is part of the analysis of a we-intention, and mutual belief entails reflexivity.

## 62 CRITIQUE: IDEAL SOCIAL ONTOLOGY

### 1.5.2 Three Central Features of the Collective Acceptance Account of Sociality

The collective acceptance account of sociality has three features, with the first being the most important: the distinction between the I-mode and the we-mode, reflexivity, and performativity. Reflexivity and performativity have been discussed by other philosophers of the social world. The general idea is that concepts that refer to institutional phenomena are self-referential or reflexive in the sense that for something to be money, it must be collectively accepted that pieces of paper of a certain kind count as money. Social entities such as money are performatively constructed by group members in the sense that the group members can collectively bring it about that certain pieces of paper count as money. This again shows that the reflexivity claim is central in Tuomela's theory. Furthermore, this shows that Tuomela is a proponent of the performativity claim as well. Recall the performativity claim— social phenomena are created and maintained by individuals who belong to a given social group through explicit performatives or acts that have the same logical structure as performatives.

In introducing the distinction between we-attitudes in the I-mode and we-attitudes in the we-mode, Tuomela introduces a new and third feature of sociality. This distinction plays a key role in his account of social institutions. The main claim is that institutions require shared we-attitudes in the we-mode to exist. This, again, is an illustration of the collective intentionality claim. For social practices, shared we-attitudes in the I-mode are sufficient, but there can be social practices based on shared we-attitudes in the we-mode.

The intuitive idea behind the distinction between acting in the I-mode and acting in the we-mode is the difference between thinking as a private person, for example by having *personal* goals, and thinking from the group's perspective, for example by having a goal as a *group* member:

THE STANDARD MODEL OF IDEAL SOCIAL ONTOLOGY    63

Thus a we-mode attitude involves *thinking and acting from the group's perspective*, and such activities are meant *for the use of members*. The members are *collectively committed* to the content of the attitude, whereas the I-mode lacks the mentioned two features of we-modeness and concerns basically the agent's self-directed (but possibly altruistic) benefit (or "utility") and action. (Tuomela 2002, 2–3, my emphasis)

For example, a number of friends decide to set up a carpool. Most have a we-attitude in the we-mode: I intend to do my part of our organizing the carpool so that we can help reduce pollution and give everyone in our group access to a car. But one group member is in it because he cannot afford his own car, and hence he has a we-attitude in the I-mode: I intend to do my part in organizing the carpool so I can have access to a car.

There are two important aspects of we-modeness: collective commitment and what Tuomela refers to as "forgroupness," which has two parts. First, it means that a certain proposition is collectively available in the group. For example, S = our carpool helps to reduce pollution is "correctly assertable" in group contexts, meaning the carpool members can use S as a premise in deciding what means of transportation to choose. The second part of forgroupness is trying to further the group's goal or interests; that is, trying to do something for the benefit and use of the group, such as taking good care of the car or buying a hybrid rather than a regular car. Tuomela writes as follows:

Basically, acting as a group member is to intentionally act within the group's realm of concern. ... What is required is that the group member in question will intentionally attempt to act in a way related to what he takes to be the group's realm of concern, such that he does not violate the group's constitutive goals, standards, values, and norms (in one word, its "ethos"). (2002, 39)

## 64 CRITIQUE: IDEAL SOCIAL ONTOLOGY

Commitment is understood as a person having bound her will in relation to performing a certain action. A collective commitment means that a person, in virtue of being a group member, has bound her will to promote the group's ethos, such as using the carpool as her primary means of transportation. More precisely, collective commitment amounts to the following:

> I take myself to be committed to s and will act accordingly, in part because I believe that I ought to do what it takes to make or keep s correctly assertable for the group; and I believe that you are also similarly committed to s and will act accordingly, in part because of your similar personal (not necessarily social) normative thoughts; furthermore, we both believe that all this is mutually believed by us. (2001, 113)

In sum, the we-mode is co-extensive with forgroupness and collective commitment. This shows the importance of deontic notions like commitment in Tuomela's theoretical framework. Recall the deonticity claim—deontic notions such as commitment, right, and obligation, are key notions and, indeed, the very glue of society. Tuomela's formal definition of the we-mode runs as follows:

> Agent x, a member of group g, has a certain attitude ATT with content p in the *we-mode* relative to group g in a certain situation C if and only if x has ATT with content p and this attitude (thus also the sentence s expressing it) has been collectively accepted in g as g's attitude, and x is functioning (viz., experiencing, thinking, and/or acting) qua a group member of g and is collectively ATT-committed to content p at least in part for g (viz., for the benefit and use of g) in C. (2002, 36–37)

To make this clearer, consider carpooling again. One of the fundamental goals of this group is to help reduce pollution to preserve the environment for future generations. This is one part of

THE STANDARD MODEL OF IDEAL SOCIAL ONTOLOGY    65

forgroupness: ethos. The belief that carpooling reduces pollution is collectively available to the group members and can be *used as a premise in reasoning*. This is the other part of forgroupness: collective availability. There is *collective commitment* to this goal in the sense that the group members believe they *ought* to preserve the carpool unit. For instance, if a member chooses another means of transportation on a regular basis, this member is boycotted or looked down upon; that is, there are *sanctions* against noncompliers. So, in this group, the goal of organizing a carpool to reduce pollution involves forgroupness and collective commitment. In other words, the group members act in the we-mode regarding this goal. This illustrates the role of deontic notions like commitments in Tuomela's theory and the deonticity claim.

Contrast this case to acting in the I-mode, as a private person. A person in this group privately questions the belief that carpooling reduces pollution. In fact, as a private person, she believes it does not. This case lacks the aspect of forgroupness; her action is not influenced by the group's goal of organizing a carpool to reduce pollution but simply by her personal goal of having access to a car. This individual does not use the group's goal as a premise in deciding what means of transportation to choose. Furthermore, she does not believe that the members of this group ought to organize the carpool to reduce pollution, so she is not committed to upholding the carpool as a group member. This scenario lacks the two aspects of acting in the we-mode: forgroupness and collective commitment. This is an illustration of the bright side of institutions in the sense that the basic concepts in Tuomela's collective acceptance account of sociality involve a reference to the group's benefit and use.

## 1.5.3  Social Practices

A social practice in its core sense is taken to consist of recurrent collective social actions performed for a shared

## 66 CRITIQUE: IDEAL SOCIAL ONTOLOGY

> social reason, expressed in the collective attitude (viz.,
> shared we-attitude) underlying the social practice.
>
> (Tuomela 2002, 3)

Standard social practices include customs and traditions, such as organic farming, eating ham for Christmas, and playing soccer on Sundays. A social practice is understood as "recurrent collective social actions performed for a shared social reason" (2002, 3). Consider a game of soccer played every Sunday; this is a social practice on Tuomela's account because the game is a collective-social action and is played every Sunday, meaning it is recurrent. Furthermore, the players' actions are performed because of a shared we-attitude, which gives them a social reason to play every Sunday. To understand what a social practice is, three concepts need to be made clear: shared we-attitude, social reason, and collective social action.

The notion of a shared we-attitude has already been discussed. A social reason amounts to having a we-attitude. If some people constitute a social practice by their shared we-attitudes, then they have a social reason to perform actions in accordance with this practice. For example, given the shared we-attitude of playing soccer on Sundays, they have a social reason to actually show up for the game.

Tuomela speaks of a *collective social action* because an action can be collective without being social—for instance, a number of people opening up their umbrellas at the same time because it starts raining—and it can be social without being collective (e.g., a single individual takes other people's beliefs into consideration). Tuomela is interested in the intersection of collective and social actions; that is, a certain number of people (collective) taking the others into consideration (social) in various ways, such as opening your umbrella at the same time as other people *because* you are all part of a theatrical performance and are aware of that fact.

# THE STANDARD MODEL OF IDEAL SOCIAL ONTOLOGY    67

Social practices play an important role in Tuomela's theory of social concepts and sociality in general: "the social world is made and maintained by people by means of their social practices" (2002, 5). This differs from Searle's account in which social institutions and institutional facts are the main objects of study. Tuomela adds social practices as an important object of study. It might be a new insight to give social practices such a prominent role in the analysis of the social world. Tuomela views social practices as the underlying building block of society, and of social institutions in particular. Note that Tuomela seems to suggest a rival proposal for the building blocks of institutions—social practices—while Searle's theory includes collective intentionality, imposition of function, and constitutive rules as the building blocks of institutional facts. However, Searle's social facts, which he stipulates are any facts involving the collective intentionality of two or more agents, are broad enough to include Tuomela's notion of a social practice. And Tuomela still regards institutions as the most important class of collective-social items. Let us consider that account.

## 1.5.4  Special Forms of Social Practices: Social Institutions

> Basically, the notion of a social institution (in a general sense) is a reflexive notion concerning a core social practice or practices governed by a system of norms based on collective acceptance for the group's benefit and use.
>
> (Tuomela 2002, 3)

On this definition of an institution, social practices are the building blocks of social institutions. Institutions are special kinds of social practices. The distinguishing features of institutions are that they are governed by a system of norms and that shared we-attitudes in the we-mode are required for the existence of institutions,

68    CRITIQUE: IDEAL SOCIAL ONTOLOGY

which can be seen by the phrase "for the group's benefit and use." On this view, institutions are essentially group phenomena in a rather strong sense because the group members must hold shared we-attitudes in the we-mode in order to constitute and maintain institutions. In connection to this, it is important to note that the feature of the bright side of institutions is built into Tuomela's account of institutions due to his including "the group's benefit and use" as part of the definition.

In addition to shared we-attitudes in the we-mode, norms are required for the existence of institutions. The general idea of a norm is this: if there is a norm in place, everyone in the group ought to perform a certain action once they find themselves in specific circumstances. For example, if there is a norm that all people in your group play soccer on Sundays, you ought to play and are expected to play soccer on Sundays. This norm gives you a social reason for action. There is an element of social power implicit in norms because the participants regard themselves and others as expected, or bound, to play soccer and risk facing sanctions for non-compliance. Here again, we see the importance of deontic notions in Tuomela's theoretical framework. Institutions can be based on two different kinds of norms: rule norms, such as when the state imposes laws on the population, or proper social norms that are based on mutual expectations, such as with the norm of gift-exchange. For full-blown institutions (see b, c, d below) on Tuomela's account, a constitutive norm is required. A constitutive norm adds a *new status* to a social practice, thus turning it into a social institution. The constitutive norm resembles Searle's constitutive rule, but it is wider. If people accept a constitutive norm, they can impose not only deontic powers on a person or object but also a new social or conceptual status. This is the sense in which Tuomela's account of institutions is wider than Searle's. This point can be made clear by considering four types of institutions:

THE STANDARD MODEL OF IDEAL SOCIAL ONTOLOGY 69

(a) institution as norm-governed social practice; (b) institution conferring a new conceptual and social status to some entity (e.g., person, object, or activity); (c) institution conferring a new deontic status and status functions to go with it to the members of the collective in question; (d) institution as an organization involving social positions and a task-right system. (2003, 141)

In our example, shifting the soccer game from a social practice to a social institution requires that the participants act in the we-mode and that there be certain norms related to the practice, such that participants are expected to play on Sundays and there are social sanctions toward non-players. This is an institution in sense (a), and Tuomela regards it as a weak case thereof; it is not a full-blown case because there is no constitutive norm. If our soccer players began to conceptualize and refer to the soccer game as "The Sunday Game" and used this notion in their thinking and acting, the game would have gained a new conceptual and social status in the sense that the use of the concept of the Sunday Game is normatively governed; that is, only soccer games of this kind are to be referred to as "Our Sunday Game," because the game and related activities have a new social and conceptual status. This is an institution in sense (b). If the game developed and became more serious—we might imagine the best players getting some special rights and responsibilities (that is to say, deontic powers)—we have an institution in sense (c). This is Searle's sense of institution. If our soccer team improved further and entered a professional league, and evolved into an organization with financial and administrative personnel, sponsors, coaches, and new players, each with distinct tasks, we would have a task-right system and an institution in sense (d).

Tuomela's account of institutions clearly illustrates the power claim—the enabling and restricting aspects of social and institutional power, such as rights and obligations, are emphasized as key phenomena. In fact, his account is the strongest expression of the power claim because this feature is built into his account of

70 CRITIQUE: IDEAL SOCIAL ONTOLOGY

institutions due to his including "the group's benefit and use" as part of the definition.

In sum, I have shown that Tuomela's account has the scope claim and the foundation claim in common with Gilbert's and Searle's account. I have also shown that this account includes the central elements picked out by Guala—collective intentionality, reflexivity, and performativity—along with two other central elements that I have identified: the deonticity claim and the power claim. Let us turn to paradigmatic features in Tuomela's examples.

## 1.5.5 Paradigmatic Features in Tuomela's Examples

The string quartet paradigm of social groups is clearly present in Tuomela's writings, especially when he develops his analysis of joint action:

> Here are some examples of such joint action: You and I share the plan to carry a heavy table jointly upstairs; to realize this plan, we sing a duet together; we clean up our backyard together; I cash a check by acting jointly with you, a bank teller; we together elect a new president for our country. (2007, 83)

Recall that the string quartet paradigm of social groups amounts to the view that small and egalitarian groups are the paradigmatic example of collective intentionality. The bright side of institutions— the emphasis on the benefits of institutions, such as solving collective action dilemmas and enabling action—is shared with Gilbert's and Searle's examples. In fact, this feature is most strongly expressed in Tuomela's theory because the bright side of institutions is built into his account of institutions due to his including "the group's benefit and use" as part of the definition. Note the use of examples of social practices, organic farming, and soccer games, in relation to the features of paradigmatic social phenomena; the

THE STANDARD MODEL OF IDEAL SOCIAL ONTOLOGY    71

dark side of the social practice of eating ham for Christmas is not mentioned at all.

There are two features of the standard model—the direct social phenomena and the visible aspects of social reality—that I have not yet explicitly addressed in relation to Tuomela's theory of sociality. The main focus of that theory are social entities that are directly dependent on the collective attitudes of a social group; that is, directly dependent on collective intentionality to exist. This is clear both from how the aims of the theory are stated and his use of examples like the Sunday Soccer Game and traveling to Naples together. But Tuomela offers interesting discussions of "derived social phenomena," and he begins to locate them in his theory: "Various unintended and unanticipated consequences (cf. the states of high inflation and unemployment, pollution of the environment) also belong to social artifacts broadly understood. It seems that they generally fall outside the scope of primary social things. Nevertheless, they are often if not in general collective-social in the derived sense, being based on things social in the primary sense" (2001, 131). For Tuomela's "derived social phenomena" I will use the term "indirect social phenomena," and I will broaden it to include intended or anticipated consequences of primary social phenomena.

It is also clear that that main focus is on transparent social phenomena. Most examples (cf., the Sunday Soccer Game, eating ham for Christmas) are of the same type as Tuomela's famous example of squirrel fur counting as money in medieval Finland; that is, social phenomena that are known to the participants in question. In this way, Tuomela's theory shares the emphasis on transparent social phenomena with Gilbert's and Searle's theories.

In sum, Tuomela's collective acceptance account of sociality shares central elements with both Gilbert's and Searle's theories. In some cases, he offers weaker versions of these elements or central claims. For instance, his account of collective intentionality is conceptually non-reductive but ontologically reductive, while Searle's account posits a separate kind of intention and Gilbert's

## 72 CRITIQUE: IDEAL SOCIAL ONTOLOGY

account is both conceptually and ontologically holistic. In other cases, Tuomela offers stronger versions of these central claims than Gilbert and Searle do. For example, that an institution is for the group's benefit and use is built into his definition of institutions which means that emphasizing the bright side of institutions and the enabling and restricting aspects of power, in contrast to its productive aspects, are conceptually related/internal to his account.

There is a model emanating from the discussion of these three theories that shaped the research field of ideal social ontology, what I refer to as "the standard model of ideal social ontology." I detail it in the next section and explain its central elements.

## 1.6 The Standard Model of Ideal Social Ontology

The standard model of ideal social ontology is detailed in the five categories below:

### MAIN AIMS

- *The scope claim:* To offer general theories of the ontology of social and institutional reality.
- *The foundation claim:* Theories in social ontology are the foundation of the social sciences, either by providing and clarifying fundamental concepts or by giving an account of the nature and existence of social phenomena.

### BASIC BUILDING BLOCKS AND FEATURES OF SOCIAL PHENOMENA

- *The collective intentionality claim:* Collective intentionality is the basic building block of social reality and a necessary

THE STANDARD MODEL OF IDEAL SOCIAL ONTOLOGY 73

condition for the existence of either all institutions or standard institutions.

- *The deonticity claim:* Deontic notions such as commitment, right, and obligation, are key notions and, indeed, the very glue of society.
- *The power claim:* The enabling and restricting aspects of social and institutional power, such as rights and obligations, are emphasized as key phenomena.
- *The reflexivity claim:* Primary social phenomena are constituted by "self-fulfilling prophecies."
- *The performativity claim:* Social phenomena are created and maintained by individuals who belong to a given social group through explicit performatives or acts that have the same logical structure as performatives.

## METHOD

- *Generic stylized facts:* Abstract examples, void of much empirical detail, are often used as paradigmatic examples in conducting conceptual analysis.[9]
- *The first-person point of view:* The social world is to be explained through the first-person intentionalist perspective.

## OBJECTS OF ANALYSIS

- *Collective intentionality*, such as walking together.[10]
- *Institutions*, such as money and private property.

---

[9] The term "generic stylized facts" comes from Guala, who urges social ontologists to test their theories against empirical evidence: "But this sort of generic 'stylized facts,' as economists would call them, carry a limited amount of useful information and can only take the ontological investigation thus far. In order to make further progress, more powerful tools of empirical investigation must enter the scene" (2007, 968).

[10] This includes social or collective action and social groups or collectivities as well.

74　CRITIQUE: IDEAL SOCIAL ONTOLOGY

- *Social and institutional facts*, such as the fact that Tom is a U.S. citizen.

### FEATURES OF THE PARADIGMATIC SOCIAL PHENOMENA

- *The string quartet paradigm of social groups:* Small and egalitarian groups as the paradigmatic example of collective intentionality.[11]
- *The bright side of institutions:* Emphasis on the benefits of institutions, such as solving collective action dilemmas and enabling action.
- *The direct social phenomena:* Nearly exclusive emphasis on phenomena that are directly dependent on collective intentionality.[12]
- *The visible aspects of social reality:* Nearly exclusive emphasis on transparent social phenomena such as being a professor.

## 1.6.1　Description of the Standard Model of Ideal Social Ontology

We turn now to a description of the elements of the standard model of ideal social ontology and some of their implications. The collective intentionality claim means that the focus is on collective beliefs understood in a strong sense; they are irreducible to individual beliefs. The implication is that much of social reality goes on in our

---

[11] The string quartet paradigm is Christopher Kutz's expression from *Complicity: Ethics and Law for a Collective Age*. Kutz writes that "philosophers studying collective action have tended to focus only on the fully cooperative form, the string quartet paradigm. Such examples inevitably generate a conception of collective action thick with mutual obligations and egalitarian dispositions: an account unsuited to the depersonalized, hierarchic, bureaucratic, but nonetheless collective institutions that characterize modern life" (2000, 11).

[12] In other words, these theories emphasize the second and third kinds of social kind, but not the first kind in Khalidi's classification of social kinds.

heads, which lessens the importance of the material circumstances of social reality.

The deonticity claim means that the standard model is either silent on or does not acknowledge forms of social power other than the deontic. For instance, there are also effects of deontic power that I call "spillover power," and there is a newly identified form of social power that I call "telic power." These forms of power also provide agents with reasons for actions that can either reinforce or conflict with the reasons for action deriving from deontic power. Neither of these important social phenomena, however, are considered by the standard model of ideal social ontology.

The power claim means that the standard model is either silent on or does not acknowledge the productive aspects of power—how norms and institutions shape our very preferences and parts of our identity in a strong sense. By contrast, the standard model is either concerned with how social practices and institutions coordinate and regulate pre-existing desires (cf., the Sunday Soccer Game and traveling together), or with how social practices and institutions create and shape preferences in a weak sense. For example, there are discussions about how institutions assign rights and obligations to people that they could not have had in the absence of the institutions in question, such as the right to vote and the obligation to pay taxes. Institutions, then, give rise to new rights, new obligations, and thus new preferences to act in accordance with them. But many philosophers and intellectual historians, like Michel Foucault, point out that norms and institutions affect us in a still stronger sense. For example, Mary Wollstonecraft analyzes how the norms of womanhood and institutions like the school system shape women's nature in contradiction to the true virtues of reason; furthermore, she vividly describes how women come to shape their preferences in accordance with a deeply unjust system (cf., the sour grapes phenomenon and the problem of adaptive preferences). Her analysis shows how norms and institutions shape our preferences and parts of our identity in a strong sense (Wollstonecraft 1792). In

## 76 CRITIQUE: IDEAL SOCIAL ONTOLOGY

short, the power claim suggests that the standard model of ideal social ontology omits the productive aspects of power.

The reflexivity claim either means that the standard model cannot account for the first kind of social kind in Khalidi's classification—say, an opaque class system—or that it is silent on such a phenomenon. Whether it cannot take the first kind of social kind into account or whether it is simply silent on it depends on the specific version of the reflexivity claim endorsed by each philosopher. I return to this issue in Chapter 2.

The performativity claim means that the central social phenomena are created and maintained by performatives or acts that have the same logical structure as performatives by a given social group. This also means that the social phenomena in question exist in relation to a social group. The "we" or social group who creates and maintains social phenomena are often taken for granted or not discussed in any depth. The implication is that controversial questions about group membership—or who is part of "we"—are often overlooked.

We turn now to the method of the standard model of ideal social ontology. The theories are developed using traditional conceptual analysis relying on intuitions and linguistic usage. They differ somewhat with respect to the aim and object of the conceptual analysis: Gilbert is primarily concerned with analyzing the intension of everyday concepts that refer to social phenomena, Searle focuses on the extension of the concept of an institutional fact, and Tuomela concentrates on developing new concepts that are useful for theory building in the social sciences.

The examples used are generic stylized facts in the sense that they abstract away from most details and differences between people, other than the phenomena directly under discussion, such as being a friend, professor, public intellectual, or president. This is certainly wise given the aim of providing detailed analyses of social phenomena whose nature it is difficult to grasp but abstracting from most differences between people means that differences of major concern for the nonideal social ontologist are quickly hidden from view. For example, using examples void of details in analyzing the social status of being president and the rights and obligations that come with that role, is silent on the fact that no woman has ever been U.S. president. Similarly, making a list of social statuses consisting of presidents, friends, and public intellectuals—and void of other details—means that patterns making it easier for members of some groups than others, even given the same abilities, to become public intellectuals will drop out of sight.

The objects of analysis are collective intentionality, social statuses or social roles ranging from formal social roles like being a citizen to informal social roles like being a friend, social practices, social institutions, and institutional facts. There is relative consensus among the three theories about what the objects of analysis are while the emphasis is slightly different: Tuomela emphasizes collective-social action and social practices, Searle emphasizes institutions and institutional facts, and Gilbert emphasizes examples of social facts like collective action in the two-person case along with social conventions. However, social phenomena that have to do with less formal institutional structures and with informal roles connected to the productive aspects of power are not among the objects of analysis. Most strikingly, gender (and race) is not taken to be a paradigmatic social phenomena in ideal social ontology. This is relevant in relation to the key question of "Which are the social phenomena?"

The string quartet paradigm of social groups means that the paradigmatic examples of collective intentionality consist of small and often egalitarian groups performing some action together, like going for a walk or making a sauce together. This means that questions about hierarchies, oppression, and domination within groups are scarcely raised.

Emphasizing the bright side of institutions, or their benefits, means that the most frequent examples involve an institution that is of value to the participants. This means that the dark side

# 78   CRITIQUE: IDEAL SOCIAL ONTOLOGY

of institutions—illegitimate power relations like oppression and domination—have not been paid much attention. The question of how an institution might benefit some and not others has also not received adequate attention, particularly when subtle factors limit, or even exclude, some groups from those benefits. Recall that a core criterion in characterizing ideal social ontology and in distinguishing between ideal and nonideal social ontology, is the third criterion—being silent on oppression. Both the string quartet paradigm of social groups and the bright side of institutions relate directly to this criterion because these two features neglect the oppressive aspects of institutions.

Focusing on direct social phenomena like money, in contrast to indirect social phenomena like a recession, again means that the first kind of social kind does not receive much attention. But many nonideal social phenomena are of the first kind of social kind.

Likewise, focusing on transparent social phenomena, such as the fact that someone is a professor, in contrast to social phenomena that might be opaque to the people in a certain society, such as the fact that having a low income is strongly correlated with reduced life expectancy, means that the latter phenomena are hidden from view.

## 1.6.2  Tendencies of Ideal Social Ontology

The standard model of ideal social ontology, developed and argued for in this chapter, only contains aims and assumptions that are shared by all three main theorists of traditional social ontology. There are some strong tendencies, or patterns, that are not shared by all three theories in all instances, but that have still shaped the field. One such pattern is emphasizing social statuses as a central object of analysis (Searle and Tuomela, but not Gilbert). Social groups, social conventions, and social practices are emphasized as objects of analysis (Gilbert and Tuomela, but not Searle).

THE STANDARD MODEL OF IDEAL SOCIAL ONTOLOGY    79

Another pattern is to view language as a basic building block of social reality or language as constitutive of social reality in the sense that language can exist without other institutions, but other institutions cannot exist without language (Tuomela and Searle, but not Gilbert). Another tendency, which stems from collective intentionality, reflexivity, and performativity is focusing on (collective) beliefs while downplaying or forgetting about material circumstances. Still another tendency, which partly stems from the feature of "the visible aspects of social reality" is to pay limited attention to what Ian Hacking calls "looping effects" (Hacking 1995). In general, debunking projects are absent from ideal social ontology. For example, the line between nature and culture is assumed to be where it appears to be (when it comes to biological sex, for instance) while some nonideal social ontologists aim to show that not only gender but also sex is socially constructed (Ásta 2018).

The frequent use of game examples illustrates the tendency of using depoliticized examples.[13] Game metaphors like playing American football and chess are frequent in Searle's writings, as are small groups of people performing actions like making a sauce, pushing a car, or dancing together, which are not obviously political. And in illustrating the complex "metaphysics of ordinary social relations," the example is ordering a beer in Paris. But most people in the world do not live in a well-ordered society like France. However, there is a clear contrast between Searle's examples on the one hand, and Gilbert's and Tuomela's examples on the other hand: more examples come from the political sphere in Searle: someone being the president, someone resigning from office, the fall of a regime, and revolutions.

These examples are often described minimally, with just a sentence or two, and are thus void of many details that would interest a nonideal social ontologist, such as the fact that no woman has

---

[13] This point is raised by Johan Brännmark in his "Contested Institutional facts" (2019a).

## 80 CRITIQUE: IDEAL SOCIAL ONTOLOGY

ever been the president of the United States. The examples of paradigmatic social phenomena are depoliticized in two different but related ways. First, most examples in ideal social ontology are not obviously political (cf., the frequent sports and games metaphors). Second, even when the examples are political, as in the existence of private property and the presidency, this dimension is not fully developed. This contrasts with most examples in nonideal social ontology, such as the civil rights movement and the women's rights movement, which are both obviously political and develop the political to a great extent.

Depoliticized examples are common in Gilbert, although there are some exceptions, including the hyper-responsible woman case, the discussion about the compatibility of coercion and the voluntaristic aspect of joining a plural subject, state of nature references, a mob storming the Bastille, a country invading another country, and whether one can understand heterosexuality as a social convention. However, the clear majority of examples are either depoliticized (cf., the conversationalists or the poetry club) or described in a depoliticized way (cf., the Father and the Sunday steak dinner).[14] The same holds for the examples against which plural subject theory and its rivals are tested (cf., the cafeteria case that is used in arguing against Lewis' account of conventions and in favor of her own account).

Furthermore, the examples used in developing the plural subject account most often share a depoliticized aspect. For instance, the case of the peaceable mushroom pickers recurs in Gilbert's account of social conventions rather than examples of the type "war against all" (1992, 39–40), the gendered dimension of the

---

[14] It should be noted that Gilbert takes her classic example of walking together as involving a political dimension in the sense that the participants' individual interests might be taken into account to varying degrees, if at all (1996, 189).

THE STANDARD MODEL OF IDEAL SOCIAL ONTOLOGY    81

restaurant case, or a country invading another country. She writes as follows of the peaceable mushroom pickers: "This places them on a par—to a degree—with those cases of families, conversationalists, discussions groups and so on, which provide our clearest, most undisputed cases" (1992, 376). This is another indication of what social phenomena are taken for granted as social phenomena. Likewise, in addressing the objection that plural subjects do not exist, Gilbert starts her response by saying, "suppose I look at my mother and my niece, who are chatting, and I say: 'There's a plural subject for you!'" (1992, 433).

## 1.7 Conclusion

The main aim of this chapter was to characterize the standard model of ideal social ontology. This standard model consists of the central elements shared by the three philosophers that shaped the research field of traditional social ontology. I have discussed their theories at some length to justify that each of them shares the central elements that I have identified as part of the standard model of ideal social ontology. An underlying picture of social reality emanates from this standard model, or more precisely, from its basic building blocks and from the features of the paradigmatic social phenomena: that social reality is built on consensus rather than conflict and contestation (cf., the first world in the two-worlds metaphor in the Introduction).

This standard model has a crucial implication: it has shaped what social ontologists take the social phenomena to be analyzed to be: direct, transparent, and deontic social phenomena built on consensus. Consequently, this model offers only a partial view of the social world while claiming it is general, and it is too limited to serve as the foundation of the social sciences. My critique of the standard model of ideal social ontology will question both the scope and foundation claims and argues that they are not fulfilled. This is an internal critique in the sense that I aim to show that the standard model of ideal social ontology's own conditions of adequacy are not met. I turn to the critique in the next chapter.

# 2

# Critique of the Standard Model of Ideal Social Ontology

## 2.1 Introduction

In the previous chapter, I developed the standard model of ideal social ontology by synthesizing central assumptions from three works that have shaped the research field of ideal social ontology. I now turn to the critique of this model. My central claim is that a paradigm shift from ideal to nonideal social ontology is underway and that this shift ought to be fully followed through. The purpose of this chapter is to argue for this central claim by criticizing the standard model of ideal social ontology. This argument is a partial defense of this central claim in the sense that I provide reasons for moving away *from* ideal social ontology here, while I turn to the reasons for moving *to* nonideal social ontology in Part II of this book. I also offer support for the claim that a paradigm shift is underway by summarizing the critique of the collective intentionality claim.

The first reason for shifting away from ideal social ontology is that one essential feature of the standard model of ideal social ontology—the collective intentionality claim—is false. Consequently, the standard model of ideal social ontology is inaccurate. The second reason for shifting away from ideal social ontology is that some essential features of the standard model of ideal social ontology—such as reflexivity and performativity—keep central social phenomena out of sight. Examples include economic classes, opaque social structures, and social power that is invisible

*Nonideal Social Ontology.* Åsa Burman, Oxford University Press. © Oxford University Press 2023.
DOI: 10.1093/oso/9780197509579.003.0003

## 84 CRITIQUE: IDEAL SOCIAL ONTOLOGY

to some or all members of a particular society. These phenomena belong to the first kind of social kind in Khalidi's classification. Neither reflexivity nor performativity holds for the first kind of social kind, so the standard model of ideal social ontology causes this first kind of social kind to simply drop out of sight and makes the social world unduly narrow.

I do not mean to say that proponents of ideal social ontology have intentionally kept these social phenomena hidden. Rather, my claim is that these assumptions—as synthesized in the standard model of ideal social ontology—have shaped the conversation in ideal social ontology in a certain way, with the effect of central social phenomena dropping out of sight. These two reasons—that the standard model of ideal social ontology is inaccurate and that it makes the social world unduly narrow—support the claim that we ought to shift away from ideal social ontology.

Another aim of this chapter is to explain *why* central social phenomena have dropped out of sight. I use the standard model of ideal social ontology as an analytical tool to offer a diagnosis of why these central social phenomena have been neglected. The upshot is that this is not accidental; it is an inevitable result of using this model. Making the analytical relationship between different elements in the model and how these elements mutually reinforce one another clearly reveals why social phenomena, such as those of the first kind of social kind, have dropped out of sight.

The structure of the chapter is as follows: I begin by summarizing objections to the collective intentionality claim to show that this essential feature of the standard model of ideal social ontology is under attack from different philosophical perspectives. I develop what I take to be the strongest objection to the collective intentionality claim—the conceivability argument—by questioning features of the standard model of ideal social ontology, showing that both institutions and institutional facts can exist without collective intentionality. Then, I explain how essential features of this model have the effect of keeping central social phenomena out of sight,

CRITIQUE OF THE STANDARD MODEL    85

such as economic classes, opaque kinds of social facts, and forms of social power other than deontic power. I conclude by drawing out the implications of this chapter: the conditions of adequacy emerging from this discussion, that social power is more central than collective intentionality in understanding the social world, and that the standard model of ideal social ontology has provided a too limited answer to the central question, "Which are the social phenomena?"

## 2.2 The Collective Intentionality Claim Is False

Recall that the second category in the standard model of ideal social ontology—the basic building blocks of social reality—involves five different claims. The most central is the collective intentionality claim. It holds that collective intentionality is a necessary condition for all institutions, or that collective intentionality is a necessary condition for standard institutions, and that collective intentionality is the basic building block of social reality.

I question the different parts separately and begin with the first. My strategy is to offer a conceivability argument which shows that paradigmatic institutions within ideal social ontology, such as money, marriage, and private property, can exist without collective intentionality. This argument aims to show that the first part of the collective intentionality claim—collective intentionality is necessary for the existence of institutions—is false. It is relevant to note that I am far from alone in questioning whether collective intentionality is necessary for the existence of institutions. This gives support to my claim that a paradigm shift from ideal to nonideal social ontology is already underway. In this section I thus describe, rather than evaluate, the various objections to the collective intentionality claim.

86   CRITIQUE: IDEAL SOCIAL ONTOLOGY

For instance, Sally Haslanger (2018) points out that much work in social ontology has overly emphasized intentionality, or what goes on in the heads of individuals, to the near exclusion of the material aspects of social reality. Similarly, Brian Epstein argues against the excessive emphasis on collective intentionality in social ontology and proposes "a more worldly—and less intellectualist—approach to social ontology"; more specifically, Epstein argues that neither collective intentions nor individual intentions are necessary for the existence of social entities such as institutions (2014, 54). Epstein invokes the distinction between grounding and anchoring to show that collective intentionality is just one way among many in which social entities can be grounded and anchored. Grounding refers to the conditions a social entity must satisfy in order to be the kind of entity it is, while anchoring refers to "the facts that put those satisfaction conditions in place" (Epstein 2014, 55). Searle's analysis of money, for instance, holds that something is a dollar bill if it is issued by the Bureau of Engraving and Printing (its grounds). This constitutive rule—bills issued by the Bureau of Engraving and Printing count as dollar bills—is anchored in collective intentionality in the sense that people must accept the constitutive rule for a particular dollar bill to be money. Epstein shows that social entities are not always grounded in intentions (either individual nor collective) and that social entities are not always anchored in collective intentions (2014, 61). Hence, collective intentionality is not necessary for institutions to exist.

Petri Ylikoski and Pekka Mäkelä (2002) reach the same conclusion by arguing that some institutions can exist based only on individual beliefs (cf., persons believing that the monetary value of coins is based on its natural properties) or on individual beliefs and common knowledge (cf., persons believing that coins have monetary value because everyone else believes so). In the same vein, Searle's most recent position (2010) argues that collective intentionality is not necessary for the existence of *institutions* because institutions can be partly constituted by individual intentionality

CRITIQUE OF THE STANDARD MODEL   87

and mutual belief rather than collective intentionality. But collective intentionality is still necessary for the existence of *institutional facts*, according to Searle's refinement of his views.

Frank Hindriks (2017) objects to the claim that collective intentionality is necessary for the existence of institutions by showing that the positive arguments in favor of this claim suggested by Gilbert, Searle, and Tuomela are invalid. One such positive argument is the "social normativity argument," which amounts to the idea that institutions partly consist in social norms and that social norms provide agents with reasons for action that are explained through collective intentionality, which is irreducible to individual intentions and mutual belief. Hence, collective intentionality is necessary for the existence of institutions.[1]

Hindriks concedes that one explanation for institutions giving rise to reasons for action is provided by the social normativity argument. However, this does not imply that collective intentionality is necessary for the existence of institutions because there can be other viable explanations of these reasons for action. For example, one might think that there is no *social* normativity and that the normativity in question is instead *moral*. Until this and other plausible explanations have been ruled out, the social normativity argument cannot establish that collective intentionality is necessary for the existence of institutions.

---

[1] Hindriks offers another objection to the social normativity argument; namely, questioning its basic assumption that norms give rise to reasons for action in the first place: "Practices can be governed by social norms without those norms as such providing people with reasons for action" (2017, 357). Another way to put this point is to say that there is no inherent social normativity in institutions; that is, the norms in question do not give rise to reasons for action. Rather, the explanation of why people follow a given norm is external to that norm, such as fear of disapproval. This, I think, sounds a lot like a sanction, and the notion of sanction is conceptually related to many accounts of norms, so this does not look like a strong objection. According to the social normativity argument, it must be that very norm that gives rise to reasons for action and not something external to the norm itself. So, it would be sufficient to argue that people, in general, follow norms due to wanting to be liked or from fear of disapproval. I think still another objection in this vein would be to grant that there is social normativity but hold that it can be explained in individualistic terms.

## 88 CRITIQUE: IDEAL SOCIAL ONTOLOGY

Johan Brännmark (2019a) offers a different line of reasoning for the same conclusion: Collective intentionality is not necessary for the existence of institutions because highly contested institutions like racist and sexist institutions can exist. These institutions might even be opaque to the people of the society in which they are found. The idea is that contestation and opacity are contrary to collective intentionality, so institutions can exist without collective intentionality. I turn to Brännmark's and Ásta's work in the next chapter on nonideal social ontology along with the works of Sally Haslanger and Katharine Jenkins, among others. In this chapter, I develop both Hindrik's and Ylikoski and Mäkelä's arguments.

### 2.2.1 The Social Construction Argument

One central argument for the thesis that collective intentionality is necessary for the existence of institutions is "the social construction argument,"[2] the short version of which is that all institutions are social constructions and social constructions require collective intentionality for their existence, so collective intentionality is necessary for the existence of institutions.[3] This argument is proposed by both Searle and Tuomela. More specifically, Searle argues that institutional facts can exist only within institutions and that institutions are systems of constitutive rules. All constitutive rules share the same form: "X counts as Y in

---

[2] This is Hindriks' name for the argument.

[3] The third argument, "the functionality argument," states that institutions have functions such as solving collective action problems and coordination problems and either the only way or the best way to solve these problems is through group reasoning, which presupposes irreducible collective intentionality. Again, collective intentionality is allegedly necessary for the existence of institutions. I will not consider this argument further because Searle and Gilbert do not share this understanding; it is only an objection to Tuomela's account and not to the standard model of ideal social ontology, per se.

context C," where the Y-term refers to the status function that is imposed on the X-term. For a status function to perform its function, it requires collective acceptance of the constitutive rules. This contrasts to physical objects like screwdrivers and hammers that can fulfill their physical functions regardless of any collective intentionality.

Hindriks' objection to the social construction argument has the same structure as his objection to the social normativity argument: until other plausible candidates to collective intentionality as the basic building block of institutions have been ruled out, the social construction argument does not establish the thesis that collective intentionality is necessary for the existence of institutions. More specifically, Hindriks objects that Searle has not offered an argument for why these attitudes must be collective for status functions to fulfill their functions. Another viable explanation would be to understand the existence of institutions and how status functions are able to fulfill their functions as consisting partly in individual attitudes and mutual belief, as is common in game theory, for example. Until this and other viable explanations have been ruled out, the social construction argument does not show that collective intentionality is necessary for the existence of institutions; the argument is simply invalid.

I agree with the conclusion that the social construction argument is invalid. But Hindriks' objection does not show that the claim that collective intentionality is necessary for the existence of institutions is false. Rather, it shows that the positive arguments in favor of the claim that collective intentionality is necessary for the existence of institutions are invalid. So, Hindriks' line of reasoning needs to be supplemented with an argument that actually establishes the negation of this claim, and the conceivability argument developed in the next section does precisely that.

90 CRITIQUE: IDEAL SOCIAL ONTOLOGY

## 2.2.2 The Conceivability Argument: Institutions Can Exist Based Partly on Individual Belief and Common Knowledge

It is noteworthy that Searle has recently offered a version of the conceivability argument (2010). The background to this argument is that there has been a major change in one of the basic building blocks between *The Construction of Social Reality* (1995) and *Making the Social World* (2010). It consists of the shift from collective intentionality to individual intentionality and mutual belief.[4] This is a major change in the sense that it is a shift to a completely individualist analysis of the central social phenomenon of institutions. This change has gone surprisingly unnoticed in the literature, with Hindriks being the exception. He emphasizes that Searle now agrees with the claim that collective intentionality is not necessary for the existence of institutions.[5]

Searle (2010) has modified his core notion of "collective acceptance" to now include individual attitudes and mutual belief, in contrast to his former position which stated that collective acceptance is an irreducible notion (1995). In *The Construction of Social Reality*, Searle argues that collective intentionality, understood as an irreducible notion, is necessary for the existence of institutions. In *Making the Social World*, Searle argues that collective intentionality is not necessary for the existence of institutions but is necessary for the existence of institutional facts. More specifically, Searle states that collective intentionality involving "cooperation" is necessary for actions within an institution, such as buying and selling or getting married, while the existence of the institution of money and marriage requires only "collective recognition." Cooperation

---

[4] I say completely individualist here because it was clear from the start that Searle is an ontological individualist, but not a conceptual individualist, in his analysis of collective intentionality.

[5] "Collective attitudes are not needed, he [Searle] argues, because institutions do not require cooperation" (Hindriks 2017, 358).

CRITIQUE OF THE STANDARD MODEL 91

requires irreducible collective intentionality, while collective recognition can be reduced to individual intentionality and mutual belief:[6]

> As a general point, institutional structures require *collective recognition* by the participants in the institution in order to function, but particular transactions within the institution require *cooperation* of the sort that I have been describing. So the couple who are planning marriage accept the institution of marriage prior to actually getting married. This is not a case of cooperating in a form of behavior but simply going along with an institution. But the actual marriage ceremony is an example of cooperation. (Searle 2010, 57)

Searle offers the following argument for changing the theory: to buy a particular house requires cooperation with the seller. The same holds for two people getting married, which requires cooperation with one's partner, so there is an irreducible notion of collective intentionality. But in buying and selling the house, both the buyer and seller must take the existence and validity of money and property for granted. Similarly, in getting married, both people must recognize the existence and validity of the institution of marriage. This requires recognition but not cooperation, according to Searle. Thus, institutions can exist without collective intentionality. In other words, the claim that collective intentionality is necessary for the existence of institutions is false.

Another way to put this point is that *types* of institutional facts such as money or marriage only require individual intentionality and mutual belief, whereas *tokens* of institutions facts, such as the fact that two people are getting married, require irreducible

---

[6] Collective recognition or acceptance is to be understood as a continuum from "enthusiastic endorsement to just going along with the structure" (Searle 2010, 57). It is important to note that collective recognition does not imply that one agrees with or approves of the institution in question.

## 92 CRITIQUE: IDEAL SOCIAL ONTOLOGY

collective intentionality. In other words, collective intentionality is no longer viewed as a basic building block of *institutions*, but it is still a basic building block of institutional *facts*.

I agree that it is conceivable that institutions can exist without collective intentionality understood in an irreducible sense. This is an important result. But the above conceivability argument needs to be strengthened to be fully convincing. In the next section, I show how paradigmatic institutions like monarchy, money, and property can exist partly based on individual intentionality and common knowledge.

### 2.2.3 Monarchy, Money, and Property as Counterexamples

Consider the following reductive account of collective intentionality: "a group $G$ believes that $p$ if and only if (1) most of the members of $G$ believe that $p$, and (2) it is common knowledge in $G$ that (1)"[7] (Gilbert 1996, 198).[8] The housing market in Stockholm serves as an example. The statement, "apartments are occupied by the legal owner or someone whom the legal owner has allowed to occupy them" refers to the institution of private property. Furthermore, nearly all people in Stockholm believe that apartments are occupied by the legal owner or someone whom the legal owner has allowed to occupy them. This is an example of common knowledge, which is understood in the following way: "It is common knowledge in $G$ that $p$ if and only if (a) p; (b) everyone in $G$ knows that $p$; (c) everyone in $G$ knows that (b), and so on, ad infinitum" (Gilbert 1996, 198). This example shows that it is conceivable that institutions

---

[7] This is Margaret Gilbert's version of one of the competitors to the plural subject account, which she refers to as, "a complex summative model: the common knowledge account" (1996, 198).

[8] This particular version is offered by Gilbert in stating a competitor to her plural subject account.

CRITIQUE OF THE STANDARD MODEL    93

like private property can exist without collective intentionality. Consequently, collective intentionality is not necessary for the existence of institutions.

Ylikoski and Mäkelä (2002) offer a similar objection to the central role collective intentionality plays in analyzing social reality: "Our main claims in this paper are that this emphasis on we-attitudes is not well-motivated and that philosophical theories of institutional reality should not restrict themselves to the analyses in terms of we-attitudes" (460). They argue for these claims by offering examples of institutions that do not require collective intentionality to exist. It is worth noting that their counterexamples are restricted to the *maintenance* of institutions as opposed to the *creation* of institutions, and that these counterexamples are directed specifically at Tuomela's and Searle's theories. But these counterexamples can be generalized to question the claim that collective intentionality is necessary for the existence of institutions.

Ylikoski and Mäkelä begin by noting that it is possible for participants to have false beliefs about the nature of an institution—they might believe that God has made the king into a king rather than their own beliefs being (at least) partly constitutive of the king being the king—according to Searle's and Tuomela's theories. They offer two types of counterexamples against the claim that collective intentionality is necessary for the existence of institutions. The first type consists of examples in which an institution can exist based only on individual belief, such as an elementary institution of authority: "A1: All members of community C believe that the authority of their leader X, is his natural property" (2002, 471). However, this is an example of an institutional fact rather than an institution, while a counterexample to an institution is required. A1 can easily be changed into being an objection against institutions, for instance by invoking individual false beliefs about the natural properties of monarchs: A1*: The authority of our past, present, and future monarchs is ordained by God. This is an example of an institution that is maintained purely by individual false beliefs. Still, one

## 94 CRITIQUE: IDEAL SOCIAL ONTOLOGY

might doubt the very maintenance of this institution due to likely instability. This instability might be caused by a lack of common knowledge, so let us add common knowledge to our example.

The second type of example that Ylikoski and Mäkelä offer is intended to show that an elementary institution of money, such as money as metal coins, can exist based on individual beliefs and common knowledge: "C2*: All members of community C believe that other members of their community believe that coins have certain monetary value because they believe that everybody else believes so also" (2002, 473). This is more convincing. It is certainly conceivable that the institution of money can exist in this way. I would even say that it is presently the case for the new cryptocurrencies like Bitcoin and Ethereum.[9] Here, we do not even have to invoke any false beliefs about the natural properties of these coins because their value rests entirely and explicitly on people having beliefs about other people's beliefs in the way stated above. All that needs to be shown is that one paradigmatic institution can exist partly based on individual intentionality and mutual belief and thus does not require collective intentionality to exist. To sum up, my example of private property and C2* offer convincing counterexamples to the thesis that collective intentionality is necessary for the existence of institutions. Hence, this thesis is false.

### 2.2.4 Collective Intentionality Is Not Necessary for the Existence of Institutional Facts

I now turn to showing that collective intentionality is also not necessary for the existence of institutional facts. If this is correct, the role of collective intentionality in analyzing the social world is

---

[9] Thanks to Peter Sahlén for suggesting this example. For illuminating discussions of the nature of money, see Eyja Brynjarsdóttir, *The Reality of Money* (2018), and Asya Passinsky's "Should Bitcoin Be Classified as Money?" (2020).

CRITIQUE OF THE STANDARD MODEL    95

further weakened because it also does not hold for paradigmatic social phenomena such as institutional facts.

I argue for the claim that collective intentionality is not necessary for the existence of institutional facts by offering a new version of the conceivability argument that builds on questioning certain features of the standard model of ideal social ontology. The short version is that it is certainly conceivable that the existence of institutional facts, such as the fact that two people are getting married, only requires individual intentionality and mutual belief. This becomes especially clear if one considers examples from nonideal social ontology.

The longer version is that it is helpful to start with features of the paradigmatic examples in the standard model of ideal social ontology. Some of these features, especially the string quartet paradigm of social groups and the bright side of institutions, have lent false credibility to the collective intentionality claim in the sense that, given these features, it is natural to assume that there is collective intentionality between, say, the parties entering into marriage. Hence, collective intentionality seems to be a necessary condition for the existence of institutional facts. If we were to shift examples from the world of ideal social ontology—in which a marriage ceremony consists of more or less equal parties voluntarily entering into a marriage—to the world of nonideal social ontology, in which there are strategic and less voluntary marriages, then it would be easier to see this. That is, shifting from the bright side of the institution of marriage to its dark side can make this clear.

In a recent historical exhibition about the development of Sweden as a nation state, the strategic nature of marriage was highlighted.[10] For royalty, marriage was often a matter of national strategic interests. In strategic marriages, it is conceivable that the queen had only individual intentionality, and the same is true for

---

[10] The exhibition, called *Gustav Vasa 2020*, was held at Kalmar Castle from April 4 to November 8, 2020.

## 96   CRITIQUE: IDEAL SOCIAL ONTOLOGY

the king. Furthermore, there can be mutual belief or common knowledge about this fact.

Let us apply the reductive account of collective intentionality to this example. A group $G$ believes that $p$ if and only if (1) most of the members of $G$ believe that $p$, and (2) it is common knowledge in $G$ that (1).[11] So, royalty of a given time believes that one gets married out of strategic interest because (1) most royals believe that one gets married out of strategic interest and (2) this is common knowledge among them. Recall the prior analysis of common knowledge: "It is common knowledge in $G$ that $p$ if and only if (a) p; (b) everyone in $G$ knows that $p$; (c) everyone in $G$ knows that (b), and so on, ad infinitum" (Gilbert 1996, 198). Let $G$ be the royalty during this time and $p$ be the statement that one gets married out of strategic interest. So, it is common knowledge among royalty that one gets married out of strategic interest because (a) one does in fact get married out of strategic interest, (b) everyone within the class of royalty knows that one gets married out of strategic interest, and (c) everyone within the class of royalty knows that everyone in that class knows that one gets married out of strategic interest, and so on, ad infinitum. This shows that it is conceivable that institutional facts can exist partly based on individual intentionality and common knowledge rather than collective intentionality. So, collective intentionality is not a necessary condition for the existence of institutional facts. This further limits the role that collective intentionality plays in the analysis of the social world.

I have shown that collective intentionality is not a necessary condition for either institutions or institutional facts to exist. The natural fallback for proponents of ideal social ontology would be to argue that collective intentionality is still a necessary condition for the existence of standard institutions. In fact, Tuomela

---

[11] This is Margaret Gilbert's version of one of the competitors to the plural subject account, which she refers to as "a complex summative model: the common knowledge account" (1996, 198).

does precisely that. Recall the collective intentionality claim that collective intentionality is the basic building block of social reality and is a necessary condition for the existence of either all or standard institutions. I turn now to showing that the latter part of the disjunction—that collective intentionality is necessary for the existence of standard institutions—is false.

## 2.2.5 Collective Intentionality Is Not a Necessary Condition for the Existence of Standard Institutions

In the previous chapter, we learned that the feature that unites Tuomela's four types of institutions is participants having shared we-attitudes in the we-mode, and I turn to considering this important claim. I argue that paying attention to certain features of the standard model, such as the string quartet paradigm of social groups and the bright side of institutions, makes Tuomela's central claim—that shared we-attitudes in the we-mode are required for the existence of institutions—look problematic at best.

We need to be clear on what this claim—that institutions require shared attitudes in the we-mode—amounts to. Is this supposed to hold for all social institutions, for the central class of social institutions, or only for some special cases of social institutions? The three features of Tuomela's collective acceptance account of sociality—reflexivity, performativity, and the distinction between the we-mode and I-mode—are relevant to answering this question. Reflexivity and performativity seem to hold for *all* social institutions. These two features are good candidates for being conceptual truths about institutions because it is hard to imagine a social institution whose participants do not regard as an institution.[12] That is, for something to be a bank or a university,

---

[12] Johan Brännmark disagrees with this conclusion in his "Contested Institutional Facts" (2019a). I discuss his view in the next chapter.

## 98 CRITIQUE: IDEAL SOCIAL ONTOLOGY

people must regard it as a bank or a university. The same holds for performativity; the institution of money is a collective social item created by actions such as our valuing and using money.

But the we-mode has a different status than reflexivity and performativity. It cannot be a conceptual truth about institutions and therefore not hold for all social institutions because we can imagine institutions that exist without the participants holding shared we-attitudes in the we-mode (cf., the conceivability arguments in the previous section). For Tuomela, this problem becomes even more apparent due to the central role that the we-mode plays in his theory. Recall that the we-mode is co-extensive with forgroupness; that is, something being for the group's benefit and use, correct assertability, and collective commitment. As an example, consider institution *a*. At one point in time, this institution was regarded as being beneficial and useful for the group members because it satisfied some of their needs. However, we can imagine background conditions changing and that the participants no longer regarding the institution as beneficial or useful (and also let us assume that it is not for their benefit and use). Still, they maintain the institution out of respect for tradition or simple habit. Consequently, the strongest interpretation, that shared we-attitudes in the we-mode are necessary for all social institutions, is false. Of course, Tuomela is free to claim that this is simply not an institution on his definition and that there is room for revising our everyday concept of an institution. But this claim risks making the phenomena fit the theory rather than the other way around. This shows that the we-mode does not have the same conceptual status as reflexivity and performativity.

Let us consider the second claim, which I think is in line with Tuomela's own view: shared we-attitudes in the we-mode are required for standard institutions, or the central class of social institutions. This is the latter part of the disjunction in the collective intentionality claim. The plausibility of Tuomela's central claim partly depends on what we take "the standard sense" of institutions

CRITIQUE OF THE STANDARD MODEL    99

to mean. My contention is that some of the assumptions Tuomela makes—assumptions that are part of the standard model of ideal social ontology such as the string quartet paradigm of social groups and the bright side of institutions—lend false credibility to the claim that the we-mode is necessary for standard institutions to exist.

Consider the string quartet paradigm of social groups and the bright side of institutions in relation to Tuomela's conception of a standard institution. For Tuomela, typical institutions create order, solve collective action dilemmas, and satisfy needs. The examples of the social institutions Tuomela chooses to discuss are generally of the same type; the group who constitutes the institution is relatively small and well defined in the sense that conflict about group membership is not an issue (cf., the string quartet paradigm of social groups), and the institution is for the benefit and use of the group (cf., the bright side of institutions). The examples appear to be chosen with the above characterization of institutions in mind: creating order, satisfying needs, and solving collective action dilemmas. The examples represent a certain type of institutions and their enabling aspects. The Sunday Soccer Game and postal systems are discussed as examples of standard institutions, while the example of a dictator who imposes laws on the population is understood as an exception (2003, 145).

But there are many other types of institutions, and if we expand the examples to include institutions of various types, some enabling and some coercive, standard institutions are not always for the benefit and use of the group. If we view institutions from a conflictual rather than a consensual perspective, the picture that emerges is different even radically so: institutions also make it possible for some groups to dominate others, for leaders to keep populations in check, and can create and reinforce profound inequalities between groups and individuals. None of these features is internal to institutions; we can imagine institutions that neither satisfy needs nor enable domination. In reality, some institutions do the former,

100 CRITIQUE: IDEAL SOCIAL ONTOLOGY

some the latter, and many do both, along with other things. What we pick out as central features of institutions and regard as typical or standard institutions depends on our perspective. If one does not pay attention to social power, then the dark side of institutions, such as their capacity to enable domination, becomes invisible. By making the coercive aspects of institutions invisible and assuming egalitarian groups with similar interests, the claim that participants regard institutions as being for their benefit and use looks unproblematic, and insufficient attention to social power lends specious support to the we-mode claim. I have argued that being attentive to social power shows that Tuomela's central claim—that the we-mode is required for the existence of standard social institutions—is simply too demanding a requirement. This means that collective intentionality is not a necessary condition for the existence of standard institutions.

The upshot of this discussion is that collective intentionality is not necessary for the existence of either institutions or standard institutions; it is also not necessary for the existence of institutional facts. Consequently, the first part of the collective intentionality claim—collective intentionality is the basic building block of social reality—is also false. To sum up, I have shown that an essential feature of the standard model of ideal social ontology—the collective intentionality claim—is false. Consequently, the standard model of ideal social ontology is inaccurate. In the next section, I turn to the second reason for moving away from ideal social ontology.

## 2.3 How the Standard Model of Ideal Social Ontology Makes Central Social Phenomena Drop Out of Sight

My aim is to show how certain features of the standard model of ideal social ontology make central social phenomena drop out of sight, such as the first kind of social kind, including economic

CRITIQUE OF THE STANDARD MODEL    101

classes and forms of social power other than deontic power. To give enough detail, I discuss economic classes in relation to Gilbert's plural subject theory, the first kind of social kind in relation to Searle's construction of social reality, and the role of social power in relation to Tuomela's collective acceptance account of sociality. I offer three specific arguments to show how this model renders central social phenomena invisible. First, plural subject theory cannot take economic classes to be paradigmatic social phenomena due to the definition of a social group upon which it relies. Second, Searle's construction of social reality cannot capture opaque kinds of social facts due to the self-referentiality of concepts that refer to social phenomena. Third, Tuomela's collective acceptance account relies on an underdeveloped notion of social power and pays inadequate attention to this central concept. I then generalize these objections to show how they target the standard model of ideal social ontology rather than only one specific theory or another.

## 2.3.1 Economic Classes Cannot Be Paradigmatic Social Phenomena

In the previous chapter, we learned that Gilbert's plural subject theory provides both a general account of social phenomena and detailed accounts of specific concepts that refer to central social phenomena, such as that of a social group. Gilbert's definition of a social group runs as follows: "Human beings X, Y, and Z constitute a collectivity (social group) if and only if each correctly thinks of himself and the others, taken together, as 'us*' or 'we*' " (1992, 147). Consequently, only sets of people that have some degree of awareness of themselves as a social group count as a social group.

Gilbert addresses the objection that her account of social groups is too narrow because it excludes the Marxian sense of class as a social group (226–230). Her reply draws on the distinction between populations who are aware of themselves as a group and those who

102 CRITIQUE: IDEAL SOCIAL ONTOLOGY

are not. The former—say, workers after consciousness-raising—count as a social group, while the latter—say, workers whose racial divisions outweigh their similar economic interests—do not. Gilbert correctly concludes, I think, that these are two significantly different kinds of phenomena. The next step in her reply is that the term "social group" should thus be reserved for groups who are aware of themselves as a group. Two types of reasons are offered. The first, which Gilbert does not consider conclusive, is an appeal to linguistic intuitions—*socius* means "ally" in Latin—and thus refers to groups that are aware of themselves as groups. The second is that populations who are not aware of themselves as groups are not on sociologists' lists of social groups.

But another, and for me more important, part of the objection remains: *what logical space is there, if any, for economic classes that are not aware of themselves as groups in plural subject theory?* This question is not answered, despite consideration of the idea that classes affect how things are in a given society and how that society's members fare. And what goes for economic classes goes for some other populations, such as women because gender also deeply affects how things are in a given society and how society's members fare.[13]

I think there is a methodological reason behind this: populations that are not aware of themselves as groups do not sit easily with the first-person intentionalist point of view. "*Intentionalism* is the view that according to our everyday collectivity concepts, individual human beings must see themselves in a particular way in order to constitute a collectivity" (Gilbert 1992, 12). This first-person intentionalist perspective contrasts with a third-person systems view that emphasizes features of the collectivity that might only be discernible to outside observers. Gilbert adopts the intentionalist

---

[13] Iris Marion Young develops a fruitful alternative to intentionalism in her "Gender as Seriality: Thinking about Women as a Social Collective" (1994).

CRITIQUE OF THE STANDARD MODEL    103

first-person point of view, along with Searle and Tuomela, and this is reflected in the standard model of ideal social ontology.

This is not to say that the first-person intentionalist view *necessarily* excludes populations that are not aware of themselves as social groups. One could, for instance, argue that these systemic features are either intended or unintended consequences of plural subject phenomena. Still, this methodological stance serves to exclude them from the list of *paradigmatic* social phenomena and thus hide them from view.

There is a related deeper problem for plural subject theory: taking economic classes and the population of women to be central social phenomena is contrary to one of Gilbert's main claims; namely, that "our general concept of a social phenomenon as equivalent to that of a phenomenon of plural subject-hood" (1992, 442). This claim *necessarily* excludes populations that are not aware of themselves as social groups—such as economic classes and women—from being core social phenomena.

Recall that Gilbert shares this first-person intentionalist perspective with Searle and Tuomela. This methodological stance is reflected in the standard model of ideal social ontology. The upshot is that this methodical stance has excluded populations who are not aware of themselves as groups, such as economic classes and women, from the list of paradigmatic social phenomena. These theories are not designed to take these types of social phenomena into account.

To generalize, a methodological feature of the standard model of ideal social ontology—the first-person intentionalist perspective— contributes to ideal social ontology making phenomena that are not discernible from the participants' own perspective invisible, such as economic classes, women who are not aware of themselves as a group, and other systemic features. Another related objection is that the self-referentiality of concepts that refer to social phenomena excludes social phenomena of which the participants are not aware: opaque kinds of social facts.

## 104 CRITIQUE: IDEAL SOCIAL ONTOLOGY

## 2.3.2 The First Kind of Social Kind Drops Out of Sight

Many social ontologists agree on and point out a peculiar feature—that concepts that describe the social world, in contrast to concepts that describe the natural world, are self-referential. This is captured by the reflexivity claim in the standard model of ideal social ontology. Searle offers the following characterization of self-referentiality:

> Logically speaking, the statement "A certain type of substance, x, is money" implies an indefinite inclusive disjunction of the form "x is used as money or x is regarded as money or x is believed to be money, etc." But that seems to have the consequence that the concept of money, the very definition of the word "money" is self-referential, because in order that a type of thing should satisfy the definition, in order that it should fall under the concept of money, it must be believed to be, or used as, or regarded as, etc., satisfying the definition. For these sorts of facts, it seems to be almost a logical truth that you cannot fool all the people all the time. (Searle 1995, 32)

In short, the self-referentiality of concepts that refer to social phenomena means that for something (S) to be an institutional fact, it must be regarded or thought of or used as S. This means that our beliefs are partly constitutive of the phenomenon in question, which explains why the relation of "what seems to be the case comes prior to what is the case" holds for institutional facts. Searle writes of observer-relative features, which include institutional facts, "for any observer-relative feature F, *seeming to be F* is logically prior to *being F* because—appropriately understood—seeming to be F is a necessary condition of being F" (1995, 13, emphasis in original).

Amie Thomasson (2003) argues that Searle's theory cannot capture power structures and economic phenomena like inflation and

## CRITIQUE OF THE STANDARD MODEL 105

recession due to this self-referentiality. She challenges the idea that all concepts that refer to social phenomena are self-referential and that it is a necessary condition for all observer-relative features, including institutional facts, that "seeming to be F is a necessary condition of being F" by pointing out that there can be social facts no one is aware of:

> But the idea that all social concepts are self-referential entails that there cannot be social facts of any *kind* whose existence members of that society do not know about—for if there are social facts of a given kind F, people must accept that certain things (or things of certain sorts) are F (and, since their collective acceptance makes it so, they must collectively be right about what things or sorts of things are F). But this severely limits the role the social sciences can play in expanding human knowledge—many of the discoveries of greatest moment in the social sciences are of things such as economic cycles, class systems, and power structures, that are capable of existing even if no one believes that anything of the kind exists, or even if no one entertains the relevant concept at all or has prior beliefs about anything of the kind. (Thomasson 2003, 275)

This objection is central. If Searle's theory cannot handle it, its potential for explaining the social world is severely limited. Furthermore, the claim that social ontology is the foundation of the social sciences is jeopardized.

In previous writings (Andersson 2007), I have argued that one can reduce macro-level phenomena, like inflation and recessions, to a collection of micro-level phenomena and thus that Searle's theory has the theoretical resources to respond to Thomasson's objection. Due to the problem of multiple realizability, I have since changed my position and now hold that macro-level phenomena are dependent on but not reducible to micro-level phenomena. This means that a "location problem" emerges for social

# 106 CRITIQUE: IDEAL SOCIAL ONTOLOGY

ontologists: macro phenomena, including opaque kinds of social facts, need to be located in our theories of the social world.

In fact, I think Thomasson's objection can be developed into an objection to the standard model of ideal social ontology rather than being only an objection to Searle's theory, and that it is even more general than hitherto assumed—it holds not only for opaque kinds of social facts but also for the first kind of social kind, whether transparent or opaque.

Let us begin with the model. I think Thomasson's conclusion that Searle's theory cannot take opaque kinds of social facts into account is correct, due to Searle's strong interpretation of self-referentiality. But Tuomela, for instance, does not interpret self-referentiality in such a strong way—holding for *all* concepts that refer to social phenomena. In this way, there is logical space for *sui generis* social phenomena of the first kind of social kind in Tuomela's theory. This weaker interpretation of self-referentiality is captured by the reflexivity claim of the standard model of ideal social ontology: primary social phenomena are constituted by "self-fulfilling prophecies" because they refer to primary social phenomena rather than all social phenomena.

The same is true of the performativity claim—it is given a weaker interpretation in the sense that it quantifies paradigmatic rather than all social phenomena. Recall the performativity claim: paradigmatic social phenomena are created and maintained by individuals who belong to a given social group through explicit performatives or acts that have the same logical structure as performatives. This means that it is not the case that the standard model of ideal social ontology *cannot* account for opaque kinds of social facts and more generally the first kind of social kind. However, the reflexivity claim and the performativity claim exclude the first kind of social kind from being among the primary and paradigmatic social phenomena because neither reflexivity nor performativity hold for these phenomena.

CRITIQUE OF THE STANDARD MODEL 107

I agree with the view that reflexive social phenomena are primary in the sense that the first kind of social kind derive from and depend on them for their existence. Because social ontology is still a comparatively new field in analytic philosophy, it is natural and sensible to start by analyzing the primary social phenomena, and the field of ideal social ontology might not yet have gotten around to analyzing the indirect social phenomena. But this means that ideal social ontology still lacks an analysis of the nature of the first kind of social kind and how it exists.

But I strongly disagree with the view that paradigmatic social phenomena are only of the second and third kinds of social kind. I take some instances of the first kind of social kind, such as economic classes and social structures, to be among paradigmatic social phenomena. In relation to this, note that reflexivity and performativity hold for the third kind of social kind and for tokens of facts belonging to the second kind of social kind, but they do not hold for the first kind of social kind. This means that the reflexivity claim and the performativity claim serve to deemphasize and thus become silent on social phenomena belonging to the first kind of social kind. In this way, the standard model of ideal social ontology makes the first kind of social kind drop out of sight.

In the next section, I show that opaque forms of power and social power in general are paid inadequate attention due to this model, which has resulted in an underdeveloped and overly narrow view of social power.

### 2.3.3 Social Power Has Played Too Small a Role in Analyzing the Social World

One important conclusion from this chapter is that the concept of collective intentionality has played too central a role in the analyses of social phenomena. In this section, I show that the opposite is

## 108    CRITIQUE: IDEAL SOCIAL ONTOLOGY

true of social power: this concept has been given inadequate attention and been afforded too small a role in analyzing social reality.

To offer more detail, let us consider this problem in relation to Tuomela's theory. In the previous chapter, we saw that social power is *implicitly* captured by Tuomela's definition of institution, although it is not singled out by the collective acceptance account. Rather, that account singles out reflexivity, performativity, and the distinction between the I-mode and the we-mode. Norms are, however, part of the definition of an institution and have both an enabling aspect that is captured by the constitutive norms and a coercive aspect, as in the form of legal and social sanctions for non-compliance. But there is no discussion of different forms of social power in Tuomela's account. It is notable, and even strange, that Tuomela does not provide a discussion of this concept in his account of social institutions because he makes many other important distinctions and classifications of institutions, collective acceptance, and norms. But there is no general account or classification of social power.

This is a limitation for various reasons. First, one of his central aims is to provide a conceptual system for theory building in the social sciences. According to his own standards, then, the account is limited because much social science is about understanding different forms of social power and what to do about illegitimate power. Of course, he has highlighted the significance of social action and social practices, which is helpful, but power, always one of the most important concepts, is missing. This puts one of his central aims into question.

Second, Tuomela claims that his account of institutions should capture social scientists' view of institutions. However, social scientists as varied as Émile Durkheim, Michel Foucault, and Pierre Bourdieu have shown an abiding interest in the relation between institutions and power. Foucault, especially, would be skeptical of any view emphasizing institutions as solutions to collective action dilemmas and satisfying needs.

CRITIQUE OF THE STANDARD MODEL 109

Any adequate account of institutions ought to capture power as an essential feature of institutions. Power is *implicitly* part of institutions in Tuomela's definition because norms are required for the existence of institutions. Norms are related to both legal and social sanctions, which are forms of coercive power. Tuomela's constitutive norm involves the enabling aspects of institutions; he focuses on how institutions make new kinds of actions possible. Searle's analysis of institutional facts as deontic powers makes explicit the idea that power is an internal feature of institutions. Searle also provides an initial characterization, definition, and classification of power, while Tuomela does not.

The general theme of Tuomela's writings is discussing cooperative cases rather than cases of conflict and contestation (cf., the first world in the two-worlds metaphor); consequently, the role and status of power is consistently downplayed in his theory. The same is true of Gilbert's writings. There is hardly any discussion of social power in Gilbert's plural subject theory. By contrast, Searle's construction of social reality emphasizes deontic power as a key theoretical component.

There are two main lessons to draw from the discussion of this objection. First, social power is a far more important concept than collective intentionality in understanding institutions. The reason is that power is an internal feature of all institutions, while collective intentionality has been shown above not to be a necessary condition for institutions or for standard institutions. The second, related lesson is that the single-minded emphasis on deontic power in ideal social ontology—captured by the power claim of the standard model of ideal social ontology—has the effect of downplaying the importance of the various forms of social power that exist, and those other forms of social power drop out of sight. In short, the conception of social power in ideal social ontology is underdeveloped and too narrow, according to its own standard because it puts the foundation claim—theories in social ontology are the foundation of the social sciences—into question.

## 110 CRITIQUE: IDEAL SOCIAL ONTOLOGY

### 2.3.4 Conditions of Adequacy Emanating from the Three Objections

To sum up, I have shown how the standard model of ideal social ontology makes central social phenomena drop out of sight, such as collectivities that are not aware of themselves as social groups but whose membership still affects the life chances of individuals to a great extent, such as economic classes and women. This is mainly due to the first-person intentionalist perspective of the standard model of ideal social ontology. These collectivities are also examples of the first kind of social kind, and I have shown how such examples, whether opaque or transparent, end up hidden from view due to the reflexivity and performativity claims of the standard model of ideal social ontology. Furthermore, I have shown how this model makes forms of social power other than deontic power drop out of sight. This is due to the following features of the standard model of ideal social ontology: the power claim, the bright side of institutions, and the string quartet paradigm of social groups. This means that there are conditions of adequacy stemming from the critique of the standard model of ideal social ontology. Showing the limits of that standard model reveals what limits need to be overcome in designing new theories.

Two conditions of adequacy emerge for my own account. The first is that the first kind of social kind needs to be captured by our theories of the social world. That is, I take some phenomena belonging to the first kind of social kind, such as economic classes (cf., the objection to Gilbert's theory) and opaque kinds of social kinds like social structures (cf., the objection to Searle's theory), to be paradigmatic social phenomena that must be analyzed and located in any complete theory of the ontology of social reality. This is related to the methodological point that one ought to choose examples of social phenomena that are varied in both content and form. The second condition of adequacy is to offer a more comprehensive theory of social power, which is needed to fulfill the

CRITIQUE OF THE STANDARD MODEL 111

two main aims of the standard model of ideal social ontology—the scope claim and the foundation claim—and that social power has been shown to be more central than collective intentionality for understanding institutions. In the next section, I turn to my diagnosis of why these central social phenomena have dropped out of sight by using the standard model of ideal social ontology as an analytical tool.

## 2.4 Using the Standard Model of Ideal Social Ontology as an Analytical Tool

How did we end up here? In other words, how did we end up with an essential claim of the standard model of ideal social ontology being false? And how do we address the issue that some of its central assumptions have the effect of making central social phenomena drop out of sight? The short answer is that there is a certain interplay between the different categories in this model—the basic building blocks in combination with the features of the paradigmatic social phenomena and the philosophical method—that makes the social domain unduly narrow. Consequently, the standard model of ideal social ontology either excludes or is silent on social phenomena taken to be central by social scientists and nonideal social ontologists.

The longer answer is this: first, consider the interplay between the category of "basic building blocks" and the category of "features of the paradigmatic social phenomena" in more detail. These two categories reinforce each other, thus making each category seem more plausible than it actually is. Take, for instance, the nearly exclusive emphasis on social phenomena that are directly dependent on collective intentionality to exist and transparent to the people in question. This emphasis results in the reflexivity and performativity claims seeming plausible because both performativity and reflexivity hold for such social phenomena, but neither performativity

## 112 CRITIQUE: IDEAL SOCIAL ONTOLOGY

nor reflexivity hold for *all* social phenomena. Consider, for example, an indirect social phenomena like a particular economy being in a state of inflation or a social phenomenon like implicit bias toward certain members of a society that is likely to be opaque to those people with the bias.

The relation also obtains in the other direction: once reflexivity and performativity are viewed as basic building blocks of social phenomena, it is natural to choose examples that display directness and transparency. Another way to put this point is to say that the one-sided diet of examples in ideal social ontology—in both content and form—has lent false credibility to the performativity and reflexivity claims. Recall the many game metaphors, such as American football, chess, and the Sunday Soccer Game, and the recurrent examples of money, presidents, and professors. It is important to note that these examples are one-sided not only in content but also in form—they are instances of the third and second kinds of social kind, but not the first kind of social kind. For the third kind of social kind, reflexivity holds for both types and tokens, and for the second kind of social kind, reflexivity holds for types of social facts. But for the first kind of social kind, reflexivity holds neither for types nor for tokens of facts. The same is true of performativity: the first kind of social kind is not performatively created and maintained by individuals who belong to a given social group. Rather, it is an intended or unintended consequence of the second and third kinds of social kind. And once reflexivity and performativity are firmly put in place as basic building blocks, then the first kind of social kind is excluded from being seen as a paradigmatic social phenomenon. Consequently, it is shown little interest.

Up to this point, I have shown how the categories of "basic building blocks" and "paradigmatic features of social phenomena" reinforce each other with two significant effects: they make each category seem more plausible than it actually is, and the first kind of social kind drops out of sight.

CRITIQUE OF THE STANDARD MODEL    113

## 2.4.1 The Culpability of the Paradigmatic Features

I now add a third ingredient—the philosophical method—to this mix to show how it also contributes to making the social world unduly narrow. Recall that the category "philosophical method" in the standard model of ideal social ontology consists in the first-person intentionalist perspective and the use of generic, stylized facts. As I have previously shown, the first-person intentionalist perspective excludes populations that are not aware of themselves as social groups from being paradigmatic social phenomena. More generally, this methodological stance contributes to excluding social phenomena that are opaque to the people in question, such as opaque social structures, from being viewed as paradigmatic social phenomena. Most of these phenomena belong to the first kind of social kind. Consequently, opaque social phenomena have been paid little attention. Again, assuming this methodological stance makes it more natural to choose examples that are known to the people in question, such as transparent social phenomena. This, in turn, supports the methodological stance because it works well for this type of social phenomenon.

It once again becomes clear how categories in the standard model of ideal social ontology reinforce each other. This time the "philosophical method" and "the paradigmatic features of social phenomena" make each category seem more plausible than it actually is, and they cause opaque kinds of social facts to drop out of sight. In relation to the philosophical method, it is also relevant to consider *how* paradigmatic examples are handled. Take, for instance, the standard examples of being a president, a student, someone's friend, or going for a walk together. Using being the president as an abstract and highly stylized example to understand the existence conditions and the nature of certain social phenomena, such as institutional facts, serves that particular purpose well: to make progress on difficult philosophical projects, it is wise to simplify where possible to highlight the aspects under investigation. But

114   CRITIQUE: IDEAL SOCIAL ONTOLOGY

presenting the examples in this way hides from view, or means that one is silent on, the fact that no woman has ever been the U.S. president. This is an example of a type of fact under scrutiny in nonideal social ontology, or more generally, how gender and race affect the life chances of individuals. And, as noted previously, gender and race are not taken to be paradigmatic social phenomena in ideal social ontology.

The generic stylized facts—characteristic of ideal social ontology—have another unfortunate consequence; they serve to hide types of social power other than deontic power. Consider the standard example of being a professor or a student, which is often used well to explain the deontic relations between professors and students. But again, using this as an abstract and highly stylized example means that other aspects of being a professor, or a student for that matter, become silenced or hidden from view, such as the likelihood that a particular student from a certain class, gender, or race starts studying at university in the first place or the likelihood that this student will pursue a degree in a particular area. A recent empirical study showed, for instance, that philosophy in Sweden attracted a disproportionate share of Swedish-born white males with a middle- or upper-class background, compared to other subjects in the humanities (Olsson-Yaouzis et al. 2018). Again, this type of fact is central to nonideal social ontology and the social sciences (even though class has been neglected up to this point in works in nonideal social ontology)[14] because it dives into the life chances of individuals; recall here the second world of social ontology. This is a different type of fact than the deontic relations between professors and students, and it is not transparent to the

---

[14] I am referring to analytic social ontology here, for instance the works of Ásta, Haslanger, Jenkins, and Dembroff, so social ontology in a rather narrow sense. If we expand social ontology to include Marxist philosophers it is certainly not true that they have ignored class, and they, along with feminist scholars, are plausibly taken as philosophers doing nonideal social ontology. Thanks to Katharine Jenkins for pointing this out.

CRITIQUE OF THE STANDARD MODEL   115

participants in questions in the way that deontic power relations are; rather, it is discoverable through statistical investigation. In this way, generic stylized facts lend specious support to the deontic power claim of the standard model of ideal social ontology.

## 2.5  Results from Using the Standard Model as an Analytical Tool

I have shown how some elements of the standard model of social ontology—the basic building blocks, the paradigmatic features of the social phenomena, and the philosophical method—have served to reinforce one another with three consequences. First, each category seems more plausible than it actually is, especially if it were considered in isolation. Second, this interplay has made the social world unduly narrow because it either excludes or remains silent on central social phenomena, such as instances of the first kind of social kind and forms of social power other than deontic power. Third, once the basic building blocks were put firmly in place, they strongly influenced the answer to the central question of which phenomena are social phenomena? Another way to put this point is that the standard model of ideal social ontology has shaped what social ontologists take the social phenomena to be analyzed to be: direct, transparent, and deontic social phenomena built on consensus. Taken together, this meant that social reality came to resemble the first world built on consensus, rather than the second world built on conflict and contestation in the two-worlds metaphor from the introductory chapter.

These consequences bear on the very purpose of the standard model of ideal social ontology. Recall that the purpose has two main aims: to offer general theories of the ontology of the social world and to be the foundation of the social sciences. Through our investigation of the standard model, we can now see how the first aim is not fulfilled: this model offers theories of one domain

116 CRITIQUE: IDEAL SOCIAL ONTOLOGY

of social reality, but it has not yet offered a general theory. Due to this, the second aim is also called into question; social scientists are often concerned with phenomena from the first kind of social kind, such as economic classes. This kind of social phenomena needs to be located in the model for it to serve as the foundation of the social sciences. Another way to put this point is to say that some social phenomena of primary concern to social scientists are not viewed as central, or paradigmatic, social phenomena in the standard model of ideal social ontology. Consequently, there is neither an account of these social phenomena nor an explanation of how they are located. This shows that the second aim also remains unfulfilled.

## 2.6 Conclusion

I have argued for the claim that we ought to move away from the standard model of ideal social ontology. The first reason is that one essential assumption of the standard model of ideal social ontology—the collective intentionality claim—is simply false, so the model itself is inaccurate. I have shown that the collective intentionality claim is false by providing conceivability arguments built on questioning various features of the standard model of ideal social ontology: examples of institutions and institutional facts taken to be paradigmatic by ideal social ontologists (cf., money, marriage, and private property) can exist partly based on individual beliefs and common knowledge rather than collective intentionality. This possibility reveals itself once one moves away from the string quartet paradigm of social groups and the bright side of institutions. In other words, the counterexamples offered in these conceivability arguments contradict two features in the standard model of ideal social ontology.

The second reason is that this model has the effect of making central social phenomena drop out of sight. Consequently, the

CRITIQUE OF THE STANDARD MODEL 117

standard model of ideal social ontology makes the social world unduly narrow. I have shown this to be a problem even by its own standards because the purpose is to offer general theories of the social world and to be the foundation of the social sciences. These two reasons—that this model is inaccurate and that it makes central social phenomena drop out of sight—mean that we ought to move away from ideal social ontology.

The standard model of ideal social ontology then served as an analytical tool. I used this model to offer a diagnosis of why we ended up with one essential claim being false and certain central social phenomena dropping out of sight: by displaying the analytic relationships between the essential elements of this model, it becomes clear that this result is not accidental but is instead an inevitable fallout of these essential elements and the interplay between them. For example, I have shown how the reflexivity and performativity claims mean that social phenomena displaying these very features are viewed as paradigmatic social phenomena. And once the standard examples used in theorizing display these features, performativity and reflexivity come to be viewed as even more central than they really are.

This interplay between the essential elements of the standard model of ideal social ontology has a significant consequence: it serves to decide which social phenomena are to be analyzed. Another way to put this point is that say that this model has decided what phenomena count as social phenomena and has decided wrongly because the phenomena chosen are too narrow and one-sided. The result is that the social world becomes unduly narrow by taking one domain of social reality to be general. This points to a central and substantial disagreement in the field of social ontology—especially between ideal and nonideal social ontologists—in their answers to the core question: Which phenomena are the social phenomena?

Three conditions of adequacy emanate from this chapter. The first is to view the first kind of social kind as a paradigmatic social phenomenon and thus locate it within my theory from the start. The second is to take the social phenomena that dropped out of sight partly due to the use of generic stylized facts as central. I am here thinking of class, race, and gender as examples of paradigmatic social phenomena. Related to these two conditions of adequacy is the third: there are forms of social power other than deontic power. Recall also that one substantial result of the analysis presented in this chapter is that social power is much more central to understanding institutions and social reality than collective intentionality is. Consequently, a general theory of the social world needs to take this into account and develop a more comprehensive theory of social power. In the coming chapters, I argue for the claim that we ought to shift to nonideal social ontology by offering an account that meets the above conditions of adequacy.

# PART II
# RECONSTRUCTION
*Nonideal Social Ontology*

# 3

# Nonideal Social Ontology

## 3.1 Introduction

A central claim of this book is that there is a paradigm shift from ideal to nonideal social ontology underway, and that this shift ought to be fully followed through. In the previous chapter, I argued for the claim that we ought to shift *away* from ideal social ontology by criticizing the standard model of ideal social ontology. In this chapter, I offer a partial argument for the claim that we ought to shift *to* nonideal social ontology. This argument requires a characterization of nonideal social ontology (cf., the second world in the two-worlds metaphor). I thus offer a characterization of nonideal social ontology—including a special branch of nonideal social ontology called emancipatory social ontology—by showing what influential accounts of nonideal social ontology have in common. I discuss Ásta's conferralism and Johan Brännmark's theory of nonideal institutions as examples of nonideal social ontology, Sally Haslanger's analyses of gender and race, and Katharine Jenkins' account of ontic injustice and ontic oppression as examples of the special subcategory of nonideal social ontology called emancipatory social ontology.

The second step in the argument for the claim that we ought to shift to nonideal social ontology is to show what important features nonideal social ontology have in common and how these features differ from the standard model of ideal social ontology. More specifically, I argue that these differences mean that nonideal social ontology can overcome some of the limitations of ideal social

*Nonideal Social Ontology.* Åsa Burman, Oxford University Press. © Oxford University Press 2023.
DOI: 10.1093/oso/9780197509579.003.0004

## 122 RECONSTRUCTION: NONIDEAL SOCIAL ONTOLOGY

ontology, such as an overemphasis on collective intentionality and too little attention to oppression.

We turn now to the first example of nonideal social ontology, namely, Ásta's conferralist account.

## 3.2 Conferralism about Social Properties

> Consider this scenario: you work as a coder in San Francisco. You go into your office where you are one of the guys. After work, you tag along with some friends at work to a bar. It is a very heteronormative space, and you are neither a guy nor a gal. You are an other. You walk up the street to another bar where you are a butch and expected to buy drinks for the femmes. (Ásta 2018, 73)

In introducing the coder example, Ásta highlights social properties which have hitherto been neglected in ideal social ontology; what she refers to as "communal properties." The new theory presented in *Categories We Live By*—the conferralist framework—promises to capture a large and crucial part of social reality with a few basic elements. It accounts for both communal properties (being cool, being a popular footballer) and institutional properties (being a professor, being a surgeon general).

*Categories We Live By* is a significant contribution to metaphysics and social theory. First, it offers a new theory of social categories.[1] In doing so, it also provides a general and systematic alternative to ideal social ontology. Second, it assigns appropriate weight to a different type of paradigmatic social phenomena—the communal—and promises to account for both institutional and

---

[1] Ásta uses "social category" and "social kind" interchangeably. On her account, *women* or *queers* are social categories, while *being a woman* or *being queer* are social properties.

communal properties. In fact, Ásta claims that, "The conferralist framework can be used to make sense of any social category. I show it in action by offering accounts of some of the most dominant social categories, but it can be used to account for any others" (2018, 4). Third, she offers an explicit and fresh stance on methodological questions with her choice of examples. Consider the coder example above: not only does it point to the centrality of communal properties that enable or restrict one's behavior, but it also represents a complex, real-world example. Ásta's choice of examples and her emphasis on communal properties are in line with her normative commitment to offer a theory that aids in fighting social injustices and oppression. She states that the book aims to provide "a deeper understanding of various social mechanics that contribute to injustice" (2018, 5). Furthermore, it is an example of feminist theorizing in the sense that the purpose is to "reveal the cogs and belts and arrangements of parts in machines that often are oppressive" (2018, 4). This contrasts with theories in traditional social ontology that seek to "describe social reality in an entirely value-neutral way, unhindered by any political commitments" (2018, 6).

We turn now to the general conferralist framework and, first, of what it is for a property P to be institutional:

**Conferred property:** P
**Who:** a person or entity or group in authority
**What:** their explicit conferral by means of a speech act or other public act
**When:** under the appropriate circumstances (in the presence of witnesses, at a particular place, etc); we can think of this as a particular institutional context
**Base property:** the property or properties the authorities are attempting to track in the conferral (Ásta 2018, 21, emphasis in original)

And, second, of what it is for a property P to be communal:

## 124 RECONSTRUCTION: NONIDEAL SOCIAL ONTOLOGY

Conferred property: P
Who: a person or entity or group with standing
What: their conferral, explicit or implicit, by means of attitudes and behavior
When: in a particular context
Base property: the property or properties the authorities [*sic*] are attempting to track in the conferral, consciously or unconsciously[2] (Ásta 2018, 22, emphasis in original)

One implication of this framework is that you have social properties in virtue of other people's beliefs about you; another is that it is other people's perception that matters, rather than you actually having the base property. Ásta writes that, "it is the *perception* that the base property (or properties) is present that matters on the conferralist account, not the *actual presence* of it, as on the constitution account" (2018, 27, emphasis in original). So, other people are trying to track a base property, and even if they are mistaken about your possessing this base property (you did not receive a college degree), you would still have the conferred property (being a college graduate). To illustrate how the conferralist framework can be used to analyze institutional properties, consider the well-known case from social ontology of being the president of the United States (Ásta 2018, 22):

Conferred property: being elected president of the United States
Who: the current US vice president, as president of the US Senate; this is the entity in authority
What: the declaration that someone has received the most electoral college votes for US President
When: on January 6, following a November election, starting at 1 p.m.

---

[2] Ásta clarifies that it should be "people with standing" here. In later works "the authorities" is replaced with "the conferrers" (Ásta 2019).

NONIDEAL SOCIAL ONTOLOGY    125

**Base property:** the majority of electoral college votes, that is, 270 or more

Furthermore, social properties—especially communal ones—are highly dependent on context.

To illustrate, consider the communal property of being cool (Ásta 2018, 22–23):

**Conferred property:** being cool
**Who:** the people in the context, collectively
**What:** their judging the person to have the base property or properties
**When:** in a particular context the person travels in, for example, one context can be at Mission High School in San Francisco, another the skate park in the Sunset District of San Francisco; someone can be cool at Mission High, but not at the skate park
**Base property:** the property or properties the conferrers are attempting to track in their conferral in each contexts; for example, having blue hair may be a base property for being cool at Mission High; having a tattoo at the skate park

There is a further central element to Ásta's account: constraints and enablements. Social properties are social statuses and are essentially tied to what you can and cannot do in a social context, in the sense that "a social property, whether institutional or communal, is fleshed out in terms of the constraints and enablements, institutional or communal, on a person's behavior and action. To have the status in question *just is* to have the constraints and enablements in question" (Ásta 2018, 29, emphasis in original). So, all social properties are constraints and enablements.

But the key notions of "behavioral constraints" and "behavioral enablements" are not sufficiently developed with respect to communal properties, and we need further clarification to fully evaluate the conferralist account. Recall that "the constraints on and

126 RECONSTRUCTION: NONIDEAL SOCIAL ONTOLOGY

enablements to a person's behavior and action" are an essential part of conferralism because social properties are defined in terms of them. But what are these constraints and enablements? Institutional properties are understood in terms of institutional rights and institutional obligations, hence are deontic in a narrow sense.[3] This is in line with ideas familiar from ideal social ontology where institutional rights are referred to as "positive deontic powers" and institutional obligations as "negative deontic powers." But there is little explanation of what the communal constraints and enablements actually are, beyond the claim that they are non-institutional powers (Ásta 2018, 20–21, 33) that are not deontic (2018, 106). What kind of powers, then, are they?

Because the purpose of the book is to account for communal properties defined in terms of constraints and enablements, the role of these non-institutional and non-deontic powers is central to the account, making it crucial to obtain a deeper understanding of them. Ásta's bully example provides greater clarity about these non-deontic constraints and enablements:

> Consider the case when Billy the bully sees that Max's grand-mother has given him the special candy from Austria, and says to Max, "Give me your candy!" Big-Tom, Big-Dick, and Big-Harry, Billy's posses, stand beside him, menacing. Max loves his Mozartkugeln and doesn't want to give Billy the candy, but he doesn't want to get the "toilet treatment" again. (Ásta 2018, 18–19)

Although Billy does not have the authority to order Max to give him the candy, he has power over Max and can make his life

---

[3] This narrow sense of "deontic"—an institutional ought following from an institutional obligation—is common in contemporary social ontology. It can be contrasted with the traditional and wider sense of "deontic" understood as what one ought to do (e.g., morally or as a matter of rationality) or the right thing to do (in a moral sense). On this narrow understanding of deontic, one's positive and negative deontic powers can be illegitimate, or morally wrong.

miserable. This power is what enables Billy to order Max to give him the candy, even though he has no institutional authority over him. In this case, Billy's power over Max has its source in Max's fear of the things Billy could do to him. Billy, then, has enough standing with Max to be able to order him to give him the candy.

I think there are two different ways—one deontic and one physical—to explain the constraints and enablements in this example. Either Billy has an informal right due to his status as the school bully and Max is under an informal obligation to give him the candy (and there are informal rights and obligations within the group of bullies), or this is a matter of (the threat of) physical force, analogous to a robber pointing a gun and "asking for" money. The group of bullies can easily outnumber Max, and Billy's social status is not needed to explain why Max hands over the candy. So, this case can be explained by deontic notions, physical force, or a combination of both. According to the conferralist framework, however, the behavioral constraints and enablements cannot be deontic because being a bully is a communal rather than an institutional property. It cannot only be about physical force either, as the example is about communal, not physical, reality. In short, these behavioral constraints and enablements are neither institutional nor about physical force in the conferralist framework. In what, then, does this category of non-institutional, non-deontic, and not purely physical power, consist?

Consider the coder in San Francisco who is expected to buy drinks for the femmes. This sounds like a deontic notion, but in this example, gender is a communal property; thus, this constraint cannot be deontic on Ásta's account. So, we need an explanation of the "communal constraints on and enablements to a person's behavior and action" to fully evaluate the correctness of the conferralist framework.

In an article published after *Categories We Live By*, Ásta clarifies what these non-deontic social powers amount to. The communal properties "do not concern rights, privileges, and obligations, but

128 RECONSTRUCTION: NONIDEAL SOCIAL ONTOLOGY

power, sway, and nondeontic restrictions" (2019, 394). Ásta's example of the female engineer illustrates this idea. In the first scenario, a female engineer intends to issue an order but, because she belongs to the social category of woman, her order is not understood as an order but is instead taken as merely a request. In the second scenario, it is understood to be an order but is openly disobeyed because she belongs to the social category of woman (Ásta 2019). These two scenarios are instances of *categorical injustice*. According to Ásta, categorical injustice "occurs when agents are systematically thwarted in their attempts at performing actions by how they are socially constructed" (2019, 392). In both scenarios there is a conflict between the engineer's institutional deontic power (she has the right to issue orders due to her institutional role) and her communal powers which, according to Ásta, are non-deontic. Ásta thus opens up a wider notion of social power than, for example, Brännmark, whose account of institutions as distributions takes the emphasis on deontic powers one step further and argues that both formal and informal (what Ásta refers to as communal) social positions are just typical bundles of Hohfeldian incidents; that is, of deontic powers. I turn to Brännmark's work in section 3.4. I think the example of the female engineer illustrates an important social dimension and that it is beneficial to view this as a form of social power. In Chapter 6, I introduce the category "structural power," and I take this example to show a conflict between the engineer's positive deontic power to issue an order, and her negative structural power.

## 3.3 Conferralism and Nonideal Social Ontology

It is time to return to the claim that Ásta's conferralism is an example of nonideal social ontology. *Categories We Live By* is an example of nonideal social ontology because it rejects at least four conditions in Mills' characterization of ideal theory; furthermore,

NONIDEAL SOCIAL ONTOLOGY 129

it is silent on the fifth. The first condition in Mills' characterization is an idealized social ontology that assumes the abstract and equal atomic individuals of classical liberalism. Recall Ásta's central examples of the coder and the bully. These examples do not abstract away from illegitimate power relations; rather, those relations are the very object of analysis. Furthermore, the agents in these examples are not the abstract, equal agents of neoclassical liberalism. Instead, it is the inequality and the very specific circumstances in which they find themselves that are the starting point of theorizing. It is also revealing that most of the examples are not completely fictional. Instead, most are drawn from current political and legal controversies and are usually richly described. So, there is a clear sense in which Ásta starts with, and pays close attention to, the actual or the nonideal. In short, conferralism rejects condition (i).

The second condition in Mills' characterization of ideal theory is attributing idealized capacities to agents. Nowhere in *Categories We Live By* are agents attributed with idealized capacities. Rather, as noted above, these agents often live in the real world (such as Ásta's recurring example of two authors, Rebecca Solnit and Guillermo Gómez-Peña, traveling through San Francisco), or the examples are inspired by real-world agents (like the coder example in the opening paragraph). Conferralism thus also rejects condition (ii).

The third condition in Mills' characterization of ideal theory is silence on oppression. As noted above, the key dividing point between ideal and nonideal social ontology is that the former is silent on oppression, whereas the latter emphasizes it. The conferralist framework is designed with oppression in mind; it seeks above all to provide a theory that can help us understand and address oppression. So, conferralism clearly rejects condition (iii), and it is illustrative to read how Ásta positions her own work with respect to oppression, particularly how normative and political commitments play a central role in her theorizing:

## 130 RECONSTRUCTION: NONIDEAL SOCIAL ONTOLOGY

> The theory presented here lies at the intersection of metaphysics, social philosophy, social ontology, and feminist theory. Camping out at that intersection can be a lonely and cold endeavor: your metaphysics friends think our job is to describe the fundamental structure of reality and the social cannot be fundamental; your social ontology friends simply want to describe social reality in an entirely value-neutral way, unhindered by any political commitments; and your feminist and social philosophy friends either think metaphysics is an ideological part of the oppressive regimes we are fighting against or simply unnecessary baggage. (Ásta 2018, 6)

The fourth condition in Mills' characterization of ideal theory is theorizing institutions in terms of the ideal-as-idealized model rather than the ideal-as-descriptive model, and *Categories We Live By* also rejects this condition. Again, the central examples in the book are instances of the ideal-as-descriptive model, like the bully in the school system. Furthermore, it is often the dark side of institutions that is emphasized, such as the conflicts between the institutional and communal properties of being a woman (cf., the North Carolina bathroom law, where the legal base property is biological sex, while the communal property, in some contexts, is genuine self-identification). In short, Ásta analyzes institutions in terms of the ideal-as-descriptive model, rather than the ideal-as-idealized model. So, conferralism also rejects condition (iv) in Mills' characterization.

To summarize, Ásta's conferralism is an example of a general theory in nonideal social ontology that clearly contrasts with the dominant theories in ideal social ontology proposed by John Searle, Margaret Gilbert, and Raimo Tuomela. In the next section, I turn to another nonideal theory in social ontology—Johan Brännmark's theory of nonideal institutions (2019a, 2019b). This theory differs from conferralism in that it allows for the existence of the first and second kinds of social kind phenomena as social properties, in addition to the third kind of social kind phenomena. Furthermore, it offers a detailed explication of the central concept of deontic power—a concept of key importance in both conferralism and ideal social ontology.

## 3.4 Nonideal Institutions and Contested Institutional Facts

> We should want a social ontology that is relevant to political theory, not one that has been turned into political theory. (Brännmark 2019a, 1062–1063)

Brännmark (2019a, 2019b) has recently developed a nonideal theory of institutions and institutional facts, making a significant contribution to social ontology by offering a new theory of institutions and institutional facts—a theory that promises to be more general than theories in ideal social ontology and conferralism—and an explication of deontic power. This work is important for my purposes in another respect, too. Brännmark explicitly refers to his theory as an example of nonideal social ontology (2019b), and I use his work for illustrative purposes because it is a clear statement of nonideal social ontology. For example, it explicitly states the purpose of theorizing, the conditions of adequacy that theories of social ontology should meet, and the need to pay attention to nonideal circumstances, such as contestation and oppression. In my power view, I also draw on his explication of deontic powers in terms of Hohfeldian incidents. The background is that the concept of deontic power is central in both ideal social ontology and nonideal social ontology, which is shown by the deonticity claim and the power claim in the standard model of ideal social ontology and the central role of constraints and enablements in conferralism. Brännmark's explication of deontic power offers a more detailed view of this central concept than has hitherto been

132  RECONSTRUCTION: NONIDEAL SOCIAL ONTOLOGY

available. This is relevant in providing a better description of social reality; it is also theoretically useful, for example, in analyzing subordinated and privileged social positions.

### 3.4.1 Institutions as Distributions

Brännmark criticizes traditional social ontology for offering an overly narrow view of social reality. Influential theories, such as Gilbert's, Searle's, and Tuomela's, cannot account for contested and opaque institutions and institutional facts like racism and sexism. This is due to their assumptions of two features: first, that there is common knowledge about the institutions that exist in one's society; and second, that social obligations follow from the existence of institutions in the sense that people have reasons to act in accordance with these obligations. Brännmark contends that these two features hold with respect to the standard examples used in traditional social ontology, which are often examples of formal and explicit institutions, like money and private property. But if we shift to other types of examples that involve informal and implicit institutions, such as racism and sexism in contemporary Western societies, these two features do not hold.[4] In fact, they are contrary to the existence of descriptively contested facts and normatively contested facts. Descriptive contestation amounts to people disagreeing about whether a certain institution exists in their society, while normative contestation amounts to people accepting that a certain institution exists but believing that this institution, due to its immoral nature, does not generate any reasons for action (Brännmark 2019a, 1051). Sexism and racism are precisely the sorts of things where there is descriptive and normative contestation in contemporary societies. Consequently, for Brännmark, the

---

[4] Brännmark points out that these institutions—racism and sexism—are also often formal and explicit.

NONIDEAL SOCIAL ONTOLOGY    133

theories in ideal social ontology cannot account for informal and implicit institutions due to their contested nature and are thus too narrow.

Brännmark's own theory—what I call institutions as distributions—is designed to overcome this limitation. His purpose is to offer a theory that is truly general in the sense of being able to account for different types of institutions and institutional facts, formal or informal and explicit or implicit. He especially wants to show "how there can be institutional facts that are deeply contested and yet still real" (2019a, 1047). Before discussing the answer to this question, I turn to the conditions of adequacy for institutions as distributions.

## 3.4.2  Conditions of Adequacy for Institutions as Distributions

According to Brännmark, a theory in social ontology should answer questions about (i) *the nature and existence* of institutions as well as their *grounds*. It is also to be (ii) *general* in the sense of capturing all institutions and institutional facts, including formal and informal and explicit and implicit institutions and institutional facts. The theory should also show how contested and opaque institutions and institutional facts, those that are informal and implicit, are possible. Furthermore, (iii) the aim of the theory is to offer a *correct description* of institutions and institutional facts:

> One consequence of this descriptive character is that, even to the extent that we do identify significant inequalities, this approach does not say anything about exactly how bad these are—or even whether they are bad at all. *Sexism* and *racism* serve as analytical terms here. Of course, given that we also happen to hold egalitarian moral and political views, an unequal distribution of informal and implicit incidents should certainly bother us,

134 RECONSTRUCTION: NONIDEAL SOCIAL ONTOLOGY

but this is still a distinct moral and political stance that we take with respect to the analysis we have made. (Brännmark 2019a, 1062–1063)

This illustrates the sharp boundary between descriptive and normative theorizing that Brännmark assumes, but normative theorizing is not completely absent from this picture. Recall Brännmark's claim (iv) that social ontology should be relevant for political theory.[5] In the next chapter, I turn to whether institutions as distributions meets the four conditions of adequacy.

### 3.4.3 Hohfeldian Incidents as the Basic Building Blocks

We have seen that ideal and nonideal social ontology disagree over which social phenomena are to be analyzed. One example of this discord is whether there can be *opaque institutions*. Ideal social ontology denies that possibility due to the performativity claim in the standard model of ideal social ontology. By contrast, one of Brännmark's main claims is that institutions that are opaque to people can exist, such as racist and sexist institutions. To argue for this point, he develops an account of the nature of institutions and institutional facts that does not presuppose the two features—identified by Brännmark—as excluding contested and opaque institutions; namely, common knowledge and the idea that institutions generate reasons for action. The key elements of institutions as distributions are as follows:

---

[5] It is not clear whether the relevance condition is intended to be separate from the third condition of adequacy: offering a correct description of institutions and institutional facts. While I treat it as a separate condition of adequacy for purposes of exposition, nothing in my argument hinges on whether it is part of the third condition of adequacy or constitutes a separate condition.

NONIDEAL SOCIAL ONTOLOGY 135

> If we take basic institutional facts to be about individuals possessing Hohfeldian incidents, institutions can be understood as *stable and structured distributions of Hohfeldian incidents.* A distribution being stable and structured can be the product of certain explicit rules being in place, but (as argued above) can also just be the product of an alignment in terms of boundary-setting and boundary-upholding micro-level behavior. (Brännmark 2019a, 1056, emphasis in original)

This quote demonstrates three central tenets of institutions as distributions. First, institutions are stable and structured distributions of deontic powers that are explicated in terms of Hohfeldian incidents.[6] Second, institutional facts, such as the fact that I am employed by Stockholm University and that Martin is my friend, are facts about "individuals possessing Hohfeldian incidents." Consequently, institutions as distributions is essentially a deontic account of institutions and institutional facts. Third, the grounds of institutions are micro-level attitudes and actions consisting of boundary-upholding and boundary-setting behavior by individuals.

Let us consider the first central tenet that institutions are stable and structured distributions of Hohfeldian incidents. The schema for Hohfeldian incidents is as follows:[7]

(1) A has a *claim* that B Φ if and only if B has a duty to A to Φ.
(2) A has a *liberty* to Φ if and only if A has no duty not to Φ.

---

[6] Frank Hindriks (2008) argues that we need a broader notion of power than Searle's notion of deontic power and introduces the term "normative attribute" to refer to Hohfeldian incidents and "actions that are deemed appropriate, or activities that are to be promoted" (2008, 133). Hindriks contends that it would be helpful to understand one kind of normative power in terms of Hohfeldian incidents.

[7] It is worth noting that Brännmark draws on Leif Wenar's interpretation of Hohfeld rather than Hohfeld's original work, which explains why (2) is referred to as a "liberty" rather than a "privilege," as in Hohfeld's original formulation.

# 136 RECONSTRUCTION: NONIDEAL SOCIAL ONTOLOGY

(3) A has a *power* if and only if A has the ability to alter her own or another's Hohfeldian incidents.

(4) A has an *immunity* with respect to B if and only if B lacks the ability to alter A's Hohfeldian incidents.

Applying this schema to a common example from ideal social ontology—that of being a property owner—illustrates how it offers a more fine-grained way of understanding this social position:

> A property right, for example, is at its core about having the liberty to use some thing as I see fit and having claims on others to keep their hands off it; but it also involves the power to transfer those liberties and claims to others (by giving them the thing in question) as well as immunities in relation to others (they cannot legitimately give away my things). (Brännmark 2019a, 1063)

By contrast, the standard model of ideal social ontology would involve a more coarse-grained view—having a property right to my home means having a positive deontic power to rent it out or sell it. The upshot is that having the Hohfeldian building blocks at our disposal means that we can more clearly understand the notion of deontic power, which is important for both ideal and nonideal social ontologists.

The second central tenet is that basic institutional facts are facts "about individuals possessing Hohfeldian incidents" (Brännmark 2019a, 1056). The relationship between institutional facts and institutions is that "the Hohfeldian incidents that make up institutions . . . tend to be ones that we hold qua occupants of some social position—they come in typical bundles" (Brännmark 2019a, 1057) Examples of social positions can be formal, such as being a prosecutor, or informal, such as being a woman. A social position is understood in terms of the typical set of Hohfeldian incidents that a holder of the social position tends to have. For example, the formal social position of being a prosecutor consists not only of claims and liberties but also the power to change other people's claims and liberties, such as convicting someone of a crime. In the Hohfeldian schema, claims and liberties are first-order incidents while power and immunities are second-order incidents. This means that the prosecutor's social position is partly characterized by holding second-order incidents, such as the power to compel people to give testimony that will convict another person of a crime and thus change that person's first-order incidents by restricting her or his liberty.

An implication of the Hohfeldian schema is that it is *relational* in the sense that one incident correlates to someone else having another incident. For example, if a person has a claim to a particular piece of property, this implies that others have a duty not to take it or use it without permission. In the literature, the relationships between different incidents are commonly represented as follows:

| A has a claim | ↔ | B has a duty |
| A has a liberty | ↔ | B has a no-claim |
| A has a power | ↔ | B has a liability |
| A has an immunity | ↔ | B has a disability |

The incidents on the left consist of being enabled in actions, while the incidents on the right consist of being constrained. Using this schema, Brännmark suggests that the social positions of being a woman or a man can be analyzed in terms of certain *patterned* distributions of Hohfeldian incidents. The informal social position of being a woman, for example, might be characterized by a typical bundle that consists of more duties and no-claims than claims and liberties, while the social position of being a man might be characterized by a typical bundle consisting of more claims and liberties than duties and no-claims. In short, the social position of being a woman might involve having more right-side incidents than left-side incidents, while the social position of being a man might involve the converse. Similarly, the social position of being

138   RECONSTRUCTION: NONIDEAL SOCIAL ONTOLOGY

black might involve more right-side than left-side incidents, while the social position of being white would likely involve the opposite. *Subordinated social positions* imply having more right-side than left-side incidents, while *privileged social positions* imply having more left-side incidents than right-side incidents. One implication of this account is that formal and informal social positions can be given the same analysis. Being a prosecutor involves having more left-side incidents than right-side incidents, while being a convicted criminal involves having more right-side than left-side incidents. But what about opaque institutions and contested institutional facts? What conceptual resources are available to explain them?

The third central tenet—that the grounds of institutions are micro-level attitudes and actions consisting of boundary-upholding and boundary-setting behavior by individuals—is needed, in addition to the other two central tenets, to explain the possibility of opaque institutions and contested institutional facts. This is a micro-level analysis in that the mark of the social is boundary-setting and boundary-upholding behavior of at least two people; as soon as we have two or more people engaging in such behavior, we have a social phenomenon.

Brännmark starts from the familiar idea that there are social expectations of how we ought to behave in various contexts. If someone fails to meet these social expectations and thereby transgresses boundaries, there will be pushback that can take different forms, such as social or legal sanctions. Our being able to engage in boundary-setting and boundary-upholding behavior means that basic institutional facts can emerge in the form of "individuals possessing typical bundles of Hohfeldian incidents" that together form institutions, which are "stable and structured distributions of Hohfeldian incidents."

The possibility of opaque and contested *institutional facts* is explained by our being mistaken about the real cues of our behavior, a type of error that is illustrated as follows:

For example, if I listen to a conversation between a man and a woman and they are taking up equal amounts of time in that conversation, I might see this woman as overstepping, as being too dominant in the conversation, and I might feel confident that others who listened to that same conversation would feel the same, perhaps even that if I did not make this assessment, those others would think that there was something amiss with my judgment. (Brännmark 2019a, 1055)

Let us call this "the gender conversation example." It shows that we might be unaware of *why* we engage in a particular boundary-setting or boundary-upholding behavior. Perhaps we think that this particular woman was aggressive, while the real cue might be that this woman did not act according to the common social expectation that women ought to yield to men. This shows how institutional facts can be opaque to ourselves and others in our society. But the standard model of ideal social ontology can also explain the possibility of opaque institutional facts because it admits to the second kind of social kind phenomena in Muhammad Ali Khalidi's classification. Recall for instance the example of the dollar bill (a token of the type of money) that is not in circulation or the citizen who is not believed to be a citizen (another token of a type).[8]

The real disagreement concerns whether opaque *institutions* can exist. The possibility of the existence of opaque and contested institutions is explained in a similar vein: We might disagree about (cf., descriptive contestation) or even be mistaken about (cf., opacity) the existence of racist and sexist institutions in our society because such institutions consist of summative attitudes at a macro level, while our everyday life takes place on the micro level (Brännmark 2019a, 1052). To return to the previous gender

---

[8] These examples come from Searle (1995) and (2010).

# 140 RECONSTRUCTION: NONIDEAL SOCIAL ONTOLOGY

conversation example, which takes place on the micro-level, one individual woman is facing social sanctions in a specific setting due to her transgressing a boundary. But this woman and other women face the same type of response at different times and in different contexts. That is, we might not understand how different behaviors in different settings add up to a pattern of a stable and structured distribution—an institution in Brännmark's sense—in which women tend to have fewer left-side Hohfeldian incidents than men. In other words, we might not see how this results in subordinated and privileged social positions for women and men, respectively. The distinction between the micro and macro levels and our not seeing clearly how actions at the micro level add up to a macro-level institution thus open up the possibility of opaque and contested institutions. For example, people might not see how behaviors at the micro level combine to create a racist and sexist institution at the macro level, or they might simply disagree about whether the sum of certain micro-level behaviors add up to a racist or sexist institution.

### 3.4.4 Meeting the Four Conditions of Adequacy

This account—institutions as distributions—aims to fulfill its own conditions of adequacy as follows: (i) *the nature and existence* of institutions is that an institution is a stable and structured distribution of Hohfeldian incidents, and its grounds are our ability to engage in boundary-upholding and boundary-setting behaviors. It is to be (ii) *general* in the sense of capturing all institutions and institutional facts, formal or informal and explicit or implicit. As we have seen, it offers the same analysis of formal (the prosecutor) and informal (being a woman) social positions in terms of typical bundles of Hohfeldian incidents. The theory should also explain how contested and opaque institutions and institutional facts are possible, as they are often informal and implicit. It explains how there can be contested and opaque institutional facts by showing how we might be mistaken about the real cues for our behavior (the gender conversation example) and explains how there can be contested and even opaque institutions by our inability to see how micro-level behaviors add up to macro-level sexist and racist institutions. The primary aim of the theory is (iii) to offer a *correct description* of institutions and institutional facts. Brännmark explicitly states that his account is to be interpreted as a naturalistic account. Moral notions are not built into the analysis, and what are usually taken to be value-laden terms like "sexism" and "racism" and "privilege" and "subordination" serve only as analytical terms. The correct description of institutions and institutional facts should also be (iv) relevant for political theory. Brännmark's main claim— that sexism and racism can be institutions in our societies—and the explanation of how there can be contested, and even opaque, institutions contribute to fulfilling conditions (iii) and (iv).

In the next chapter I argue that it is unclear whether this theory can meet its own conditions of adequacy. The reason is economic class—a key nonideal phenomenon relevant both for offering a correct description and for political theory—which cannot be a social position and thus not an institution on this account.

## 3.5 Apparent and Real Disagreements between Ideal and Nonideal Social Ontology

Shifting perspective from the specifics of the nonideal theories of conferralism and institutions as distributions to the debate between ideal and nonideal social ontology serves to uncover one apparent and two real disagreements. The apparent disagreement concerns institutions and the danger of social ontologists talking past one another with respect to institutions and institutional facts. Brännmark's conception of an institution is much broader than the one used in ideal social ontology. For example, customs

142 RECONSTRUCTION: NONIDEAL SOCIAL ONTOLOGY

and traditions and some contested and opaque phenomena all count as institutions for him. Ideal and nonideal social ontologists could agree that contested and opaque social phenomena exist but disagree about whether these phenomena should be called "institutions." Brännmark is open to referring to these phenomena as "institutions" or "social structures." I take this to be a verbal dispute and thus only an apparent disagreement. I retain the narrow sense of "institution" and "institutional facts" from ideal social ontology and refer to some of the contested and opaque social phenomena as "social structures" rather than "institutions" in Chapter 6. The central question is whether the nature and existence of these social phenomena can be explained, regardless of how we refer to them.

One of the real disagreements between ideal and nonideal social ontology is the social phenomena that are picked out as central. Brännmark uses racism and sexism as primary examples of social phenomena and explicitly states that gender is *the* paradigmatic example of a social construction; Ásta makes the same point. Indeed, as the next section makes clear, much of the work in emancipatory social ontology is about race and gender.

Another real disagreement between ideal and nonideal social ontology concerns which conditions of adequacy a theory should fulfill. More specifically, there is substantial disagreement about whether moral and political commitments should play any role at all. In the ideal social ontology tradition, the ontological investigation is to proceed in an "entirely value-neutral way," to borrow Ásta's phrase. By contrast, Ásta explicitly states that conferralism is a work of feminist theory and that part of the motivation behind her work is to offer a theory that is useful in understanding oppression. Brännmark meanwhile, not only states that a theory of social ontology should be relevant to political theory—a field in which questions of legitimate and illegitimate power relations are central—but also that it is the responsibility of the theorist to not contribute to reproducing ideology, with ideology understood in a pejorative sense (Brännmark 2019b). So, ideal social ontologists deny that moral and political commitments should play any role in the ontological investigation, while their nonideal counterparts are open to moral and political commitments playing a limited role, either in the negative sense of not reproducing ideology or in the positive sense of contributing to understanding oppression.

Still, there is an important similarity between ideal social ontology and the two versions of nonideal social ontology—conferralism and institutions as distributions—discussed thus far: they are all projects of descriptive social ontology. Emancipatory social ontology, on the other hand, is not content with a merely descriptive social ontology. In fact, the *primary aim* of emancipatory social ontology is to offer theories that are useful for social change. Moral and political commitments thus play a different and larger role in this branch of social ontology.

Emancipatory social ontology is at the other end of the spectrum from ideal social ontology. A central aim is to contribute to fighting social injustices like gender and race oppression. This tradition is thus much more likely to have the theoretical resources needed to account for racism and sexism than ideal social ontology because its theories are often designed with these kinds of social phenomena in mind.

Brännmark, however, distances himself from emancipatory social ontology just as he does from the ideal form. I thus interpret institutions as distributions as occupying a middle position between ideal and emancipatory social ontology. He does this by assuming and defending a boundary between social ontology understood as a descriptive enterprise and political theory understood as a moral enterprise: "We should want a social ontology that is relevant to political theory, not one that has been turned into political theory" (2019a, 1062–1063). A clear division of labor is taken for granted: theories in social ontology should offer an accurate description of social reality, while the different project of normative theorizing should offer an analysis of what is morally wrong with,

## 144 RECONSTRUCTION: NONIDEAL SOCIAL ONTOLOGY

say, certain inequalities. This points to a substantial difference—indeed, the central disagreement—between nonideal ontology and emancipatory social ontology. The former holds that social ontology is primarily about describing, rather than changing, social reality, while the latter regards social ontology as not only describing social reality but primarily offering theories and concepts that are useful for social change. This disagreement translates into different conditions of adequacy for nonideal social ontology and its special subcategory of emancipatory social ontology.

## 3.6 Emancipatory Social Ontology

Examples of emancipatory social ontology, a subcategory of nonideal social ontology, include Sally Haslanger's Marxist-inspired analyses of gender and race (2000), Katharine Jenkins' work on ontic injustice and ontic oppression (2016, 2020, 2023), and Robin Dembroff's work on ontological oppression and critical gender kinds (2020). This branch is characterized by the activist purpose to offer theories or theoretical tools that are useful in fighting specific forms of oppression in one's society or, more generally, that are useful in combatting social injustice.

I use Haslanger's influential analyses of gender and race and Jenkins' recent work on ontic injustice and ontic oppression to illustrate the central elements of this branch of social ontology. I follow Jenkins in calling it "emancipatory social ontology." I pay special attention to the role of social power and economic class in my discussion of these accounts.

### 3.6.1 Haslanger on Gender and Race

> At the most general level, the task is to develop accounts of gender and race that will be effective tools in the fight against injustice. (Haslanger 2000, 36)

NONIDEAL SOCIAL ONTOLOGY    145

Sally Haslanger has provided one of the most influential analyses of gender and race to appear in the last two decades. For the purposes of this volume, Haslanger's account is used as an illuminating example of a specific subcategory of nonideal social ontology—emancipatory social ontology—and how this tradition differs from ideal social ontology and the other versions of nonideal social ontology discussed so far. In addition, I consider the role that social power and economic class play in Haslanger's account. I do not cover the central debates and objections to this account, which are beyond the scope of this book.

Haslanger's ameliorative project differs in both aim and method from ideal social ontology. The goal of her project is to offer theoretical tools that are useful in the fight against social injustice. This contrasts starkly with the aim of ideal social ontology to offer an accurate description of social reality. Her method is a conceptual analysis of a certain type, known as analytical or ameliorative. The ameliorative method is closely connected to the purpose; if our current concepts do not contribute to the fight against social injustice, the theorist need to stipulate new meanings. Thus, there is an explicit stipulative component built into this method.

More specifically, Haslanger (2000) offers an illuminating discussion of three different philosophical projects with respect to conceptual analysis: one might be interested in explicating our everyday concept of X by focusing on the intension of the concept (the conceptual project), one might be interested in tracking a social kind by focusing on the extension of the concept (the descriptive project), or one might be interested in designing a concept to play a certain theoretical or political role (the analytical or ameliorative project). Ideal social ontology is mostly concerned with the descriptive project and, in some cases, the conceptual project, while Haslanger's version of emancipatory social ontology employs the ameliorative project.[9] With that in mind, let us turn to Haslanger's ameliorative analyses of gender and race:

---

[9] The analytical project is referred to in later works as "ameliorative," a term I use in the pages that follow.

146  RECONSTRUCTION: NONIDEAL SOCIAL ONTOLOGY

S *functions as a woman* in context C iff$_{df}$

> i) S is observed or imagined in C to have certain bodily features presumed to be evidence of a female's biological role in reproduction;
> ii) that S has these features marks S within the background ideology of C as someone who ought to occupy certain kinds of social position that are in fact subordinate (and so motivates and justifies S's occupying such a position); and
> iii) the fact that S satisfies (i) and (ii) plays a role in S's systematic subordination in C, i.e., *along some dimension*, S's social position in C is oppressive, and S's satisfying (i) and (ii) plays a role in that dimension of subordination. (Haslanger 2000, 42–43, emphasis in original)

For the definition of "S functioning as a man," female is replaced with male in all instances above, while subordination and oppression are replaced with privilege (for the full definition, see Haslanger 2000, 42–43). This analysis entails that functioning as a woman or functioning as a man is about belonging to a social class; that is, one's gender is a social position. This contrasts with views that treat gender as an intrinsic feature of an individual. It also entails that current genders are *necessarily hierarchical* because functioning as a woman or functioning as a man is partly analyzed in terms of subordination and privilege. Consequently, the concept of illegitimate social power is at the core of the analysis because subordination and privilege—variants of illegitimate social power—play this central role.

Haslanger proposes one virtue of her account is that it offers a parallel to race, and her definition of being racialized is as follows: A group G is *racialized* relative to context C iff$_{df}$ members of G are (all and only) those:

NONIDEAL SOCIAL ONTOLOGY 147

  iv) who are observed or imagined to have certain bodily features presumed in C to be evidence of ancestral links to a certain geographical region (or regions);

  v) whose having (or being imagined to have) these features marks them within the context of the background ideology in C as appropriately occupying certain kinds of social position that are in fact either subordinate or privileged (and so motivates and justifies their occupying such a position); and

  vi) whose satisfying (i) and (ii) plays (or would play) a role in their systematic subordination or privilege in C, i.e., who are *along some dimension* systematically subordinated or privileged when in C, and satisfying (i) and (ii) plays (or would play) a role in that dimension of privilege or subordination. (Haslanger 2000, 44, emphasis in original)

The parallels to her analysis of gender are clear: gender and race are analyzed as social classes, current genders and races are necessarily hierarchical and consist partly in illegitimate relations of social power (subordination and privilege), and perceptions of bodily features play a central role in that subordination and privilege.

### 3.6.2 Class and Gender and Race

I have emphasized the central role of social power in this account. I turn now to economic class, which plays three distinct roles. First, the Marxist sense of class is used as a *theoretical starting point*— Haslanger's account draws explicitly on critical theory and work in feminist theory. Second, economic class serves as an *analytical tool* in that genders and races are analyzed as social classes. Furthermore, the notion of a "background ideology" figures in Haslanger's definitions of both gender and race, and ideology is a key element in Marxist thinking and critical theory. The very definition of gender includes as a component a modified version of

148   RECONSTRUCTION: NONIDEAL SOCIAL ONTOLOGY

the Marxist idea that one's relation to the means of production determines one's social position—women's subordination is partly explained by women's role in *re*-production. Third, class figures in one of the *conditions of adequacy*, which states that an account of this kind ought to be able to take intersectionality into account, and the intersection of gender, race, and class is explicitly referred to (Haslanger 2000, 36).

However, the role class does *not* play in Haslanger's account is notable—economic class itself is not the *object of analysis*. This decision is understandable, as her aim is to provide accounts of gender and race that are useful in the fight against injustice, which is already a complex enough challenge. Given Haslanger's broader critical project, however, economic class is important in the fight against injustice. Recall that a stated virtue of her account is that it offers parallel analyses of gender and race, so one cannot help but wonder: Can we extend these analyses of gender and race to economic class? I return to this question and its answer in Chapter 4. I turn next to Jenkins' version of emancipatory social ontology.[10]

## 3.6.3  Jenkins on Ontic Injustice

Jenkins' recently developed account of ontic injustice is explicitly moral, as it is aimed at a specific type of moral wrong that operates through social ontology, hence the term "ontic injustice":

---

[10] The account of ontic injustice is different from the other theories discussed in one important respect: it is not an account *of* the ontology of social kinds, rather it relies *on* an ontology of social kinds in identifying a new kind of injustice. I still think it makes sense to include it here for two main reasons: first, emancipatory social ontologists often do not draw a very sharp line between the social and the moral; second, there is a trend in both ideal and nonideal social ontology to use social ontological accounts as the basis for understanding moral phenomena (cf., Gilbert's *Rights and Demands*, Searle's account of human rights as status functions, and Ásta's categorical injustice).

I show that an individual can be wronged by the very fact of being socially constructed as a member of a certain social kind—kinds such as *wife, slave, woman, black person*. Since this wrong operates through social ontology, I term it *ontic injustice*. (2020, 188, emphasis in original)

The key idea is that a person suffers ontic injustice when that person is a member of a social kind and there is a negative mismatch between the social constraints and enablements that partly constitute that social kind and the person's moral entitlements. Jenkins' primary example is the social kind "wife" in England and Wales until just a few decades ago. Before 1991, there was a marital rape exemption in place such that the social kind wife partly consisted of not having the social (including legal) enablement of saying no to sex with one's husband. But all persons are owed the moral entitlement to have full control over their bodies in this respect. Hence, there is a negative mismatch between social and moral entitlements. Consequently, being a member of the social kind wife in England and Wales before 1991 implied that one was suffering ontic injustice. The marital rape exemption was removed in 1991. Assuming that there were no other immoral constraints or enablements in which the social kind wife partly consisted, being a member of the social kind wife after 1991 implies that one is not suffering ontic injustice. In this example, there has been a change in the social constraints and enablements that partly constitute the social kind. But we are still talking about the social kind "wife," according to Jenkins. In other words, one is still a wife in both scenarios, and only in the former do women who belong to the social kind wife suffer ontic injustice. Accordingly, Jenkins distinguishes between social kinds that are contingently "sites of ontic injustice" and those that are necessarily so. "Wife" is an example of the former, while "slave" is an example of the latter. Jenkins points out that for the social kind "slave," the severe immoral constraints cannot be removed without the social kind itself ceasing to exist. Consequently, combating

# 150  RECONSTRUCTION: NONIDEAL SOCIAL ONTOLOGY

ontic injustice requires different strategies for different social kinds; some social kinds—those that are contingently unjust—can be changed to remove the ontic injustice (as with "wife" before and after 1991), while other kinds—those that are necessarily unjust—need to be abolished to remove the injustice, such as "slave."

The theoretical value of ontic injustice, according to Jenkins, is that it emphasizes the role that social kinds play in enacting injustice, that it opens up the possibility of resolving certain disagreements about gender kinds, and that it serves to analyze and fight oppression (2020, 188). Let us turn to Jenkins' definition of ontic injustice:

> An individual suffers ontic injustice if and only if they are socially constructed as a member of a certain social kind where that construction consists, at least in part, of their being subjected to a set of social constraints and enablements that is wrongful to them. (2020, 191)

An important part of this definition is "wrongful." This should be interpreted as a moral wrong, as is further explicated using Jean Hampton's concept of a "moral injury," which is *damage to the realization of a victim's value, or damage to the acknowledgement of the victim's value, accomplished through behaviour whose meaning is such that the victim is diminished in value*" (Hampton 1992, 1679, emphasis in original). Jenkins broadens this notion of moral injury in two respects: first "behavior" is replaced with "treatment" to refer not only to the behaviors of individuals but also to "the product of human social arrangements," and second, there is a shift from human beings to sentient beings to allow for the possibility that beings other than humans can suffer ontic injustice.[11]

---

[11] The notion of moral injury presupposes that there is a gap between one's social and moral value. That is, it excludes a metaethical view that equates the moral with the social where value is concerned.

It is important to note that the notion of a social kind referred to in the definition of ontic injustice is compatible with different theories in social ontology because most accounts agree that social constraints and enablements partly constitute social kinds. In fact, Jenkins shows that there is an implicit consensus in social ontology such that, "what it is to be a member of a certain social kind is, at least in part, to be subject to certain social constraints and enablements" (2020, 188–189). This implicit consensus is relevant to my point that social power is a central concept, perhaps even *the* central concept, in social ontology.

Having clarified what morally wrongful means in this context, and that social constraints and enablements partly constitute social kinds, opens a gap between the social and the moral, and it is this gap, or negative mismatch, between social constraints and enablements and moral entitlements that constitutes ontic injustice. This gap has an interesting and important consequence; namely, that someone can suffer ontic injustice without knowing it. Jenkins makes clear that ontic injustice is separate from being subjected to an act that is harmful, which is partially explained by the social constraints of the social kind "wife" (actual rape within marriage). Ontic injustice is also separate from the psychological damage of knowing about the immoral constraints to which one is subjected due to being a member of the social kind, even if that particular act never happens (the possibility of rape without legal sanctions). So, one can suffer ontic injustice without ever being subjected to a specific act that is morally wrong. Jenkins writes that the wrong in which she is interested "is the mere fact that an individual *is* a certain kind of social being, where what it means to be that kind of social being is to be subject to morally inappropriate constraints and enablements" (2020, 191, emphasis in original). The claims that ontic injustice is separate from actual acts so that one can suffer ontic injustice without knowing it is relevant for economic class.

## 152 RECONSTRUCTION: NONIDEAL SOCIAL ONTOLOGY

I return to this topic in the next chapter. In the next section, I turn to Jenkins' version of emancipatory social ontology and hence the larger project of which ontic injustice is part.

### 3.6.4 Jenkins on Emancipatory Social Ontology

> I write this book primarily because I want to understand race and gender oppression, and I want to understand them because I want to end them. Understanding the ontological aspects of race and gender strikes me as useful given this aim. (Jenkins 2023, Introduction)

The concept of ontic injustice is part of a larger social ontological project that is referred to as "an instance of emancipatory theory" (Jenkins 2023, Introduction). This version of social ontology is a far cry from ideal social ontology. Recall the two aims of the standard model of ideal social ontology: to provide a general theory of the ontology of the social world and to offer a theory that is the foundation of the social sciences. Jenkins' work is in opposition to these aims: her main aim is not to offer a general theory of the social world but to analyze specific social phenomena such as gender and race kinds, with special attention to gender and race oppressions in a specific social situation (the contemporary United Kingdom). And the primary aim of her theory and her role as a theorist are not to describe social reality and thus provide a foundation for the social sciences, but to move her society in a more just direction. This aim of contributing to social justice is translated into a condition of adequacy for the theory: "A further feature of the emancipatory approach I adopt here is to build the aim of contributing to positive social change into the theorist's endeavour as a success condition" (Jenkins 2023).

> To take one example, I will attend not only to the truth or falsity of various claims about the ontology of race and gender, but also to the practical implications of articulating those claims in particular speech contexts. If the theory has adverse consequences in this regard, I shall consider that a defect of the theory *as* a theory. (Jenkins 2023)

This contrasts sharply with the descriptive approach to social ontology adopted by ideal social ontology and conferralism and institutions as distributions alike. For Jenkins, there is no clear boundary between questions belonging to ontology as traditionally understood and questions belonging to moral and political philosophy as traditionally understood. Rather, theorizing is supposed to be useful for helping to end gender and race oppression.

In relation to this, recall that Mills' characterization of ideal theory includes the criterion of silence on oppression. One central difference between ideal and emancipatory social ontology concerns oppression; the former is silent on oppression, whereas the latter is vocal on the matter. To illustrate this emphasis, consider the role of oppression in Jenkins' work. It serves at least three roles: First, it is an explicit aim of the theory to contribute to ending gender and race oppression, so it figures in the conditions of adequacy. Second, gender and race oppression are the very objects of analysis or social phenomena that should be explained. So, oppression is clearly visible in Jenkins' choice of examples and the social kinds that are analyzed; wife, woman, black person, trans person, and slave. In relation to this, note that the concept of moral injury—a key component of ontic injustice—can include nonhuman animals. The investigation is extended from human social kinds to other animals, which opens up the possibility that being a member of the social kind animal means suffering ontic injustice. Third, oppression figures in the epistemology in the sense that Jenkins assumes that knowledge is situated. On this view, the oppressed have different and better ways of gaining knowledge about their oppression: "Accordingly, I will treat attending to what oppressed people have to say about oppression, either individually or collectively, as an especially important route to knowledge" (Jenkins 2023, Introduction). So, once again, it is clear that oppression is a key dividing line in contemporary social ontology.

## 3.7  Two Remaining Disagreements in Contemporary Social Ontology

Let us turn to the two ends of the spectrum—ideal and emancipatory social ontology—in relation to Brännmark's previously stated four conditions of adequacy. Ideal social ontology agrees with the first condition of adequacy that a theory in social ontology should answer questions about the nature and existence of institutions along with their grounds. It also agrees with the second condition of adequacy—that the purpose is to offer a general theory of institutions—but departs from the view that institutions can be opaque, so there is disagreement about what counts as an institution and thus disagreement about what it means to have offered a general theory of institutions. Ideal social ontology accords with the third condition of adequacy that the aim of the theory is to offer a correct description of institutions and institutional facts. This is revealed in the main aims of the standard model of ideal social ontology—to offer general theories about the ontology of the social world that can be the foundation of the social sciences—because these are to be interpreted as descriptive metaphysics and offering a general theory of institutions is part of offering a general theory about the ontology of the social world. But ideal social ontology does not agree with the fourth condition that theories in social ontology should be relevant for political theory in any other sense not already captured by the other conditions of adequacy: for example, that political theory singles out phenomena that are part of the correct description of the social world.

NONIDEAL SOCIAL ONTOLOGY 155

Emancipatory social ontology, on the other hand, agrees with the first condition and adds that social phenomena other than institutions are of central importance, most notably the human social kinds linked to oppression. With respect to the second condition of adequacy, emancipatory social ontology cautions against general theories and general claims, arguing that one needs to consider the wide diversity of human experiences and human societies. The main point of disagreement concerns the third condition of adequacy: that the primary aim is to offer a correct description of institutions and institutional facts. For emancipatory social ontology, the primary aim is to offer theories that are useful for changing immoral institutions and, more generally, fighting social injustices and oppression.

The upshot of this discussion is that two real disagreements between ideal, nonideal, and emancipatory social ontology have surfaced. One is which conditions of adequacy a theory should fulfill, and the other involves which social phenomena are to be analyzed: Institutions? Opaque institutions? Human social kinds, especially those linked to oppression?

## 3.8 Conclusion

The main aim of this chapter has been to characterize nonideal social ontology. This is relevant to my main claim that there is a paradigm shift from ideal to nonideal social ontology underway and that this shift ought to be fully followed through because we need to know what it is we are, and ought to be, shifting to. Returning to Mills' distinction between ideal and nonideal theory, it became clear that the key dividing line is oppression: ideal social ontology is mostly silent and nonideal social ontology is vocal about it. In fact, there is a scale that runs from an ideal social ontology that is silent on oppression to a nonideal social ontology that emphasizes oppression in its descriptive projects and an emancipatory theory that aims to contribute to ending specific forms of oppression.

Oppression is one form of illegitimate social power. I showed that the concept of social power is central in, and unifies, all these accounts: For conferralism, social constraints and enablements play a central role, and institutions as distributions is an essentially deontic account that helps to clarify this important notion through its explication in terms of Hohfeldian incidents. In Haslanger's analyses of gender and race, social power is essential because subordination and privilege are built into the definitions—an illegitimate form of social power. And Jenkins identifies ontic injustice that consists of the mismatch between the moral entitlements and the social constraints and enablements—social power—that partly constitute social kinds. So, in all these accounts, social power is an essential component.

Another key difference between ideal and nonideal social ontology concerns the use of examples. Ideal social ontology often uses generic stylized facts, and nonideal social ontology uses fully fleshed-out examples from our nonideal circumstances, such as a wife in pre-1991 England and Wales.

Interestingly, there are central similarities between ideal social ontology and the two theories of nonideal social ontology somewhere in the middle of the spectrum; that is, conferralism and institutions as distributions. One similarity relates to the purpose of the theory: It is descriptive metaphysics, and the aim is to offer a general theory of social properties (conferralism) or institutions (institutions as distributions). Another similarity concerns the basic building blocks, with reliance on other people's attitudes as a condition of existence for social phenomena. This is relevant in relation to the important anomaly that I have discerned in nonideal social ontology: that economic class is not a phenomena of concern in nonideal social ontology, despite the fact that it is a key nonideal social phenomena, and that it is crucial for meeting the conditions of adequacy of nonideal social ontology. I turn to this challenge in the next chapter.

# 4
# Critique of Nonideal Social Ontology

## 4.1 Introduction

In the previous chapter I characterized nonideal social ontology, including the special subcategory of nonideal social ontology called emancipatory social ontology. I also showed how nonideal social ontology differs from the standard model of ideal social ontology and I argued that these differences mean that nonideal social ontology can overcome some of the limitations of ideal social ontology, such as an overemphasis on collective intentionality and too little attention to oppression.

In this chapter, I discover an anomaly within nonideal social ontology: that economic class, despite being a major factor in oppression, is hidden from view. This is troubling given that these theories are explicit about not serving an ideological role (understood in a pejorative way) or fighting social injustice. I show that one reason behind this anomaly is, in fact, that nonideal social ontology has not moved far enough from the standard model of ideal social ontology in one key respect; theories like Ásta's, Johan Brännmark's, and Sally Haslanger's all rely on other people's attitudes in their analyses of social phenomena. This excludes economic class because it does not depend on attitudes in this way. According to its own standards, not paying enough attention to economic class is a serious limitation of nonideal social ontology.

Another limitation is that there is still not a theory of social power, which is the central concept in nonideal social ontology. The upshot is that a comprehensive theory of social power and a descriptive analysis of economic class are both missing in nonideal

*Nonideal Social Ontology.* Åsa Burman, Oxford University Press. © Oxford University Press 2023.
DOI: 10.1093/oso/9780197509579.003.0005

158 RECONSTRUCTION: NONIDEAL SOCIAL ONTOLOGY

social ontology. I seek to overcome these limitations by developing my own version of nonideal social ontology. The completion of the argument for the claim that we ought to shift to nonideal social ontology requires my power view presented in Chapters 5 and 6.

We turn now to economic class and the conferralist framework.

## 4.2 A Critique of the Conferralist Framework: Categories We Don't Know We Live By

I take the conferralist framework to be the central innovation in *Categories We Live By*, but I must pose an objection to this framework: conferralism cannot account for *all* social properties of individuals, such as the opaque aspects of class. This shows that, contrary to conferralism's central claim, conferral by others is not a necessary condition for a social property of an individual to exist. I then discuss an implication of this objection, which is that it calls into question whether conferralism can meet its *own* conditions of adequacy, such as providing a theory that can aid us in understanding injustice and oppression, as class is central to understanding these phenomena. My diagnosis is that this objection points to an underlying methodological problem: Ásta and other social ontologists have been fed on what Wittgenstein called a "one-sided diet" of *types* of examples of social phenomena. This methodological problem results in an overly limited view of the paradigmatic social phenomena, which in turn, makes conferralism too narrow to fulfill its intended role.

### 4.2.1 What Are the Paradigmatic Social Phenomena?

It is important to answer the question, "What are the paradigmatic social phenomena?" because what we understand as examples of

CRITIQUE OF NONIDEAL SOCIAL ONTOLOGY 159

such paradigms profoundly influences our theorizing. For example, our view of the paradigmatic social phenomena determines what phenomena we ought to be able to explain and what examples to use as starting points in developing our theories. These exemplars have various sources, such as the philosophical tradition (cf., the many game analogies), our own experiences, and our preconceptions of the social world. Furthermore, the examples of paradigmatic social phenomena are often *theory-driven* and drawn from *particular domains*, such as legal reality. For instance, Ásta states that *Categories We Live By* is a work in feminist theory, which makes gender and oppression central phenomena to explain, and her examples are chosen along these lines. She also emphasizes that she is especially interested in the categories that are protected in various jurisdictions, such as gender, race, disability, sexual orientation, and religion (Ásta 2018, 69, 93).[1] Consequently, many of her examples come from the legal domain. But these are still mere differences in the content (games, gender, law) of examples of paradigmatic social phenomena, and it is the kind, or type, of examples chosen that is even more important. Consider Wittgenstein's warning in *Philosophical Investigations* (§593): "A main cause of philosophical disease—a one-sided diet: one nourishes one's thinking with only one kind of example." Proceeding in a piecemeal fashion in choosing examples might thus result in a failure to acknowledge crucial social phenomena. Much work in social ontology, including Ásta's, has relied on a one-sided diet of kinds of examples. To avoid this pitfall, I think it would be useful to systematize our choice of examples in terms of type rather than content, using the fundamental dimension of mind-dependence to do so.

Returning to Muhammad Ali Khalidi's (2015) classification of social kinds is useful for this purpose. He starts from the familiar

---

[1] Ásta analyzes social properties of individuals, for example, being a woman or being queer, in order to give a theory of the nature of social categories, for example, women, queers (2018, 1).

# 160 RECONSTRUCTION: NONIDEAL SOCIAL ONTOLOGY

idea that social properties depend on our propositional attitudes in different ways and then asks us to consider two questions to clarify those differences (Khalidi 2015, 103, emphasis in original):

(i) Does the existence of the *kind* depend upon our having certain propositional attitudes towards it?

(ii) Does the existence of *instances of the kind* depend on our having propositional attitudes towards them, namely that they are instances of that kind?

The answers to these questions result in a three-fold classification (Khalidi 2015, 104):

|  | (i) | (ii) |  |
|---|---|---|---|
| First kind of social kind | NO | NO | racism, recession |
| Second kind of social kind | YES | NO | war, money |
| Third kind of social kind | YES | YES | permanent resident, prime minister |

The shift from top to bottom in the classification is a shift from weaker to increasingly stronger mind-dependence. The first kind of social kind is mind-dependent in the sense that some mental states about other social phenomena need to exist for the kind to exist, but these mental states need not be about the kind itself. For example, money or some kind of trading must exist (the second kind of social kind) for a recession to exist (the first kind of social kind). The second kind of social kind is mind-dependent in the sense that there must be mental states about the kind itself for it to exist, but there need not be mental states about each individual token for the token to exist. For example, for the kind money to exist, there must be mental states about money, but an individual token, say a coin, can exist even if there are no mental states about that particular coin. The third kind of social kind is mind-dependent in the

CRITIQUE OF NONIDEAL SOCIAL ONTOLOGY 161

sense that there must be mental states about both the type and the token for each to exist. Khalidi writes that the "third kind are social kinds whose very existence depends on specific attitudes towards the kind itself, and whose individual instances must also be deemed by at least some people to be members of the kind for them to be members of the kind" (Khalidi 2015, 104).

Ásta approvingly cites Khalidi's classification in clarifying a central difference between conferralism and John Searle's theories of social reality (1995, 2010). The former takes social properties to be of the third kind, while the latter admits to social properties of both the second and third kinds:

> Conferralism about social categories of people is committed to the claim that such social categories are of type 3 on the Khalidi scale, that is, both the existence of the corresponding category and membership in the category depend on subjects in the way that conferralism outlines. (Ásta 2018, 28)

But this central tenet of conferralism—that social categories of people are of the third kind—results in the theory being too narrow, even by its own standards. Ásta states that *Categories We Live By* is a work in social theory that should be useful for certain purposes in the humanities and the social sciences: "Doing so also serves to support work done in the humanities and social sciences on the role of social construction in generating and upholding oppressive practices and institutions" (Ásta 2018, 4). However, much work in the social sciences, especially about oppression, is concerned with phenomena of Khalidi's first type. Consider economics, which studies recession, inflation, economic inequality, and the effects they have, or sociology, which studies social stratification and class. Starting one's theorizing from only phenomena of the third type involves a risk of not getting as far as these cases (they are to be dealt with later) and/or regarding them as less central than the other two types of social phenomena.

## 4.2.2 The First Kind of Social Kind: Economic Class

One of the main contributions of *Categories We Live By* is to offer a general account of social categories guided by a normative commitment: providing a theory that can aid in fighting social injustices and oppression.

Throughout the book, Ásta applies the conferralist framework to categories like sex, gender, race, disability, sexual orientation, and religion, all of which show (evidence of) a base property that either is or is taken to be transparent to the conferrers, whether on the body, in manners, or in speech. In each example, the conferrers attempt to track something they can observe. There are other social categories, like class, that also involve constraints and enablements but are discussed only in a few short passages in the book. Recall my earlier point that what are considered paradigmatic social phenomena highlight some aspects of social reality while hiding others. This is relevant in relation to Ásta's examples, nearly all of which involve (evidence of) some transparent base property. Furthermore, her choice of examples suggests that they are drawn from anti-discrimination law and thus involve a person's sex, gender, race, disability, sexual orientation, or religion. In fact, Ásta writes that "the categories that are legally protected in various jurisdictions are of special importance to my analysis" (2018, 4) and that she applies "the conferralist framework to some of the other 'usual suspects', that is, to some of the other categories that are protected classes in various jurisdictions, such as race, religion, and disability" (2018, 93). But class is not a category that is protected in law, so the anomaly that class is not given the same attention as the other social categories in Ásta's work—despite its significant and often governing contribution to injustice and oppression—might be due to the fact that the social properties in her examples of paradigmatic social phenomena come from anti-discrimination law.

It is thus both interesting and important to consider whether the conferralist framework can accommodate a person's class,

CRITIQUE OF NONIDEAL SOCIAL ONTOLOGY 163

especially the opaque dimensions of class. The latter would be an example of the first kind of social kind. The conferralist analysis can easily be applied to certain aspects of class. Ásta offers the historical example of a group of people with standing referring to the use of certain words and not others as upper class; hence, conferring this property on some people: "The Sloane Set decided what was U and non U (this is code for 'upperclass'). Using certain words was U, others non-U. Using cloth napkins was U; paper napkins non-U. And so on" (Ásta 2018, 50). Call this the Sloane Set example.

Here again, there is a transparent feature that is taken as (evidence of) the base property of being upper class. With respect to the Sloane Set example, it is instructive to quote the introduction by Alan S. C. Ross: "Today, in 1956, the English class-system is essentially tripartite—there exist an upper, a middle, and a lower class. It is solely by its language that the upper class is clearly marked off from the others" (1956, 11). This is clearly a different sense of class than the Marxist sense. It also tracks a transparent base property (language). This is further emphasized in the subtitle of the book which refers to transparent, or identifiable, characteristics: *Noblesse Oblige: An Enquiry into the Identifiable Characteristics of the English Aristocracy.*

But there are other aspects of class that work in other ways, such as one's relation to the means of production. This category differs from the other social categories considered so far: its constraints and enablements are not due to the perceptions of the conferrers but rather to one's place in the capitalist system.

We can call the Sloane Set example "social class" and the latter Marxian notion "economic class." The first can be captured within the conferralist framework, but the second cannot. Still, economic class is a social property that impacts, often profoundly, what one can and cannot do by setting behavioral constraints and enablements, but it is not a conferred property. In fact, economic class *cannot* be a conferred property because it conflicts with the central tenets of the conferralist account: that the conferrers are

164  RECONSTRUCTION: NONIDEAL SOCIAL ONTOLOGY

attempting to track a base property, that their perception is essential to the conferral, and that the constraints and enablements are tied to a person's perceived social status. It might even be that class is an opaque kind of social fact to the conferrers.[2] It would then be, due to its very opacity, in conflict with the central idea of conferralism, which is that the perception of other people is essential for a social property of an individual to exist. In short, conferrals by others is not a necessary condition for a social property of an individual to exist. Still, economic class is a social property that significantly impacts one's life chances and a key component of social injustice and oppression. Thus, it is central to Ásta's project. In summary, the conditions set out in the conferralist framework are not necessary for a social property of an individual to exist because some social properties, such as one's economic class, can exist without being conferred.

### 4.2.3 The Normative Commitment: Understanding Injustice and Oppression

One might think that our disagreement is merely verbal: should we or should we not call "class" in this Marxian sense a social category? I think, however, that the disagreement goes deeper and comes back to the question, "What are the phenomena we ought to be able to explain?" Given that a central motivation for *Categories We Live By* is to provide tools helpful for understanding injustice and oppression and tools that are useful for the humanities and social sciences, class is of utmost importance. Ásta writes:

---

[2] Amie Thomasson (2003) first introduced opaque kinds of social facts in a powerful objection to Searle's theory of social reality (1995). Thomasson distinguishes between epistemic and conceptual opacity: "Call a kind F of social entities 'epistemically opaque' if things of that kind are capable of existing even if no one believes that anything of kind F exists, and 'conceptually opaque' if things of that kind are capable of existing even if no one has any F-regarding beliefs whatsoever" (Thomasson 2003, 275–276).

CRITIQUE OF NONIDEAL SOCIAL ONTOLOGY   165

> My motivation for giving a metaphysics of social categories is fueled by the awareness that, while social categories can be a positive source of identity and belonging, they often are oppressive, and membership in them can put serious constraints on a person's life options. So, in offering my theory of social categories, the aim is to reveal the cogs and belts and arrangements of parts in machines that often are oppressive. Doing so also serves to support work done in the humanities and social sciences on the role of social construction in generating and upholding oppressive practices and institutions. (Ásta 2018, 4)

Call this "the normative commitment." Recall also that this is a work in feminist theory. Ásta notes that another condition of adequacy for her theory is to make sense of intersectionality. Much influential work in feminist theory has been about the intersection of class and gender (e.g., Skeggs 1997; Hill Collins 1990). The implication of not being able to account for the opacity of class is that conferralism fails to meet its own conditions of adequacy: providing tools helpful for understanding oppression and injustice, accounting for the intersection of class and gender central to feminist theory, and providing tools for the humanities and the social sciences in understanding the role of social construction in upholding oppressive regimes. So, is Ásta really identifying the categories we live by? In short, class can sometimes be a category that we don't know we live by but that still matters a great deal for Ásta's purposes. The upshot is that conferralism is too narrow, according to its own standard.

## 4.2.4  Reply: Conferralism Is a Theory of All Socially Salient Categories

One possible reply to this objection would be to claim that conferralism is an account of *most*, rather than *all*, social properties

## 166   RECONSTRUCTION: NONIDEAL SOCIAL ONTOLOGY

of individuals. Ásta has undoubtedly already greatly expanded our theories of the social world by giving communal properties their proper place, and it might simply be greedy to ask for more. Ásta claims, however, that her theory is an account of *any* social category: "The conferralist framework can be used to make sense of any social category. I show it in action by offering accounts of some of the most dominant social categories, but it can be used to account for any others" (2018, 4). Given this textual evidence, I take it that restricting the scope of the theory would not be Ásta's preferred choice of response.

Another related reply is to say that conferralism is an account of all *socially salient* properties of individuals and that economic class, especially opaque class, is not a socially salient category. There is textual evidence to support this response: "the main aim of the account I am offering is to account for socially salient categories and properties, phenomena that *make a social difference*" (Ásta 2018, 108, emphasis in original). The phrase "make a social difference" is used interchangeably with "social significance." In other words, the theory is meant to capture what it is for a feature of an individual to have social significance, understood as follows:

> for a feature B to have *social significance* in a context is for another feature F to be conferred upon people taken to have B. F is then the socially constructed feature. Let's take the example of disability again. For disability to be socially constructed, on this conception, is for a feature, physical impairment, to have *social significance* in a context such that people taken to have the feature get conferred onto them extra social constraints and enablements that are over and above the constraints and enablements that mere physical impairment brings. (Ásta 2018, 44)

Ásta offers the examples of laws that bar people with physical impairments from driving, even if they can physically drive safely (an example of an institutional constraint), and not taking someone

## CRITIQUE OF NONIDEAL SOCIAL ONTOLOGY 167

with a speech impairment seriously (an example of a communal constraint). One's economic class, if socially significant in the above sense, would then be a conferred property and hence captured by conferralism. If one's economic class is not socially significant in this sense (and the opaque dimensions of class would not be because they are not conferred), it would not on this view be a social property of an individual. It might rather be a material property or a material relation that has social consequences.[3] Thus, it would not be a counterexample to the claim that conferralism can accommodate all socially salient properties of individuals.

But the same problem shows up again: this sense of social significance is simply too narrow given the motivation of *Categories We Live By* and its normative commitment because it excludes properties that greatly impact one's life chances and contribute to social injustices and oppression. Distinguishing between two senses of "making a social difference" reveals the problem. The first is making a social difference in the sense of *affecting one's life chances* and contributing to injustices and oppression, even if one is unaware of it. The second is Ásta's sense of social significance, detailed above, which is conceptually related to conferrals by others. But social significance as affecting one's life chances is an important and intuitive sense given the motivation of this work and the normative commitment. Consequently, claiming that one gives an account of social properties that are socially significant in this narrow sense remains in conflict with the normative commitment. In short, to understand injustice and oppression that are not due to

---

[3] This was Ásta's response to this objection at the *Social Ontology 2019* conference in Tampere, Finland. This response is further developed as one of two possible routes Ásta considers in responding to this objection (Ásta 2020). The first route is to maintain that economic class is not a social category of individuals but rather a material category. The second route is to maintain that economic class is a social category of individuals. In addition to institutional and communal categories of individuals there is a material category of individuals. Conferralism concerns institutional and communal but not material categories of individuals. Ásta notes difficulties with both routes; that the first risks excluding a central social phenomenon that the theory ought to be able to explain and that the second limits the scope of conferralism (2020).

## 168  RECONSTRUCTION: NONIDEAL SOCIAL ONTOLOGY

conferrals by others we need another sense of social construction than "social construction as social significance."

Social significance plays an important role in the book as it is Ásta's preferred conception of social construction. This means that neither the conferralist framework nor social construction as social significance can accommodate opaque class. Consequently, neither of the two central conceptual resources of *Categories We Live By* can do this.[4] Note that this is not to say that Ásta's theory *cannot* handle opaque class in some way. Rather, my claim is that Ásta's account will remain *incomplete* until she has shown how to capture the first kind of social phenomena, or more precisely, the social categories of individuals that belong to the first kind of social phenomena.[5]

I believe this discussion points to a deeper methodological concern for social ontologists: in constructing our theories of the social world, we need to start from examples of all three of Khalidi's types of phenomena, not only the second and third types.

### 4.3  Institutions as Distributions and Economic Class

I now turn to Brännmark's theory of institutions as distributions, and whether it can accommodate economic class. This theory might be thought to overcome the above limitation of conferralism because it allows for the existence of the first and second kinds of social kind phenomena as social properties, in addition to the

---

[4] My preferred option would be to analyze opaque class as an indirect phenomenon that is dependent on the second and/or third types of social phenomena to exist, and that can be captured by another sense of social construction than social construction as social significance. I turn to this solution in Chapter 6.

[5] Ásta correctly points out, in responding to my objection, that the scope of conferralism is not to explain all social categories and therefore not to explain the general category of the first kind of social kind (for example recessions) but rather the social categories *of individuals* (Ásta 2020). I have thus changed the incompleteness claim in the main text to hold for social categories of individuals belonging to the first kind of social kind (e.g., economic class).

CRITIQUE OF NONIDEAL SOCIAL ONTOLOGY   169

third kind of social kind phenomena. Furthermore, it is explicitly designed to accommodate opaque kinds of social phenomena.

However, I argue that it is unclear whether this theory can meet its own conditions of adequacy. The reason is economic class—a key nonideal phenomenon relevant both for offering a correct description and for political theory—which cannot be a social position and thus not an institution on this account. And it has not yet been demonstrated that there are other theoretical resources to take economic class into account, so the theory is, at best, incomplete at this point.

### 4.3.1  Critique: Class Cannot Be a Social Position and Thus Not an Institution

The phenomenon of economic class poses a problem. In fact, the institutions as distributions approach has the same difficulty as conferralism in taking economic class into account because it takes other people's attitudes or conferrals to be a necessary condition for occupying a social position. Recall that *social position* is a core concept, understood as "how people are categorized as belonging to a certain class of agents or persons" (Brännmark 2019a, 1057). Note that, as with conferralism, other people's conferrals are relevant here. Brännmark expands on the idea of a social position:

> The necessary element is that there must be ideas in play about what qualifies someone as holding a certain social position. This can involve someone else having exercised Hohfeldian *powers* in a relevant way. For instance, if I want to become a legitimate medical doctor, I need to attend a school that has the power to confer on me the set of Hohfeldian incidents involved in being a doctor. But with many social positions there are instead informal rules of recognition in place which mean that if I fulfill certain criteria, anyone can (and is expected to) recognize me as occupying

170 RECONSTRUCTION: NONIDEAL SOCIAL ONTOLOGY

> the relevant position and, hence, as holding the relevant set of Hohfeldian incidents. For instance, in order to be recognized by your peers as having parental duties you do not need an official ruling that you are a parent. (Brännmark 2019a, 1058, emphasis in original)

A necessary condition, then, for someone to occupy a social position is that other people either formally or informally recognize one as occupying that position. This means that one's economic class cannot be a social position because social positions are grounded in other people's attitudes and behavior, while economic class is about one's relation to the means of production. So, these grounds exclude economic class from being a social position. Consequently, economic class cannot be an institution. This is dubious because both race and gender can be institutions. Economic class shares central features with gender and race, such as often informal and implicit and contested and opaque. In short, economic class is a key nonideal social phenomenon of great relevance to political theory. It thus needs to be captured according to Brännmark's own conditions of adequacy. But economic class is necessarily excluded from being a social position due to the assumption that the grounds of institutions and institutional facts are other people's attitudes and behaviors. This means that it is excluded from being an institution because the definition of an institution contains the notion of a social position.

I am *not* claiming that there are no theoretical resources within institutions as distributions to take economic class into account. Rather, I have shown that class cannot be a social position and hence not an institution according to the institutions as distributions account. One way to try to include economic class in this theory would be to understand social reality as layered and argue that class depends on other social phenomena to exist. So, institutions are grounded in micro-level attitudes and behaviors of individuals, in which case economic class can be grounded in

CRITIQUE OF NONIDEAL SOCIAL ONTOLOGY 171

institutions, like private property and corporations. However, there is not yet such an explanation. Like conferralism, then, the theory of institutions as distributions is incomplete—according to its own standards—until economic class is located.

## 4.4 Class and Gender and Race

I now turn to economic class in emancipatory social ontology. More specifically, let us return to the question from the previous chapter: Can we extend Haslanger's analyses of gender and race to economic class?

The short answer is no. Economic class cannot be given a similar analysis. One reason why economic class is necessarily excluded from Haslanger's account of gender and race is the reference to other people's attitudes in the first condition. But economic class works differently than many other social kinds because attitudes are not a necessary condition for belonging to a certain economic class. Another reason why this analysis cannot be extended to economic class is the reliance on bodily features (whether observed or imagined) in the first condition of respective analysis, but bodily features are not relevant in the same way in relation to economic class; the relationship to the means of production is what matters, not bodily features. This is not to say that economic class cannot affect bodily features; on the contrary, it often does to a great extent; indeed, access to dental care in Sweden is currently a class issue. So, for economic class, the relation obtains in the other direction from most other social kinds; membership in a certain economic class often affects bodily features, while for most social kinds, perception of presumed or real bodily features partly constitutes being a member of a social kind like gender and race.

I would like to make clear that I do not view the fact that Haslanger's account of *gender and race* cannot be extended to economic class as a criticism. Rather, my point is that there is an

## 172 RECONSTRUCTION: NONIDEAL SOCIAL ONTOLOGY

important asymmetry between gender and race on the one hand and economic class on the other, an asymmetry that is revealed by the fact that economic class cannot be given the same analysis as race and gender. The reason is the reliance on other people's perceptions present in the analyses of race and gender. That the account of gender and race cannot be extended to economic class is indeed relevant to the broader project of providing theoretical tools that are useful in fighting social injustice. In relation to this, recall that one of Haslanger's own conditions of adequacy refers explicitly to the importance of an intersectionalist analysis of gender, race, and class. So, once again, the upshot is that economic class is relevant to nonideal social ontologists (including the emancipatory version of nonideal social ontology), and the cause for exclusion is the same: the reliance on other people's attitudes. Jenkins' concept of ontic injustice does not rely on other people's attitudes in the same way as the theories discussed above and thus opens up the possibility of capturing economic class.

## 4.5 Class and Ontic Injustice

What about ontic injustice and class? Can economic class be an example of ontic injustice? Let us review Jenkins' definition of ontic injustice:

> An individual suffers ontic injustice if and only if they are socially constructed as a member of a certain social kind where that construction consists, at least in part, of their being subjected to a set of social constraints and enablements that is wrongful to them. (2020, 191)

An implication of this view is that one can suffer ontic injustice without knowing, which is relevant for economic class. Although Jenkins (2020) does not explicitly apply this analysis to class, it has

CRITIQUE OF NONIDEAL SOCIAL ONTOLOGY   173

the theoretical resources to state that being a member of a certain economic class, say the working class, is an example of ontic injustice. The reason is that this approach does not rely on attitudes in the same way as the other approaches do. Jenkins' approach to social kinds does rely on other people's attitudes because these social kinds are partly constituted by social constraints and enablements. But it is the negative mismatch between one's social constraints and enablements and one's moral entitlements that constitutes ontic injustice, and people might not even be aware of this gap. The fact that someone can suffer ontic injustice without knowing about it is a strength of this account because it opens up the possibility of accounting for the first kind of social kind phenomena as "sites of ontic injustice." The upshot is that Jenkins singles out another type of opacity—that just being a member of a social kind can, in and of itself, constitute a moral wrong.

For example, there was most likely a negative mismatch between the social constraints and enablements of being a factory worker in nineteenth-century Britain and a person's moral entitlements. It is possible to extend Jenkins' analysis to economic class and say that being a member of this social kind means, *ipso facto*, that one suffers ontic injustice. Note, however, that this is not a descriptive account of the nature of economic class and how it exists; rather, it is a moral critique. My last point assumes a boundary between social ontology and moral and political matters—a boundary that Jenkins and other emancipatory social ontologists might question.

## 4.6  Conclusion

In the previous chapter, I pointed out a central similarity between ideal social ontology and the two theories of nonideal social ontology somewhere in the middle of the spectrum (conferralism and institutions as distributions) concerning the basic building blocks—reliance on other people's attitudes as a condition of

# 174 RECONSTRUCTION: NONIDEAL SOCIAL ONTOLOGY

existence for social phenomena. This is relevant in relation to the important anomaly that I have discerned in nonideal social ontology: that economic class is not a phenomena of concern in nonideal social ontology despite the fact that it is a key nonideal social phenomena, and that it is crucial for meeting the conditions of adequacy of nonideal social ontology. I suggested the following theoretical explanation of this anomaly: Any type of analysis that directly rests on people's attitudes cannot be extended to economic class because class does not depend on other people's attitudes in the same way that many other social kinds do. This relates to the standard model of ideal social ontology. Because nonideal social ontology has not moved far enough away from it, economic class is excluded from being a social kind and has thus dropped out of sight in this tradition too.

Now, there is a specific and influential subcategory of nonideal social ontology—emancipatory social ontology—that has moved further away from the standard model of ideal social ontology in the sense that it does not share the same purpose and method. For emancipatory social ontology, the primary aim is social change rather than descriptive metaphysics. With respect to Haslanger's analysis of gender and race, I have shown that class was used as a theoretical starting point, an analytical tool, and a condition of adequacy, but that no analysis of economic class was offered here either. In fact, Haslanger's analysis could not be extended to economic class for the same reason as the other theories; its reliance on other people's attitudes is built into the definition. Jenkins' concept of ontic injustice is different; here, economic class can be said to be ontically unjust because this analysis does not rest on other people's attitudes in the same way as the other theories. However, we still do not have a purely descriptive account of economic class; that is, an account of the nature and existence of economic class. This is relevant because economic class is important to all these branches: for ideal social ontology, in obtaining an accurate description of social reality and in providing a foundation for the social sciences;

for nonideal social ontology, for the same reasons, and either to not contribute to ideology understood in a pejorative sense, or to understand oppression and thus also contribute to ending it; and for emancipatory social ontologists, in offering theoretical tools that are useful in the fight against oppression.

In Chapters 5 and 6, I develop a pluralistic account of social power and propose a taxonomy of social facts that can accommodate economic class. Part of developing this pluralistic account of social power is to show that we need another building block in our ontology: telic power. This is the topic of the next chapter.

# 5

# Telic Power

## 5.1 Introduction

In previous chapters, I have shown that *deontic power* is a central concept in both ideal and nonideal social ontology. I have also shown that it is *the* central form of power in ideal social ontology, which is illustrated by the deonticity claim of the standard model of ideal social ontology. In this chapter, I argue that deontic power, however, is too narrow to capture a central dimension of the social world exemplified by certain aspects of gender and class. One reason why this category has been neglected in social ontology is a one-sided diet of examples and consequent emphasis on deontic power. More generally, my point is that works in ideal social ontology tend to assume a consensus-oriented view of social phenomena, rather than regarding them in terms of conflict and contestation. This impacts what are taken to be paradigmatic social phenomena, which is a central theory choice that highlights some aspects of social reality while hiding others. As a methodological point of departure, I take gender and class as paradigmatic social phenomena and thus as central examples from which to start. I will argue that shifting from the standard examples of being a citizen or a professor to being a woman or of a certain class means that a distinct central dimension of the social world can reveal itself.

I introduce another category of power—telic power—which has hitherto been overlooked. I provide a definition of telic power before giving two reasons for introducing this new concept. First, it captures a distinct central dimension of the social world, previously neglected due to the one-sided use of examples and the subsequent

*Nonideal Social Ontology.* Åsa Burman, Oxford University Press. © Oxford University Press 2023.
DOI: 10.1093/oso/9780197509579.003.0006

emphasis on deontic power. Second, it is theoretically useful because, among other things, telic power can both conflict with and reinforce our deontic powers. Consequently, I offer a pluralistic account of social power that consists of telic power and deontic power among others.

## 5.2 Deontic Normativity and Deontic Power in Social Ontology

To illustrate dimensions of the social world that are usually hidden, it is helpful to first examine the sole emphasis on the deontic exemplified by the main proponents of the early debate in ideal social ontology. Raimo Tuomela views *social practices* as a core concept and an agent's position within these social practices are defined in terms of deontic powers. He writes: "A (social) position in a given social system will be understood here basically as a set of obligations and rights" (2002, 223). In her pioneering work *On Social Facts*, Margaret Gilbert's main claim is that many of our everyday collectivity concepts, such as collective action, social groups, and social conventions, have the notion of *a plural subject* at its core. And Gilbert offers the following analysis of a plural subject, "Generalizing: for any set of people, $P1, \ldots Pn$, and any psychological attribute $A$, $P1, \ldots Pn$ form the plural subject of $A$-ing if and only if they are jointly committed to $A$-ing as a body" (1996, 8). Note that a key notion is *joint commitment*; that is, a deontic notion. Furthermore, a core concept in John Searle's theories of social reality is *deontic power* (1995, 2010). This focus on the deontic is represented by the deonticity claim in the standard model of ideal social ontology. A recent interesting development in ideal social ontology is the emphasis on *moral deontic notions* such as human rights. Both Searle (2010) and Gilbert (2018) have developed an account of human rights. This development illuminates the same focus on the deontic.

## 178   RECONSTRUCTION: NONIDEAL SOCIAL ONTOLOGY

Recall the notion of deontic power and the distinction between positive and negative institutional deontic power that Searle (1995, 100) describes:

> The first [positive deontic power] is where the agent is endowed with some new power, certification, authorization, entitlement, right, permission, or qualification granting the ability to do something he or she could not otherwise have done; and the second [negative deontic power] is where the agent is required, obligated, in duty bound, penalized, enjoined, or otherwise compelled to do something he or she would not otherwise have had to do—or, what amounts to the same thing, prevented from doing something that would otherwise have been doable. Roughly speaking, the two major categories are those of positive and negative powers.

Deontic power is understood as a dispositional concept or an ability, as this quote makes clear. Viewing deontic power as an ability means that an agent can have power without exercising it, in contrast to the view that power only exists when it is exercised. Positive deontic powers are institutional rights, while negative deontic powers are institutional obligations. There is a connection between status functions, deontic powers, and reasons for action on Searle's account: status functions are meant to regulate behavior and expectations and have deontic powers tied to them to fulfill this role. Recognizing these deontic powers creates desire-independent reasons for action. So, according to Searle's (2001) theory, the mere recognition of a status function as binding gives rise to reasons for action. This means that deontic power works through the perception of *normative reasons* because agents regard themselves as normatively bound to act in certain ways.[1]

---

[1] In the case of desire-independent reasons for action, the reason is prior to the desire, and the reason is the ground of the desire. In the case of desire-dependent reasons for action, the desire is prior to the reason, and the desire is the ground of the reason.

In Chapter 3, I showed that deontic power is also a central concept in nonideal social ontology. For example, the conferralist view analyzes institutional properties in terms of deontic powers, whereas communal properties are non-deontic social powers. Ásta thus opens up a wider notion of social power than, for example, Brännmark, whose account of institutions as distributions takes the emphasis on deontic powers one step further and argues that both formal and informal (what Ásta refers to as communal) social positions are just typical bundles of Hohfeldian incidents; that is, of deontic powers.

Deontic power is also a central form of social power in the special subcategory of emancipatory social ontology. For example, Haslanger's analysis of gender and race involves hierarchy as an essential element and deontic power is plausibly a key component of hierarchies. Jenkins, too, uses deontic power in her central example of ontic injustice—that of being a wife in England and Wales before 1991—and as a key component in the constraint and enablement framework she has recently developed (Jenkins, 2023).

The upshot of these developments in nonideal social ontology is twofold: first, most of these accounts plausibly suggest that there are other central forms of social power than deontic, and it is thus important to identify and analyze these other forms of social power.[2] Second, there is a clearer understanding of deontic power available than has hitherto been the case; namely, the explication of deontic powers in terms of Hohfeldian incidents. In Chapter 6, I will show

---

For example, a promise creates a desire-independent reason for action in Searle's analysis: "promises are by definition creations of obligations; and obligations are by definition reasons for action" (2001, 193). Nothing in my argument hinges on there being desire-independent reasons for action (in contract to desire-dependent reasons for action).

[2] Note that Brännmark's account of institutions is essentially deontic and that no other forms of social power are needed to give a general account of *institutions*. This is still compatible with holding the view that there are other forms of social power in social reality.

180   RECONSTRUCTION: NONIDEAL SOCIAL ONTOLOGY

how this more fine-grained notion of deontic power can be useful for both ideal and nonideal social ontologists.

There are, however, some accounts of teleological normativity in social ontology. Examinations of teleological normativity with respect to social action and institutions include Seumas Miller's *Social Action: A Teleological Account* (2001) and, more recently, Frank Hindriks and Francesco Guala's "The Functions of Institutions: Etiology and Teleology" (2021). Charlotte Witt and Sally Haslanger use the idea of teleological normativity in novel ways with respect to gender and gender norms. In the following sections, I take their views of gender norms and teleological normativity one step further by explicitly identifying and defending a new form of general social power.

## 5.3  Teleological Normativity

Returning to the standard examples of being a citizen or a professor used in ideal social ontology, I want to draw attention to a noteworthy feature. Having imposed this status function on someone implies that one can *evaluate* how well this person fulfills this status function: is she an excellent, good, or bad professor? The possibility of evaluating people in this way suggests that there is a different type of normativity than deontic in the social world, namely, teleological normativity.[3] In this section, I clarify this notion with an example about a certain aspect of class and gender.

Sociologist Beverley Skeggs investigated gender and class norms in *Formations of Class and Gender: Becoming Respectable* (1997) by conducting interviews with British working-class women. Many of them worked in the home as housewives. Skeggs refers to the norm of good housewife in this context as someone who has an

---

[3] I claim that the sole focus in the early debate in ideal social ontology has been deontic normativity and that the *main* focus in social ontology has been on deontic normativity.

TELIC POWER    181

impeccably clean home, respectable clothes, refined language, and shows care and concern for others.

*Housewife example:* One of the women interviewed shared her thoughts with Skeggs (1997, 3) after a Health Visitor inspected the interviewee's home:

> You know they're weighing you up and they ask you all these indirect questions as if you're too thick to know what they're getting at and you know all the time they're thinking "she's poor, she's no good, she can't bring her kids up properly" and no matter what you do they've got your number. To them you're never fit, never up to their standards.

The woman notes a standard that she fails to live up to in the eyes of the Health Visitor—and perhaps even herself—and that thus she is not a good housewife. Consider a fact specific to this example:

> (i) The fact that housewife H was perceived to fail to meet the standard of a good housewife by the Health Visitor (and herself).

The housewife example illustrates one important sense of a "norm," which is that of an *existing ideal* or *standard* against which objects and individuals can be measured. Being perceived as living up to the ideal means that you are perceived as a *good instance of that kind*, in this case a housewife, while being perceived as not living up to the ideal means that you are perceived of as a *bad instance of that kind*. Here, the interviewee is well aware of the standard to which she is held and notes her failure to live up to it.

This quote and fact (i) point to another aspect of being a housewife than what can be expressed in terms of deontic normativity and deontic power. One key aspect of being a housewife can be understood in terms of rights and obligations. For example, she might have the right to certain governmental benefits due to her social role, which is a positive deontic power, but she also mentions

## 182 RECONSTRUCTION: NONIDEAL SOCIAL ONTOLOGY

not being good and never being able to reach a certain standard. Consequently, employing only deontic power to describe this case would mean missing at least one of its crucial aspects and thus mischaracterizing it: the Health Visitor does have the *right* to visit the home, but she does not have the right to visit an impeccably clean home. Meanwhile, the interviewee does not have an *obligation* to have an impeccably clean home, although she does have an obligation to pay taxes on her benefits and take care of her children. So, to describe fact (i) adequately, social ontologists need other conceptual resources than deontic normativity and deontic power, which I call teleological normativity and telic power.

To explain the notion of teleological normativity, I begin by contrasting it with deontic normativity, which concerns what we can demand of each other. Teleological normativity concerns ideals that we (sometimes) try to live up to and others expect us to live up to. Consider that some functions of being a housewife or a woman are defined in terms of a purpose or goal rather than in terms of rights and obligations, which means that there is an ideal measuring how well we live up to this purpose. This ideal provides agents with reasons for action; for example, a woman perceives that she ought to live up to a certain ideal and that others are expecting her to do so.

### 5.3.1 Haslanger on Teleological Normativity and Gender Norms

To continue to clarify these concepts and the connection between them, it is helpful to consider Sally Haslanger's work on gender norms, which "are clusters of characteristics and abilities that function as a standard by which individuals are judged to be 'good' instances of their gender; they are the 'virtues' appropriate to the gender" (2012, 42). Haslanger illustrates her notion of a gender norm with an example of a paring knife:

Something counts as a paring knife only if it has features that enable it to perform a certain function: it must be easily usable by humans to cut and peel fruits and vegetables. We can distinguish, however, between something's marginally performing that function and something's performing that function excellently. A good paring knife has a sharp blade with a comfortable handle; a poor paring knife might be one that is so blunt that it crushes rather than cuts a piece of fruit, it might be too large to handle easily, and so on. Those features that enable a paring knife to be *excellent* at its job, are the "virtues" of a paring knife. (2012, 42–43)

Applying this idea to the housewife example shows that some aspects of the social role of a housewife involve being measured against an ideal: the role consists not only of the constitutive rules that specify our rights and obligations but also of an ideal or a standard, so what counts as having succeeded as a housewife is measured against that ideal. In Skeggs' study, the ideal consists of having an impeccably clean home, respectable clothes, refined language, and care and concern for others, and the interviewee is viewed as far from excellent in this respect. She falls short of the ideal.

The upshot is that social reality also consists of ideals that we sometimes want to live up to and that others expect us to live up to. The main focus in ideal social ontology to date has been on status functions defined in terms of rights and obligations and thus on deontic normativity. However, once we have imposed status functions on people, it becomes possible to judge whether or not they are excellent at their jobs, whether or not they demonstrate the "virtues" of that role. So, for example, one might measure a particular professor against the ideal of professorship, and one might conclude that she is an *exemplar of that kind* or that she falls short of the ideal and is thus *substandard.* The same holds for individual women and men, whom we often measure against ideals of femininity and

## 184 RECONSTRUCTION: NONIDEAL SOCIAL ONTOLOGY

masculinity. Haslanger continues to use the analogy of the paring knife to clarify gender norms:

> In general, our evaluation of the goodness or badness of a tool will be relative to a function, end, or purpose, and the norm will serve as an ideal embodying excellence in the performance of that function. Likewise, masculinity and femininity are norms or standards by which individuals are judged to be exemplars of their gender and which enable us to function excellently in our allotted role in the system of social relations that constitute gender.... For each role there are performances that would count as successes and others that would count as failures; in general, one could do a better or worse job at them. The suggestion is that gender roles are of this kind; gender-norms capture how one should behave and what attributes are suitable if one is to excel in the socially sanctioned gender roles. (2012, 42–43)

Haslanger points to an important feature of gender norms; they capture how one should or *ought* to behave, and there are sanctions ranging from strange looks to ostracism if one does not conform to gender norms. This can be explained in terms of reasons for action. If an agent, say the housewife, recognizes an ideal, she experiences an "ought," which gives her reasons for action to try to live up to the ideal.[4] The interviewee above might spend a lot of time on cleaning the house before the inspection by the Health Visitor and pay extra attention to clothes and language. Hence, these ideals provide reasons for action which can come into conflict with reasons for action deriving from deontic powers. To use another example: a professor might experience a conflict between

---

[4] On the other hand, if an agent recognizes but opposes a certain ideal, it might generate reasons for action in opposition to the ideal, as when there exists a norm that women should not speak up in public, and a woman speaks up to protest to that norm. This might, however, generate reasons for action for some other people in the group, who might impose a social sanction by not inviting her to the next meeting.

the telic and the deontic aspects of her status function as professor. She might experience a conflict between her deontic powers, such as administrative obligations, and standards of excellence or ideals connected to the status function of being a professor, such as publishing high-quality work beyond what is strictly required. This is a conflict between two different types of "ought"; there appear to be at least two different types of social "oughts," and this discussion adds the "ought" of teleological normativity. To further clarify how this "ought" differs from the deontic "ought" it is helpful to draw on Charlotte's Witt original account of gender essentialism for social individuals, and more specifically, her defense of the ascriptivist account of social normativity.

### 5.3.2 Witt on Social Normativity and Gender as a Mega Social Role

Witt develops and defends a new version of gender essentialism using an Aristotelian framework. She changes and weakens the general formulation of gender essentialism—roughly, that there is some feature all women have in common that makes them belong to the category of woman—in two ways. First, gender essentialism is a view about *individuals* rather than kinds; second, it is about *social* individuals in contrast to human organisms or persons. Witt's main claim is that "gender is uniessential to social individuals" (2011, 30). Unification essentialism, or uniessentialism, offers an answer to the ontological question "what is it?" in terms of constitution; more specifically, what makes an individual object or person into that particular individual is its functional essence. "A functional essence is an essential property that explains what the individual is for, what its purpose is, and that organizes the parts toward that end" (Witt 2011, 14). For example, the functional property of a house is to provide shelter, and it is this function that makes the material parts into the whole that is the house. Likewise,

## 186 RECONSTRUCTION: NONIDEAL SOCIAL ONTOLOGY

gender plays a unifying role and makes us the social individuals we are (Witt 2011, 18). Witt argues that gender is a mega social role in the sense that it is prior to and organizes our other social roles such as being a parent or a professor (Witt 2011, 78–80).

Witt's work is a substantial and novel contribution to social ontology and feminist theory. For my purposes, the ascriptivist account of social normativity that she develops and defends is especially important. According to Witt, social normativity differs from ethical normativity in at least two ways: first, social normativity relates to us as occupiers of social positions in particular cultures, presumably in contrast to ethical norms relating to us as persons; second, it is the assessments of others that ground social normativity, in contrast to the agent herself accepting a norm (Witt 2011, 76). Witt writes:

> For social normativity, therefore, it is the assessment by others that establishes or grounds its normative pull rather than the individual's acceptance or endorsement of a norm, which is often thought to ground ethical obligation. Hence, social normativity, while a genuine and important kind of normativity, is different from ethical normativity. (Witt 2011, 76)

The key idea for my purposes is that once others view a person as having a particular social role, that person becomes "responsive to and evaluable under a social norm" (Witt 2011, 19). It is important to note that it is other people's perception or recognition that matters and, as Witt convincingly argues, that we are always stuck with these evaluations, even if we detest the norms behind them; there is simply no escape. Thus, even if we protest against an unjust gender norm, we are still responsive to it and evaluable under it, including by the act of protesting.

I also agree with the view that social normativity is genuine and different from ethical or moral normativity, but I draw the distinction between social normativity and moral normativity differently than Witt. According to the ascriptivist account of social normativity, the social ought is understood as a *normative pull* coming from our social roles, while the moral ought is understood in terms of *obligation*. Witt writes, "I use the phrase 'responsive to and evaluable under' to describe the normative pull of social roles rather than the language of obligation, which is more appropriate to describe ethical normativity" (2011, 32). Rather than understanding the social ought in terms of a normative pull and the moral ought in terms of obligation, as Witt does, I think there are two separate dimensions at play here. One dimension is social versus moral normativity, and the other dimension is teleology versus deontology. These two dimensions can cut across one another. For example, occupants of social roles often have institutional rights and obligations (deontic powers) due to their social roles, and these institutional rights and obligations can be morally justified or unjustified. So, there is a social ought deriving from our negative deontic powers; that is, our obligations. This social ought can be compatible with or in conflict with a moral ought.[5] Additionally, occupants of social roles are "responsive to and evaluable under" a norm and thus experience the normative pull of that social norm, a norm that can be morally justified or unjustified. Witt offers the example of the defective bank robber as an example of being evaluated under a social norm that is morally unjustified (2011, 17). So, there can be a social ought deriving from the social norms that we fall under as occupants of various social roles. In addition to the teleological social ought, then, I think that there is a deontic social ought.[6]

---

[5] This narrow sense of "deontic"—an institutional ought following from an institutional obligation—is common in contemporary social ontology. It can be contrasted with the traditional and wider sense of "deontic" understood as what one ought to do (e.g., morally or as a matter of rationality) or the right thing to do (in a moral sense). On this narrow understanding of deontic, one's positive and negative deontic powers can be illegitimate, or morally wrong.

[6] There might be a moral obligation to develop our talents (deontic normativity), but there might also be aspects of moral norms pertaining to us as persons, say developing our talents, that are about teleological normativity. I do not take a stand as to whether there can be instances of the fourth category: a teleological moral ought.

188  RECONSTRUCTION: NONIDEAL SOCIAL ONTOLOGY

My definition of telic power has some similarities with Witt's view: it is other people's perceptions or assessments that matter; the telic power of an individual partly refers to being evaluable under a social norm, and the normativity in question is social and not moral.[7] I depart from Witt's view in two ways. First, I draw the distinction between social and moral normativity in a different way, as explained, and second, I identify and define a distinctive form of general social power built on teleological normativity. I now turn to my definition of telic power.

## 5.4  Telic Power

This teleological "ought" is relevant for social power. Some forms of social power, such as deontic power, work through agents' perceiving that, due to deontic normativity, they ought to perform a certain action as a result of recognizing a status function. Other forms of social power work through agents' perceiving a different kind of ought (teleological normativity) related to an ideal. This involves a *coercive dimension* (cf., gender norms) as well as a certain kind of "pull-effect" in the sense that agents *strive* to fulfill some of the ideals they embrace (cf., being an excellent scholar). The coercive dimension and the pull-effect is related to social power. The evaluation of an agent by other agents and the effects of these evaluations can thus give rise to telic power.

> TELIC POWER: An agent A has telic power if and only if there exists an ideal such that agent A can be measured against it, and the distance perceived by other agents of A from the ideal affects A's ability to effect certain outcomes.

This category of power is inherently social in two respects: there must exist a shared norm or ideal in the community in question,

---

[7] This differs from Seumas Miller's (2001) teleological account of norms, which is a moral account; it includes a "moral ought" in the conditions (139).

and it is the judgment of other people that is partly constitutive of a given agent's telic power. This category thus shares a central feature with deontic power: an agent's telic power is partly constituted by the intentionality of other agents, just like an agent's deontic power is partly constituted by the intentionality of other agents. The ideals are related to functions in the way previously suggested; once we have imposed a function on someone or something—either assigning the status function of a professor or assigning the function of a paring knife—it becomes possible to evaluate that person or thing according to a standard.

Let us return to the housewife example. The interviewee noted that she was perceived as far from fulfilling the housewife ideal, which is likely to restrict her actions in certain ways. In contrast, if she were perceived as fulfilling the ideal, that would most likely enable her actions. For instance, we might imagine that the Health Visitor inspection was part of a process of determining whether the parents should be allowed to keep custody of their children. In one scenario, the interviewee is perceived as a good housewife, and this piece of information might tip the case in the parents' favor, allowing them to retain custody. In another scenario, she is perceived as a bad housewife, as substandard, and this piece of information might tip the case in the opposite direction and cause the parents to lose custody. This suggests that telic power can both reinforce and conflict with deontic power because how well someone is perceived as fulfilling an ideal can impact that agent's deontic powers. Consequently, and as with deontic power, it is theoretically useful to make a distinction between positive and negative telic power, understood as a variation of the general formula of telic power above:

POSITIVE TELIC POWER: An agent A has positive telic power if and only if agent A is perceived as living up to the ideal; she is viewed by other agents as a good exemplar of the relevant kind, and this positively affects or enhances A's ability to effect certain outcomes.

# 190 RECONSTRUCTION: NONIDEAL SOCIAL ONTOLOGY

> NEGATIVE TELIC POWER: An agent A has negative telic power if and only if agent A is perceived as not living up to the ideal; she is viewed by other agents as substandard or as a bad exemplar of the relevant kind, and this negatively affects or restricts A's ability to effect certain outcomes.

Even though the definitions of positive telic power and negative telic power handle the custody example well, they are open to a serious objection: an agent's positive telic power can restrict, rather than enhance, his ability to effect certain outcomes, and an agent's negative telic power can enhance, rather than restrict, her ability to effect certain outcomes. Consider the following example.

*The muscular quantum physicist.* Quentin is a former professional bodybuilder and currently a hard-working quantum physicist. He is still active in the gym and admired by his peers there for his bodily features; he is elected a new board member of the gym. He struggles, however, to gain acceptance among his university colleagues. He learns that, once again, a scrawny junior colleague has been selected over him as department chair.

Assume that the explanation behind Quentin's new status function and deontic power as a gym board member is due to his positive telic power, which he has because he is viewed as an exemplar of the masculinity ideal shared among his gym peers. However, this is also the explanation behind not being selected department chair because this same masculinity ideal is in conflict with the quantum physicist ideal (not unlike Sheldon Cooper in *The Big Bang Theory*).

The ability to effect certain outcomes thus needs to be understood as domain-specific; it is in the specific domain relevant to the social role as bodybuilder or quantum physicist, respectively, that an agent's positive telic power enhances his ability to effect certain outcomes and an agent's negative telic power restricts his ability to effect certain outcomes. I propose the general definition of telic power and its two variations as:

TELIC POWER*: An agent A has telic power in a domain if and only if there exists an ideal such that agent A can be measured against it and the distance perceived by other agents of A from the ideal affects A's ability to effect certain outcomes in that domain.

POSITIVE TELIC POWER*: An agent A has positive telic power in a domain if and only if agent A is perceived by other agents as living up to the ideal, as a good exemplar of the relevant kind, and this positively affects or enhances A's ability to effect certain outcomes in that domain.

NEGATIVE TELIC POWER*: An agent A has negative telic power in a domain if and only if agent A is perceived by other agents as not living up to the ideal; she is viewed as substandard or as a bad exemplar of the relevant kind, and this negatively affects or restricts A's ability to effect certain outcomes in that domain.

## 5.5  A Distinct Central Dimension of the Social World

The definitions of deontic and telic power reveal both similarities and differences. They are alike with respect to power being an ability that is directly dependent on the intentionality of other agents; agents (rather than structures) have power, and there is positive power that enables action and negative power that restricts action. However, there are key differences that make clear that telic power is distinct from deontic power.

One difference is that a person can be seen as fulfilling an ideal to a greater or lesser degree: there is a gradual scale. In contrast, having an institutional right, a positive deontic power, is binary; a person either has the right to receive a salary in virtue of being an employee or does not.

## 192 RECONSTRUCTION: NONIDEAL SOCIAL ONTOLOGY

Another difference is that deontic power and telic power have different existence conditions. Telic power requires ideals, rather than institutions and status functions, to exist.[8] Telic power can exist without deontic power; imagine, for instance, a society with only ideals but no institutional rights and obligations.[9] Telic power, in contrast to deontic power, does not necessarily depend on institutions to exist, as there can be non-institutional social statuses displaying teleological normativity and telic power, such as the social status of being a woman or man. In our context, there are no institutional rights and obligations attached to the social role of being a woman or a man, but there are certainly ideals of femininity and masculinity. The examples regarding gender norms present a noteworthy difference between telic and deontic power. Telic power is not dependent on institutions to exist; rather, it is dependent on social norms to exist. Telic power having different existence conditions from deontic power points to a separate telic dimension.

Still another reason pointing to telic being separate from deontic is the possibility of an "ought-remainder." Recall the earlier example of the professor who experienced a conflict between her deontic powers, such as administrative obligations, and standards of excellence or ideals connected to the status function of being a professor, such as publishing high-quality work *beyond what is required*. Assume that she has fulfilled all her institutional obligations but still believes that she ought to do more with respect to her role as professor. Deontic power cannot explain this "ought" because she has already fulfilled all her institutional obligations. This "ought" is separate from deontic power. To explain this case, it is

---

[8] I understand "institution" in the rather narrow sense defined by Searle as "a system of constitutive rules" (1995).

[9] One might question that telic power exists. But it should be clear that it has causal powers in the same sense as deontic power has, which is a common criterion for existence. But as this example illustrates, they do not have the same causal powers (cf., also the professor example).

useful to invoke the category of telic power, because this "ought" is related to an ideal. Examples of acts that go beyond what is required point to the telic category. Consider an analogy with supererogatory acts. The etymology of the word "supererogatory" is "paying out more than is due," and the idea refers to a class of actions that go beyond the call of duty, actions that are morally "praiseworthy though non-obligatory acts" (Heyd 2002). This example illustrates actions that are socially (and sometimes morally) praiseworthy but not institutionally required. Let us return to the conflict between the two different "oughts": once she has fulfilled all her administrative obligations, our professor still feels that she ought to do things that are socially (and sometimes morally) praiseworthy but not required by virtue of her institutional role. This possibility of an "ought-remainder" after one has fulfilled all one's deontic requirements (obligations) points to a separate telic dimension.

## 5.6 Theoretical Usefulness

In this section, I argue that viewing gender and class as paradigmatic social phenomena shows that social ontologists need conceptual resources other than deontic power, such as telic power, to capture important aspects of the social world.

*The research funding case:* Christine Wennerås and Agnes Wold decided to investigate potential sexism and nepotism in the postdoctoral fellowship research funding process of the Medical Research Council (MRC), a key agency supporting biomedical research in Sweden. They found a significant *gender bias* and *affiliation bias* in the funding system: "a female applicant had to be 2.5 times more productive than the average male applicant to receive the same competence score as he" (1997, 342). Similar results were found for being affiliated with someone on the committee: "the affiliation bonus was of the same magnitude as the 'male gender' bonus" (1997, 342). They reached these conclusions by comparing

## 194 RECONSTRUCTION: NONIDEAL SOCIAL ONTOLOGY

the scientific competence score each applicant received from the MRC with the number and quality of each applicant's scientific publications. The authors were able to access the competence scores for each applicant due to Sweden's Freedom of Press Act, which grants access to documents held by official bodies. Consider a fact specific to this example:

> (ii) the fact that "a female applicant had to be 2.5 times more productive than the average male applicant to receive the same competence score as he." (Wennerås and Wold 1997, 342)

The outcome of the funding process was that four women and sixteen men were awarded a postdoctoral fellowship by the MRC. Another fact related to this case is (iii) the fact that male applicant M was awarded a postdoctoral fellowship by the MRC, which is an institutional fact. There are many other institutional facts with accompanying deontic powers in this case. For instance, it is an institutional fact that the chair of the committee has a PhD, and it is another institutional fact that postdoctoral applicant M has a PhD, or he would not have been eligible for the fellowship. Applying key concepts from the standard model of ideal social ontology is helpful in analyzing (iii).

However, (ii) has a different character than (iii). It is not the case that a male applicant has a *right* to receive a "gender bonus" or that an applicant who knows someone on the committee has a *right* to receive an "affiliation bonus." The members of the MRC certainly do not have an *obligation* to give competence scores based on gender, affiliation, or both. By contrast, the applicants might have a right to receive a decision within three months, and the members of the MRC might thus have an obligation to process all applications to meet that deadline. Hence, it would be a mischaracterization to describe (ii) in terms of institutional facts and deontic powers. Social ontologists interested in explaining social phenomena other than the institutional rights and obligations of citizens and professors, such as the distribution of deontic powers among different social groups or how our social roles as women or men or our class affect our life chances, need other conceptual resources, such as telic power.

The category of telic power can be theoretically useful in clarifying *feedback loops* between the different categories and can thus increase our understanding of the research funding case and similar examples.[10] One part of the explanation for the female applicants' lack of positive deontic power and the male applicants' positive deontic power might lie in telic power: women on average are more likely to be perceived as substandard and men as exemplars of the researcher ideal. In this way, telic power can impact the competence score of the applicants and result in a lack of positive deontic powers for women, which in this case results in not being awarded a postdoc. That is, the negative telic power of female applicants can partly explain their limited access, compared to male applicants, to the positive deontic powers of a postdoctoral fellowship. This outcome reinforces the negative telic powers of female researchers while enhancing the positive telic powers of male researchers because one aspect of being perceived as an exemplar of a researcher is being awarded this kind of prestigious fellowship. In short, the telic powers of agents can impact their deontic powers, and their deontic powers can impact their telic powers.

In addition to providing explanatory tools for cases in which telic and deontic powers reinforce or conflict with each other, there are conflicts between different ideals, leading to cases of *conflicting standards*. First, imagine a businessperson whose work requires significant amounts of travel. This individual is often absent from the everyday lives of family and friends. Achieving excellence in one's career might conflict with being a good partner, friend, or parent, which requires a regular presence in the everyday lives of those to whom one is close. The two standards are incompatible in

---

[10] For an actual case of this kind, see Malmström, Johansson, and Wincent (2017).

## 196 RECONSTRUCTION: NONIDEAL SOCIAL ONTOLOGY

the sense that one cannot achieve excellence in both, or even be viewed as a good instance of both, standards. However, one can be considered good or excellent according to one standard. So, a person can fall short (or even fail) according to one standard precisely by achieving excellence with respect to another.[11]

Second, imagine a case in which the conflict between different standards is irresolvable in the sense that whatever a person does, she will be perceived as substandard. Marilyn Frye writes of the "double bind" as "situations in which options are reduced to a very few, and all of them expose one to penalty, censure, or deprivation" (1983, 2). Frye continues with an example: "It is common in the United States that women, especially younger women, are in a bind where neither sexual activity nor sexual inactivity is all right." If a young woman is sexually active, she may be punished (in the form of criticism or snide remarks) for being "loose" and an "easy lay," while she may be punished for being "uptight" and "frigid" if she is sexually inactive (1983, 3). So, being a young woman means, according to the norms Frye describes, being perceived as substandard and a bad instance of a woman, no matter what she does. This conflict is irresolvable. Another, more contemporary, example involves female managers. According to some norms and ideals of femininity, women should not be assertive, but according to norms of leadership, leaders should or must be assertive. So, if a female manager is assertive and thus fulfills the business ideal of a good manager, she is perceived as substandard with respect to femininity; by contrast, if she fulfills a feminine ideal by not being assertive, she is perceived as a substandard manager.

Another version of the double bind is the unavailability of standard types of cases, that is, cases where a person's experience and life plan cannot be made sense of because there is either no

---

[11] Witt offers a similar example of the single mother who is a medical doctor. She experiences a conflict between her social role as mother and her social role as a doctor that includes working night shifts (2011, 84).

standard to measure oneself against and strive for or only bad standards are available. It is helpful here to consider Miranda Fricker's notion of "hermeneutical injustice" and her example of gay men in the United States in the 1950s. Fricker understands "hermeneutical injustice" as instances "wherein someone has a significant area of their social experience obscured from understanding owing to prejudicial flaws in shared resources for social interpretation" (2007, 147). Fricker discusses passages from Edmund White's *A Boy's Own Story* (1982) to show how hermeneutical injustice can affect a person's self-understanding and even damage that very self. For Fricker, White lacks "the hermeneutical resources" to understand his own experience because the only available constructions of homosexuality at the time treated it as a passing phase, a sickness, or the like. Put another way, the lack of telic power based in, say, a neutral or positive construction of homosexuality can be a significant disadvantage. Furthermore, the fact that the only standards (sickness, perversion, etc.) available were bad standards means that falling into this category would necessarily imply that one was a substandard human being.[12]

## 5.7 Conclusion

In sum, I have introduced a new concept—telic power—into social ontology and argued that it captures a distinct central dimension of the social world and that it is theoretically useful. This new concept of power shares certain features with deontic power—power is an ability that agents have, it is partly and directly dependent on other

---

[12] In relation to this, consider Charles Mills' (2017) critique of personhood in Immanuel Kant's writings, especially his critique of Kant's racial hierarchy. Mills uses textual evidence to show that Kant viewed different races on a gradual scale of personhood (Mills 2017, 95–97). Only whites could be full persons, whereas other races were seen as substandard persons, or what Mills dubs "subpersons." This is an extreme case of the positive and negative telic powers of individuals, affecting their deontic powers.

## 198 RECONSTRUCTION: NONIDEAL SOCIAL ONTOLOGY

agents' intentionality, and there is both positive and negative power. However, there are also important differences that distinguish telic power from deontic power. First, the respective definitions illuminate different characteristics, such as telic power being gradual rather than binary. Second, the two types of power have different existence conditions because telic power is dependent on ideals rather than institutions and status functions to exist. This shows that telic power is separate from deontic power. Third, there is the possibility of an "ought-remainder" which points to a separate telic dimension.

I have argued for the theoretical usefulness of telic power by providing three types of cases. The research funding example showed how telic power can both conflict with and reinforce our deontic powers and that there thus are important feedback loops between the two types of power. Furthermore, it showed how some standards are inherently gendered in the sense that men received a gender bonus and women a gender penalty. The businessperson example illustrated how telic power can be invoked to explain cases where agents find themselves torn between conflicting standards. However, this type of conflict is resolvable. By contrast, the double bind cases illuminated irresolvable conflicts in the sense that an agent will be viewed as substandard regardless of what she or he does. In short, this shows that social ontologists interested in explaining cases of conflict and contestation—in addition to examples based on consensus—would benefit from invoking the category of telic power.

# 6

# A Taxonomy of Social Facts

## 6.1 Introduction

In Chapter 5, I introduced the category of telic power, arguing that it is both distinct from deontic power and theoretically useful. This means that I offer a pluralistic account of social power consisting of telic, deontic, and other powers. In this chapter, I offer a more comprehensive account of social power. I distinguish between social power that is directly dependent on the intentionality of agents and social power that is indirectly dependent on the intentionality of agents. Telic power and deontic power are direct forms of social power. I introduce and define two indirect forms of social power—"spillover power" and "structural power"—and show how they can accommodate central social phenomena, such as those belonging to the first kind of social kind, including an opaque gender and class structure.

The reasons for and relevance of expanding the account of social power are the two main criticisms that I have pointed out throughout this work: first, that social power is a central social concept in both ideal and nonideal social ontology but that this central notion is underdeveloped and too narrow. We thus need a more detailed and comprehensive account of social power. The second point is that the first kind of social kind, especially class, has dropped out of sight, even though that it must be accommodated because it is a central social phenomenon. My power view, as detailed in the previous chapter and in this chapter, is thus in part a response to these shortcomings.

*Nonideal Social Ontology.* Åsa Burman, Oxford University Press. © Oxford University Press 2023.
DOI: 10.1093/oso/9780197509579.003.0007

## 200 RECONSTRUCTION: NONIDEAL SOCIAL ONTOLOGY

There is an important implication of developing the power view with its four categories of social power; it can be used as a basis for a taxonomy of social facts. The key idea is that social power is the central social concept and nearly all the social facts in which we are interested contain one form of social power or another. Hence, I offer a taxonomy of social facts in virtue of social power. In the next section, I provide some background to the relevance of offering a taxonomy in social ontology and distinguish my taxonomy from other proposals.

## 6.2 A Taxonomy of Social Facts in Virtue of Social Power

How many types of social facts are there? The purpose of this chapter is partly to develop a taxonomy of social facts to answer that question, but one might wonder why we need a taxonomy of social facts in the first place. One reason is that providing a taxonomy is an important theoretical development in any field and is thus a way to further improve our understanding of the social world. Building a taxonomy is undertaken in many of the sciences: taxonomies are central to biology, while a taxonomy of different types of speech acts, for example, has been proposed in philosophy (Searle 1969). Influential works in social ontology have improved our understanding of collective intention and action, along with central social phenomena such as social practices, institutions, gender, race, and power. Much attention has been paid to social facts, especially the subcategory of institutional facts, and the type of power accompanying institutional facts; that is, deontic power.

But, as I argue, both direct forms of social power, deontic and telic, are insufficient to capture important dimensions of social reality and explain, for example, cases of power that are *opaque* to agents, such as the development presented below of the research funding case that appeared in Chapter 5. Consequently, we need a fine-grained view of different types of social facts for our theories of the social world both to capture important dimensions of the social world and to analyze cases where different types of power reinforce or conflict with each other. I thus argue for two related claims: that this taxonomy can capture central dimensions of social reality, and that it has explanatory value and is thus theoretically useful.

Before turning to the arguments for these two claims, let me briefly consider alternative proposals and explain why I think a taxonomy of social facts should use social power as its central feature. In the literature, two taxonomies have been offered. One is a broad taxonomy of certain types of facts ranging from brute facts to institutional facts by virtue of different functions, including a more fine-grained account of the special subcategory of social facts—institutional facts—by virtue of different types of deontic power (Searle 1995, 121). The other is Khalidi's (2015) tripartite distinction between three kinds of social facts in virtue of the different ways that they are belief-dependent.

There are three reasons for providing a taxonomy of social facts with power as the fundamental feature. First, power is a central dimension of social reality, as influential works in the field of social ontology recognize. Second, it is theoretically useful for analyzing important phenomena, such as the research funding case, by distinguishing between social facts which are facts about different types of power. Third, using gender and class as paradigmatic social phenomena means that certain facts become salient; these facts are often about power. Consequently, I suggest understanding social facts in terms of the main types of social power rather than in terms of functional facts (as we find in Searle's taxonomy of social facts) or belief-dependence (as we find in Khalidi's taxonomy of social kinds). I propose to shift from functions or belief-dependence to social power as the fundamental feature in which to give a taxonomy of social facts. It should be noted that the taxonomy is not constructed purely in terms of social power because I include one category of social facts that is not about social power. The suggested

## 202    RECONSTRUCTION: NONIDEAL SOCIAL ONTOLOGY

taxonomy contains categories that are taken to be mutually exclusive. It remains a tentative proposal in that it may not be exhaustive because there might be other categories of social power.

### 6.2.1  A Test Case for the Taxonomy of Social Facts

Let us return to the research funding from Chapter 5 and develop it further. Recall that Wennerås and Wold found a significant *gender bias* and *affiliation bias* in the funding system: "a female applicant had to be 2.5 times more productive than the average male applicant to receive the same competence score" (1997, 342). Similar numbers held for being affiliated with someone on the Medical Research Council (MRC) committee: "the affiliation bonus was of the same magnitude as the 'male gender' bonus" (Wennerås and Wold 1997, 342). Now, suppose that before the publication of this article in *Nature*, no one knew about the fact that a female applicant had to be 2.5 times more productive than the average male applicant to receive the same competence score. Call this an opaque social fact because (presumably) no one knew this fact prior to the publication. Suppose also that it is part of a general pattern. Consider a fact specific to this modified research funding case:

> (i) The fact that "a female applicant had to be 2.5 times more productive than the average male applicant to receive the same competence score" (Wennerås and Wold 1997, 342) is part of a general pattern.

This clearly contrasts with one of the facts discussed in the previous chapter:

> (ii) The fact that the male applicant M was awarded a postdoctoral fellowship by the MRC.

It is relevant to bring up Thomasson's (2003) objection that Searle's early theory cannot account for opaque kinds of social facts: roughly speaking, the kinds of social facts that members of a particular society do not know about. This objection was discussed at length in Section 2.3.2. Thomasson's objection draws attention to types of social facts other than the standard examples used in ideal social ontology and points toward a central difficulty for Searle's theory; namely, that it can account for facts of type (ii) but not facts of type (i). This indicates that we need a category for social facts of type (i). More generally, what categories do we need to account for social facts of this type? I argue that we need the category of "structural power." Before turning to that concept, however, I introduce the central distinctions that are used in developing the taxonomy along with a visual image of the taxonomy.

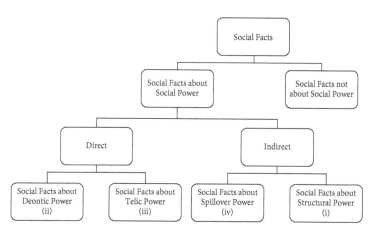

Figure 6.1 A Taxonomy of Social Facts

## 6.2.2 Central Distinctions

Thomasson's objection is based on what I take to be a *fundamental distinction* between social facts that are *directly* dependent on the

204    RECONSTRUCTION: NONIDEAL SOCIAL ONTOLOGY

intentionality of agents to exist and social facts that are *indirectly* dependent on the intentionality of agents to exist. In the former case, our beliefs about that very kind of social fact, such as money, are partly constitutive of the social phenomenon in question, while the latter exist due to our beliefs about other social phenomena. For example, a recession can exist without any beliefs that the economy is in a state of recession, but it cannot exist without any beliefs about money or a similar system of exchange. To ensure terminological clarity, I refer to the former as "direct social facts" and the latter as "indirect social facts." My taxonomy builds on this fundamental distinction. The social facts that fall into the two categories on the left-hand side of Figure 6.1 are directly dependent on the intentionality of agents to exist, while social facts falling into the two categories on the right-hand side of Figure 6.1 are indirectly dependent on the intentionality of agents to exist. After clarifying key terms and distinctions in the section below, I turn to the two categories of direct social facts: "social facts about deontic power" and "social facts about telic power."

## 6.3  Non-Power-Related and Power-Related Social Facts

First, consider the distinctions between brute facts, social facts, and institutional facts. Brute facts require neither institutions nor collective intentionality for their existence, social facts are stipulatively defined as "any fact involving collective intentionality,"[1] and institutional facts require institutions for their existence (Searle 1995, 38). For instance, the existence of a mountain is a brute fact, two people going for a walk together is a social fact, and the existence

---

[1] "By stipulation, I am using the expression 'social facts' so that all and only cases of collective intentional facts are social facts. Institutional facts are then a special subclass of social facts, and our problem has been to specify exactly the features that define this subclass" (Searle 1995, 122).

A TAXONOMY OF SOCIAL FACTS 205

of money is an institutional fact. I retain these understandings of brute and institutional facts but change the stipulative definition of social facts to "any fact involving the intentionality of two or more agents" due to the objection I raised in Chapter 2 about taking collective intentionality as a fundamental notion.

To begin characterizing social power, we can distinguish it from brute power; social power depends on the intentionality of agents, whereas brute power does not. Brute power depends on and works through the intrinsic features of a person, while social power depends for its existence on the intentionality of agents, whether directly or indirectly. In this context, I take the relevant senses of dependence to be both existential and essential. It is not only the case that social power requires intentionality of agents for its existence (i.e., existential dependence), but it is also the case that the intentionality of agents partly makes social power what it is by determining its very nature (essential dependence). Furthermore, there is a hierarchy or fundamentality involved in the sense that, for example, the intentionality of two or more agents is more fundamental than social power because there can be intentionality of two or more agents without social power, but there cannot be social power without the intentionality of agents. So, the statement "social power is dependent on the intentionality of two or more agents to exist" should be interpreted in terms of both existential and essential dependence and as involving a hierarchy.[2] That is, our beliefs

---

[2] There are different senses of "ontological dependence" (cf., Correia 2008; Fine 1995). Correia writes of dependent objects: "A dependent object, so the thought goes, is an object whose ontological profile, e.g. its existence or its being the object that it is, is somehow derivative upon facts of certain sorts—be they facts about other particular objects or not" (2008, 1013). Generally, when I refer to "dependence" in this chapter it is to be understood in terms of both *existential* and *essential* dependence and as involving a *hierarchy*. Correia states that claims regarding existential dependence usually take this general form: "(1) $x$ cannot exist unless $y$ does" (2008, 1014), which is interpreted as a form of metaphysical modality, and distinguishes between different interpretations of (1). For our purposes, generic necessitation is relevant because it "captures a notion of an object's existence requiring the existence of an object *of a certain sort*. Where 'F' is a general term, '$x$' generically necessitates an 'F' is defined as . . . $x$ cannot exist unless something is an F" (Correia 2008, 1014). So, for example, the statement "deontic power is dependent on institutions to exist" should be interpreted in terms of both existential

## 206  RECONSTRUCTION: NONIDEAL SOCIAL ONTOLOGY

are directly or indirectly constitutive of social power. For instance, a person using raw strength to open the heavy door to a conference room is an exercise of brute power, while someone being awarded a postdoctoral fellowship is an exercise of social power. I consider social power in what follows. It is important to note that deontic power is a subcategory of social power on this view, but it is *not* the only relevant subcategory. So, for example, fact (ii) that the male applicant M was awarded a postdoctoral fellowship by the MRC is a social fact about deontic power and thus a social fact about both social power and deontic power, while fact (i) that "a female applicant had to be 2.5 times more productive than the average male applicant to receive the same competence score" (Wennerås and Wold 1997, 342), and that this is part of a general pattern is a social fact about social power but not deontic power.

Given the stipulative definition of a social fact above, this category is broad indeed, ranging from hyenas hunting a lion to the U.S. Congress passing legislation.[3] Given the aims of an investigation, one singles out different subcategories of social facts as significant. A zoologist might be mostly interested in the intentionality of two or more primates, while some social ontologists' main concern may be a special subcategory of social facts; namely, institutional facts and their accompanying deontic powers. My main concern is social facts that are facts about social power.[4] This focus should be viewed in light of my earlier discussion of the paradigmatic

and essential dependence and as involving a hierarchy, where the intentionality of two or more agents is more basic than deontic power.

[3] These are Searle's examples. The latter—that the U.S. Congress passes a certain law L—is an institutional fact. The category of institutional facts is a special subcategory of social facts.

[4] Social ontologists as different as Haslanger and Searle will presumably agree on making this the main concern. Haslanger analyzes gender as one's position in a hierarchical structure (a system of power), and Searle claims that social reality is essentially a system of deontic power. More specifically, in *The Construction of Social Reality*, Searle argues that all institutional facts (other than honorific ones) can be framed in terms of different conventional powers by performing operations on the "basic formula": "We accept (S has power (S does A))" (1995, 104). In later works, Searle argues that even honorific institutional facts can be framed in terms of conventional power (2010, 24).

social phenomena in social ontology: Shifting from the standard examples in ideal social ontology to gender and class as paradigmatic social phenomena means that social facts about different types of social power become salient and stand out as significant.

The first distinction in the taxonomy is thus between "non-power-related social facts" and "power-related social facts." An example of the first category is the fact that two people, who stand in no relation of power to each other, spontaneously start a conversation or go for a walk together. Interestingly, some of the social facts that do not *seem* to be about power, such as the fact that two people go for a walk together, might on closer inspection actually be about social power. For instance, imagine that two other people agree to go for a walk together. Assume that there are no formal relations of power between them; for example, they might both be tenured professors in the same department, but they do not have equal social standing in the sense that one is a much more respected academic. The fact that the person with higher social standing is the person who decides on the time and location for the walk would be a fact about social power, given that the decision is partly due to her higher social standing. Still, there are cases of social facts that are not about social power, and I call this first category in the taxonomy "social facts not about social power."

The other distinctions in the taxonomy are between different types of social power. To provide a taxonomy of social facts in virtue of social power, one needs to answer the question, "What types of social power are there?" Another way to put this question is to ask, "What types of power can be created by the intentionality of agents?"

## 6.4 Direct Social Power: Deontic and Telic

We begin by reviewing the two main types of direct social power—deontic and telic—that can be created by the intentionality of

## 208    RECONSTRUCTION: NONIDEAL SOCIAL ONTOLOGY

agents. These forms of power depend *directly* on the intentionality of agents to exist. Another relevant similarity is that deontic and telic power both work through perceptions of normative reasons to be explained. Consider a power-holder making the statement, "Let x happen!" This can be understood in a reason-giving sense ("x *ought* to happen") or in a non-normative sense ("x *will* happen").[5] An example of the reason-giving sense is when a power-holder uses her status function as the MRC chair to offer a certain candidate the postdoctoral fellowship. She can give *reasons* for offering the fellowship to a certain candidate, such as the Council voting in favor of the candidate and her duty to inform the successful candidate. When normative forms of social power are exercised, power-holders and subjects of power regard themselves as *normatively bound*; that is, they *ought* to act in certain ways, which creates reasons for action. For example, the chair now has the *right* to offer candidate M the postdoctoral fellowship, and the MRC members now have an *obligation* to stick to their decision. Some aspects of the research funding case thus illustrate this type of normative power involving rights and obligations; it is because of her status function as chair that she can offer candidate M the fellowship. And fact (ii) that the male applicant M was awarded a postdoctoral fellowship by the MRC is indeed a social fact about normative power, and more specifically deontic power, because candidate M now has the new status function of postdoctoral fellow, which means that he has new normative powers such as the right to receive a salary and funding for his laboratory, while other relevant agents regard themselves as normatively bound to fulfill their obligations with respect to M. These aspects of the research funding case can thus be explained by invoking the notion of positive deontic powers (rights) and negative deontic powers (obligations). Consequently,

---

[5] Eerik Lagerspetz refers to a similar distinction in his analysis of authority in *Opposite Mirrors* (1995, 72).

the second category in the taxonomy is "social facts about deontic power."

## 6.4.1 Deontic Power

I use the notion of deontic power and the distinction between positive and negative deontic power as described below:

> The first [positive deontic power] is where the agent is endowed with some new power, certification, authorization, entitlement, right, permission, or qualification granting the ability to do something he or she could not otherwise have done; and the second [negative deontic power] is where the agent is required, obligated, in duty bound, penalized, enjoined, or otherwise compelled to do something he or she would not otherwise have had to do—or, what amounts to the same thing, prevented from doing something that would otherwise have been doable. Roughly speaking, the two major categories are those of positive and negative powers. (Searle 1995, 100)

Given the importance of deontic power, it is worth considering in more detail. It is helpful to distinguish between *resources* for power, power as an *ability*, and the *exercise* of power. Money is sometimes referred to as a positive deontic power, but this risks blurring the distinction between a resource for power and power as an ability. The two usually go together, but they do not have to, as an agent can have money but still be unable to transform that resource into an ability. For instance, there could be restrictions in place such that certain agents cannot buy things even if they have enough money. Distinguishing between resources for power and power as an ability and understanding deontic power in terms of the latter is

210  RECONSTRUCTION: NONIDEAL SOCIAL ONTOLOGY

one way of clarifying the notion and making it less broad.[6] On the other hand, distinguishing power as an ability from its exercise and understanding deontic power in terms of the former means that it is not unduly narrow because it is important to be able to say that an agent can have power without exercising it. If one thinks that power exists only when it is exercised, one is not able to account for, for example, domination as a form of power, which is problematic, given that domination is fruitfully used to characterize gender relations (cf., Halldenius 2001; Pettit 1997). Deontic power is thus understood a dispositional concept, or ability, in line with the quote above.

## 6.4.2  Deontic Power and Hohfeldian Incidents

In Chapter 3, I noted that there is a clearer understanding of deontic power available than has hitherto been the case; namely, the explication of deontic powers in terms of Hohfeldian incidents. To illustrate the theoretical fruitfulness of this more fine-grained account of deontic powers, let us return to Jenkins' example of the marital rape exemption. Today, a wife in England and Wales has an institutional right not to be sexually assaulted by her husband, just as he has an institutional obligation not to sexually assault her. Given the extremely low conviction rates in sexual assault cases,

---

[6] In the philosophical debate on power, it is common to make a distinction between the *power-to* do something and having *power-over* others. Some theorists, such as Peter Morriss (2002), argue that power-to is the relevant notion; while others, such as Steven Lukes (2005), argue that power-over is the relevant notion. On this latter view, Searle's notion of deontic power would be too broad because it would view simply buying groceries as an exercise of deontic power. However, what we take the relevant notion of power to be depends partly on our purpose. Given the purpose of providing a taxonomy of social facts, rather than focusing only on analyzing hierarchical power relations and inequalities, I take the former notion to be the most important for two reasons. First, it is frequently employed in the debate on social ontology; second, and more importantly, the former notion is more general because having power over others can be construed as having the power to decide for or about those others, while not all forms of power-to can be construed as having power-over others.

A TAXONOMY OF SOCIAL FACTS   211

however, it seems odd to say that wives and husbands have these institutional rights and obligations, respectively. The coarse-grained notion of deontic power from ideal social ontology has trouble handling these and similar cases where there is a substantial difference between one's formal rights and those rights in practice.

One option would be to say that wives and husbands do indeed have these institutional rights and obligations in a formal sense, but they do not have these rights and obligations in an informal sense. So, we need to distinguish between and operate with both formal and informal notions of deontic power.[7]

My preferred route would be to employ the basic elements of rights—Hohfeldian incidents—to describe this case. A wife has a *claim* that her husband will not sexually assault her if and only if a husband has a duty to his wife not to sexually assault her. This is a first-order incident. But given the extremely low conviction rates, we might say that the husband has a Hohfeldian *power*—a second-order incident—that alters the first-order incident of his wife. Recall that power in the Hohfeldian schema is understood as follows: A has a *power* if and only if A has the ability to alter her own or another's Hohfeldian incidents. So, the husband has the power to alter (i.e., ignore) his own obligation and his wife's right to bodily integrity. This example illustrates that the more fine-grained notion of deontic power can be useful for ideal and nonideal social ontologists, including emancipatory social ontologists. Thus, the notion of deontic power used in my taxonomy is the original formulation of deontic power coupled with the specification in terms of Hohfeldian incidents, which means that a deontic power

---

[7] Another, related option would be to distinguish between different senses of a "right" in terms of different kinds of claims. For example, Susan James (2003) argues that understanding rights as effectively enforceable claims has advantages over understanding rights as formal entitlements. The wife, then, does not have the right not to be sexually assaulted by her husband in the sense that she does not have an effectively enforceable claim, despite her formal entitlement. I think that this is not the route to take because this view of rights becomes too narrow and does not uphold the distinction between formal entitlements and effectively enforceable claims.

## 212 RECONSTRUCTION: NONIDEAL SOCIAL ONTOLOGY

is an ability that an agent has to effect a specific outcome and that the basic elements of this ability can be further specified using Hohfeldian incidents.[8]

We are now able to state some central features of the second category—social facts about deontic power—in the taxonomy: M's positive deontic power is partly constituted by the intentionality of agents, which means that his ability to effect certain outcomes, say, receiving a salary and funding for his laboratory, is *directly dependent* on the intentionality of agents and thus a direct social phenomenon. In general, our beliefs about this type of power are partly constitutive of it. Consequently, deontic power is necessarily visible or transparent. This kind of power imposes *external constraints* on agents and works through the perceptions of normative reasons. Finally, deontic power is dependent on institutions to exist.

This latter feature is relevant in relation to Barry Barnes' work on power. In *The Nature of Power*, Barnes' aim is to understand the nature and basis of social power. He notes that in our commonsense thinking, we often try to understand power in terms of its basis and that certain forms of power, such as the power of engines or artifacts, are well understood in this way; others, however, such as willpower and social power, are not well understood due to an insufficient understanding of the nature of their basis:

> In our common sense thinking we tend to assume that power can be understood by reference to the nature of its source, that the constitution of the source makes intelligible the capacity to work or act that inheres in it. Different kinds of powers are thought to inhere in differently constituted sources. (Barnes 1988, 4)

---

[8] My position differs from Brännmark's view of deontic power; it is, for example, narrower in being a normative form of power, as described in Section 6.4 on deontic power.

A TAXONOMY OF SOCIAL FACTS  213

Recent works in social ontology have clarified important concepts such as institutions and social norms, which also means that the different sources of power have become clearer. I draw on Barnes' insight in developing the taxonomy, pointing out what the different types of power depend on to exist. The next category—telic power—differs from deontic power in its basis, among other things, as it requires social norms rather than institutions to exist.

### 6.4.3  Telic Power

Interestingly, having imposed the status function of being a postdoctoral fellow on M implies that we can *evaluate* how well M fulfills this status function: Is M an excellent, good, or bad postdoctoral fellow? In Chapter 5, I argued that the possibility of evaluating M and other agents in this way suggests that there is a different type of normativity in the social world than deontic; namely, teleological normativity. Furthermore, I showed that there is a different type of normative power than deontic; namely, telic power. Recall the housewife example and a fact specific to this example: (iii) The fact that the housewife H was perceived to fail to meet the standard of a good housewife by the Health Visitor (and herself). This is a social fact about telic power. Furthermore, to adequately account for (iii) and similar facts such as the fact that M was perceived as a good postdoctoral fellow by the relevant agents, we need the category of telic power. In addition to capturing another dimension of social reality, this category is useful for explanatory purposes because an agent's telic power can reinforce and/or conflict with her deontic power, as the housewife example suggests. Let us review the definitions of telic power:

TELIC POWER*: An agent A has telic power in a domain if and only if there exists an ideal such that agent A can be measured against it and the distance perceived by other agents of A from the ideal affects A's ability to effect certain outcomes in that domain.

# 214 RECONSTRUCTION: NONIDEAL SOCIAL ONTOLOGY

> POSITIVE TELIC POWER*: An agent A has positive telic power in a domain if and only if agent A is perceived by other agents as living up to the ideal, as a good exemplar of the relevant kind, and this positively affects or enhances A's ability to effect certain outcomes in that domain.

> NEGATIVE TELIC POWER*: An agent A has negative telic power in a domain if and only if agent A is perceived by other agents as not living up to the ideal; she is viewed as substandard or as a bad exemplar of the relevant kind, and this negatively affects or restricts A's ability to effect certain outcomes in that domain.

We are now able to state some central features of the third category, "social facts about telic power." This category shares some central features with deontic power: An agent's telic power is partly constituted by the intentionality of agents, which means that her ability to effect certain outcomes is directly dependent on the intentionality of agents and is thus a direct social phenomenon. In general, our beliefs about this type of power are partly constitutive of it. Consequently, telic power is necessarily visible or transparent. Telic power cannot exist without the existence of social norms understood as ideals or standards; it is thus dependent on social norms to exist. Like deontic power, it is a normative form of power because it works through the perceptions of normative reasons; that is, it works by virtue of agents recognizing an ought connected to the ideal and that this ought gives them reasons for action. However, there is an important difference from deontic power. This type of power, unlike deontic power, does not depend on institutions but on social norms to exist. In Barnes' terms, it has a different basis. However, the social world does not consist only of direct social phenomena and normative powers, so it is time to turn to indirect social phenomena and non-normative powers.

## A TAXONOMY OF SOCIAL FACTS   215

## 6.5  Indirect Social Power: Spillover and Structural

Deontic and telic power are direct forms of power that also share the feature of working through the perceptions of normative reasons; that is, by agents recognizing a social ought. However, there are also indirect forms of social power. I turn now to describing the two indirect forms of social power: spillover power and structural power, which differ from deontic and telic power because they do *not* work through the perceptions of normative reasons. When non-normative forms of social power are exercised, the subjects do not regard themselves as normatively bound to act in certain ways.

## 6.5.1  Spillover Power

To illustrate this type of power, consider the following case.

*The start-up example:* Imagine that the head of a country's central bank declares that interest rates will increase, which is an exercise of deontic power, but imagine that he also happens to mention some interesting new start-ups, including his friend's company. By virtue of his status function as the head of the central bank, an institution-dependent property, this person can effect a certain outcome— here, increasing the share price of his friend's company—not by exercising his deontic powers but still in virtue of his status function: making a statement S about a particular start-up as interesting has the effect of people buying shares in that start-up. More specifically, consider:

> (iv) The fact that the head of the central bank, by making statement S, increased the share price of his friend's start-up.

To explain this fact, it is helpful to note that his status function has certain spillover effects; he has the ability to effect outcomes other

## 216    RECONSTRUCTION: NONIDEAL SOCIAL ONTOLOGY

than those that fall within his deontic powers. This visible type of non-normative power can thus be seen as a spillover effect of deontic power.

This form of power is indirect in the sense that it depends on deontic power to exist, and it does not work through the perceptions of normative reasons in the same manner as deontic power. The head of the central bank cannot create a new institutional fact, such as requiring people to buy shares in his friend's start-up, and the individuals in the audience presumably do not feel that they *ought* to buy stocks in the start-up. In fact, he cannot give this type of reason because he has not been assigned any deontic power in this matter. The kinds of reasons he can provide are instrumental reasons; if you want to become rich, buy shares in this particular start-up. Still, this is an exercise of social power—non-normative rather than normative—in the sense that the head of the central bank has an ability, which is indirectly dependent on the intentionality of agents and more specifically indirectly dependent on institutions and deontic power, to effect certain outcomes. I call this type of power spillover power:

> SPILLOVER POWER: An agent A has spillover power if and only if agent A has a status function with accompanying deontic powers and this affects agent A's ability to effect certain outcomes beyond those deontic powers.

To capture both the negative and positive spillover effects of having a certain status function, it is useful to distinguish between positive and negative powers within this subcategory. For example, the spillover effects of the head of the central bank having this status function involve a *positive spillover power* in the sense that it positively affects his ability to effect certain outcomes; for example, he can encourage people to buy shares in his friend's company, while the spillover effects of having the status function of a former inmate involve a *negative spillover power* in the sense that it negatively

A TAXONOMY OF SOCIAL FACTS 217

affects one's ability to effect a certain outcome, beyond his already negative deontic powers, such as convincing an audience to buy something.

Again, this definition can be varied to accommodate positive and negative forms of spillover power; replacing "affects" with "enhances" gives us positive spillover power, while replacing "affects" with "restricts" gives us negative spillover power:

> POSITIVE SPILLOVER POWER: An agent A has positive spillover power if and only if agent A has a status function with accompanying deontic powers and this enhances agent A's ability to effect certain outcomes beyond those deontic powers.

> NEGATIVE SPILLOVER POWER: An agent A has negative spillover power if and only if agent A has a status function with accompanying deontic powers and this restricts agent A's ability to effect certain outcomes beyond those deontic powers.

Generally, how we set up our institutions and which status functions we assign to different people affect the indirect powers that different individuals and groups have in relation to one another; that is, the distribution of deontic power affects the distribution of indirect power. In a more interesting example of spillover power that shows how the distribution of deontic powers can impact agents' spillover powers, consider Philip Pettit's work on domination as being subject to someone's arbitrary will:

> The grievance I have in mind is that of having to live at the mercy of another, having to live in a manner that leaves you vulnerable to some ill that the other is in a position arbitrarily to impose; and this, in particular, when each of you is in a position to see that you are dominated by the other. . . . It is the grievance expressed by the wife who finds herself in a position where her husband can beat her at will, and without any possibility of redress; by the employee

218 RECONSTRUCTION: NONIDEAL SOCIAL ONTOLOGY

who dare not raise a complaint against an employer, and who is vulnerable to any of a range of abuses, some petty, some serious, that the employer may choose to perpetrate. (Pettit 1997, 4–5)

This quote points to an asymmetric relation between power-holders and the subjects of power and can plausibly be explained partly as a spillover effect of the distribution of deontic powers. While considering Pettit's quote, let us consider a more specific example.

*The wedding example*: Two employees, E and S, work as servants for family F, their only employer. All agents know that the area has an abundance of servants and that E and S would have enormous difficulties securing new positions if they were to lose their jobs and that it would be nearly impossible to get new jobs without a reference letter from F. Furthermore, all agents know that there are no unemployment benefits or unions, and that the relevant legislation is biased against employees. In short, the distribution of deontic powers is highly unequal, and it would be accurate to describe the relation between the family F and the servants as one of domination, no matter how benevolent the family members might be. So, E and S are in a situation where not fulfilling F's wishes, however inappropriate, involves a significant risk of losing their jobs without any possibility of redress. Now, imagine that the employment contract clearly states all the rights and obligations of E, S, and F, by which F has a right to have dinner cooked each night for the four family members and E and S are under an obligation to prepare that meal. One day, a member of F says, "There will be a big dinner for all one hundred guests at my daughter's wedding," and E and S begin to prepare for the wedding dinner.

If the agents were pressed about this case, the member of F would not say that she had a right to have the wedding dinner cooked and E and S would not say that they were under an obligation to cook the wedding dinner. In fact, the member of F could not give any reasons involving her deontic powers but rather a different type of reason—an instrumental and blunt—reason: "If you want to keep your jobs, cook the wedding dinner." This illustrates how the distribution of deontic power can give rise to non-normative power, because the family member can decide on matters that are outside her deontic powers to decide due to the spillover effect of her status function as employer in combination with the distribution of deontic power in this society.

We are now able to see the usefulness of this fourth category, "social facts about spillover power." Both the fact (iv) that the head of the central bank, by making statement S, increased the share price of his friend's start-up, and the fact that E and S prepare the wedding dinner are social facts about spillover power. With this category in place, we are now able to capture this type of social fact, domination as a form of social power, and how deontic power can affect indirect power.[9]

This enables us to state some central features of spillover power. This type of power is necessarily transparent because it works through the perception of instrumental reasons. In addition, it is indirectly constituted by the intentionality of agents; that is, it exists partly by virtue of our beliefs about direct social phenomena such as deontic power. Consequently, it is an indirect social phenomenon, and its basis is deontic power.

The previous categories of social facts about different types of social power all share the feature of transparency. However, as Thomasson's objection pointed out, there are also opaque kinds of social facts. To be able to take these into account, I need to introduce the last category, "social facts about structural power."

[9] It is important to note that agents can be dominated without knowing about it. The category "structural power" is thus needed to accommodate the aspects of domination that are opaque.

220 RECONSTRUCTION: NONIDEAL SOCIAL ONTOLOGY

## 6.5.2 Structural Power

Let us return to the modified research funding case and the fact (i) that "a female applicant had to be 2.5 times more productive than the average male applicant to receive the same competence score" (Wennerås and Wold 1997, 342), and that this is part of a general pattern. Suppose now that fact (i) is opaque to people in this society. Interestingly, there are types of social facts and forms of power that are opaque, or invisible, to all parties.[10] This type of power presupposes the existence of a social structure that is itself opaque. To clarify the kind of opacity I have in mind, it is helpful to consider Thomasson's notions of *epistemic* and *conceptual* opacity:

> Call a kind F of social entities "epistemically opaque" if things of that kind are capable of existing even if no one believes that anything of kind F exists, and "conceptually opaque" if things of that kind are capable of existing even if no one has any F-regarding beliefs whatsoever. (2003, 275–276)

So there can also be indirect types of social power of which neither power-holders nor subjects of power are aware, such as the fact that "a female applicant had to be 2.5 times more productive than the average male applicant to receive the same competence score" (Wennerås and Wold 1997, 342) prior to the publication of this article. Given that the relevant agents already had beliefs about gender bias in other contexts but were not aware of the effect of this bias in the presumed meritocracy of research funding, it is most

---

[10] There is another relevant distinction regarding opacity; namely, the distinction between type and token, or between kinds of social facts and instances of that kind. Thomasson's objection concerns kinds of social facts. Opaque instances of a kind would not pose a problem to Searle's theory because there could be a dollar bill never in use or a counterfeit dollar bill (instances of a kind) unknown to all agents, but money as a kind could not be opaque, or unknown to all agents, on his analysis, due to the self-referentiality of social concepts. Fact (i) is to be interpreted as exemplifying an epistemically opaque kind of social fact.

plausibly described as an example of epistemic opacity. After the publication, this fact became known to the relevant parties and thus transparent. Now let us use the modified research funding case and more precisely the fact that female researchers have their opportunities systematically restricted in Swedish society. To be able to analyze this fact, notions of "social structure" and "structural power" are needed. One can understand a social structure in the following way:

SOCIAL STRUCTURE: A social structure exists if and only if members of a collectivity, by virtue of that membership, systematically have their opportunities (as individuals) restricted or enhanced.[11]

Given the existence of a social structure, in this case a gender structure, a man has certain abilities to effect certain outcomes by virtue of his social status as a man, abilities that women therefore lack.[12] In this case, men have their opportunities enhanced and women have their opportunities restricted in ways that are in disproportion to their relevant abilities. Adding the clause "in ways that are in disproportion to their relevant abilities" means that we have an instance of an unjust social structure. For example, if Wennerås and Wold's result is part of a general pattern, then there is a social structure in place: Female researchers have their opportunities to receive research funding systematically restricted and male researchers have their opportunities systematically enhanced in ways that are in disproportion to their relevant abilities. Due to the existence of this social structure, the male applicant M's ability to receive

---

[11] This characterization is a development of a view I presented earlier (Andersson [now Burman] 2007). I have changed the terminology from "social group" to "collectivity" to more clearly capture this broader understanding of a collectivity. A substantial difference is that I now omit "in ways that are in disproportion to their relevant abilities" to not assume by definition that all social structures are morally unjust. In this way, we can distinguish between social structures that are morally unjust and those that are not.

[12] For recent accounts of social structure, see Haslanger (2016) and Ritchie (2020).

## 222  RECONSTRUCTION: NONIDEAL SOCIAL ONTOLOGY

research funding was in fact shown to be partly about social power rather than purely about research merits due to the gender bias discovered by Wennerås and Wold. This illustrates the possibility of an agent having social power, even if this agent and others are unaware of it, due to the existence of opaque social structures. I call this type of social power "structural power":

> STRUCTURAL POWER: An agent A has structural power if and only if there exists a social structure and this affects agent A's ability to effect certain outcomes.

Note that the above definition does not include opacity as a condition because this type of power can be either transparent or opaque to the relevant agents. If the social structure is known to the relevant agents, then we have a form of transparent structural power, while if the social structure is unknown to the relevant agents, then we have a form of opaque structural power. This is a matter of degree because there are varying degrees of transparency. The social structure could be unknown to all the relevant agents (opaque), known to most or some agents (varying degrees of transparency), or known to all agents (transparent). It is also important that the notion of a collectivity be understood in a broad sense, including both social groups whose members are aware of themselves as a social group and members who are not aware of themselves as members of a social group or collectivity. This makes it possible to include an economic class structure as an example of a social structure.

It is useful to distinguish between positive and negative powers within this subcategory to analyze the modified research funding case more precisely. One can describe the research funding case as male applicants having a *positive structural power* and female applicants having a *negative structural power* due to their gender, as the social status of being a man increased men's ability to effect certain outcomes, such as receiving research funding, while the social status of being a woman reduced women's ability to effect the same outcome:

POSITIVE STRUCTURAL POWER: An agent A has positive structural power if and only if there exists a social structure and this enhances agent A's ability to effect certain outcomes.

NEGATIVE STRUCTURAL POWER: An agent A has negative structural power if and only if there exists a social structure and this restricts agent A's ability to effect certain outcomes.

Consequently, the fact (i) that "a female applicant had to be 2.5 times more productive than the average male applicant to receive the same competence score" (Wennerås and Wold 1997, 342) is part of a general pattern is a social fact about the negative structural power of female researchers. Prior to the authors' investigation, this fact would be best described as a social fact about opaque negative structural power, which shifted to increasing transparency after the publication. Now, after publication, fact (i) is best described as a social fact about transparent negative structural power. In short, the category of structural power is theoretically useful in analyzing social facts of this type and having this category in the taxonomy offers the important advantage of being able to account for opaque kinds of social facts.

This category is also useful in analyzing how structural power can reinforce or conflict with the deontic powers of agents, as exemplified by fact (i). For example, one can partly explain the low share of research funding for female applicants in the following way: Their negative (epistemically opaque) structural power restricted their positive deontic powers stemming from receiving a postdoctoral fellowship. Furthermore, this negative structural power could also restrict their telic power because not being awarded a prestigious fellowship contributes to being perceived as not meeting the standard of excellence in research and thus being

## 224 RECONSTRUCTION: NONIDEAL SOCIAL ONTOLOGY

further away from the ideal researcher, which might in turn reinforce future female applicants' negative structural power. In short, structural power can impact both the deontic and telic powers of agents; put another way, indirect social power can impact direct social power.

Let us turn to another example of structural power. During the most intense phases of the pandemic, Swedish newspapers reported that the risk of being infected with COVID-19 and the risk of dying from such an infection varied widely—as much as three times—across different areas of Stockholm. The Public Health Agency of Sweden launched an information campaign about COVID-19 in several languages after statistics showed that people from an immigrant background were significantly overrepresented in those infected with and dying from COVID-19. However, some reporters and people from these neighborhoods pointed out that the issue was not language; rather, many people living in these areas could not work from home. Their jobs, such as working in eldercare and driving buses or metro trains to get other people to and from work, required them to leave home and mix with others. In addition, it was noted that there is a high degree of cramped housing accommodation in these neighborhoods. One reporter concluded that what appeared to be an issue about language, race, and ethnicity was really about economic class.

This example reinforces the importance of material conditions and their connection to a person's chances in life—or even of staying alive, as with COVID-19. One's relationship to the means of production determines whether or not one could work from home and hence whether or not one has an increased likelihood of becoming infected due to the need to work elsewhere (and perhaps take public transportation to get there). One's relationship to the means of production will also affect one's likelihood of being able to afford a car and thus decrease the likelihood of getting infected. Finally, it also profoundly affects one's living situation and how crowded it is. Some facts about this case are examples of institutional facts: the fact that someone is employed as a bus driver or a university professor. These are social facts about deontic power. Other facts about this case are examples of structural power, such as the fact that an individual belonging to the working class in Stockholm has a greater risk of becoming infected with and dying from COVID-19 than individuals belonging to Stockholm's upper class. This fact falls into the category of social facts about structural power.

## 6.6 Testing the Taxonomy of Social Facts

There is a taxonomy of social facts emanating from this discussion, summarized in Figure 6.1. The suggested taxonomy consists of five main types of social facts: social facts not about social power, social facts about deontic power, social facts about telic power, social facts about spillover power, and social facts about structural power.[13]

I have used gender and class as paradigmatic cases to argue for the claims that this taxonomy can capture the central dimensions of social reality and that it is theoretically useful. Shifting from the standard examples of money and presidents to gender and class meant that types of social facts other than institutional facts were emphasized and showed that there are relevant distinctions other than the distinction between social and institutional facts, such as the distinction between direct and indirect social facts, to be drawn within the broad category of social facts. Consequently, there are important subcategories other than institutional facts, as shown in the taxonomy, and these other dimensions of the social world are captured in the suggested taxonomy.

---

[13] The latter four categories share a common feature of social power understood as "an agent A has social power if and only if A has an ability, which is existentially and essentially dependent on the intentionality of two or more agents, to effect certain outcomes." This is a refined version of my definition of social power (Andersson [now Burman] 2007).

226  RECONSTRUCTION: NONIDEAL SOCIAL ONTOLOGY

Applying this taxonomy to our initial examples—research funding, housewife, and start-up—and the related social facts, results in the following picture: the fact (ii) that the male applicant M was awarded a postdoctoral fellowship by the MRC is a clear-cut example of an institutional fact and is thus a social fact about deontic power; more precisely, it is about positive deontic power for applicant M. However, describing fact (iii) that the housewife H was perceived to fail to meet the standard of a good housewife by the Health Visitor (and herself) and the fact (iv) that the head of the central bank, by making statement S, increased the share price of his friend's start-up, as social facts about deontic powers would be inaccurate. Instead, the fact that H is perceived as substandard is a social fact about (negative) telic power, while (iv) is a social fact about the (positive) spillover power of the head of the central bank. Meanwhile fact (i) that "a female applicant had to be 2.5 times more productive than the average male applicant to receive the same competence score" (Wennerås and Wold 1997, 342) and additionally assuming that this is part of a general pattern is a social fact about the (negative) structural power of female applicants. Having this latter category of structural power means that we can account for opaque kinds of social facts.

Furthermore, making fine-grained distinctions within the category of social facts offers access to new and expanded conceptual resources that are helpful in explaining complex cases such as the research funding case. I have argued for the theoretical usefulness of this taxonomy by showing how the different types of powers can reinforce or conflict with each other. The housewife example illustrated how an agent's (positive or negative) telic power can impact her deontic power (keeping or losing custody of her children).

The taxonomy can also clarify how an agent's direct power can affect that agent's indirect power. The distribution of deontic power in a society, for example, can impact the spillover power of agents, as illustrated by the wedding example. But the relation also obtains in the other direction because an agent's indirect powers can affect an agent's direct powers. Structural power can, for instance, impact an agent's deontic powers, as illustrated by the research funding example and the fact that it is part of a general pattern; that is, the negative structural power of female applicants can partly explain their limited access to the positive deontic powers of a postdoctoral fellowship enjoyed by some male applicants.

Furthermore, applying the taxonomy to complex cases can clarify *feedback loops* between the different categories. For example, one part of the explanation for the female applicants' negative structural power and the male applicants' positive structural power might be telic power: Women on average are more likely to be perceived as substandard and men as excellent, or as exemplars of a kind, when it comes to the ideal standard of a researcher (consider the gendered picture of the absentminded professor). Telic power can thus impact the competence score of applicants and result in negative structural power for women, which in turn translates into fewer positive deontic powers. This outcome reinforces the negative telic powers of female researchers while enhancing the positive telic powers of male researchers because one aspect of being perceived as an exemplar of a researcher is being awarded a prestigious fellowship. This in turn fortifies the perception of male researchers as closer than female researchers to the ideal standard of a researcher.[14]

Because the indirect powers of agents can impact their direct powers and their direct powers can impact their indirect powers, the taxonomy presented here can also be useful in clarifying these possible feedback loops. It can thus also be used as an analytical tool to help explain ideal social phenomena and the persistence of nonideal social phenomena such as deep inequalities, oppression, and domination in a given society.

---

[14] This is another way in which I go beyond Witt's work on gender norms and social normativity. I show how telic power conflicts with and/or reinforces other forms of social power such as deontic power and structural power. I also clarify the feedback loops between the different forms of social power.

## 6.7 Conclusion

This chapter is a crucial part of the power view, the core framework which I develop in this book while acknowledging that the issues it addresses are so complex and important that it will be open to refinement in the future. The power view consists of the pluralistic account of social power and the associated taxonomy of social facts that draws on a fundamental distinction between social facts that depend directly on the intentionality of agents to exist and social facts that depend indirectly on the intentionality of agents to exist. This distinction carries over to the account of social power. There are two direct (deontic and telic) and two indirect (spillover and structural) forms of power. The structural power category is especially important because it can accommodate social facts belonging to the first kind of social kind, such as social facts about opaque gender and class structures.

An important implication of the pluralistic account of social power is that it can be used as the basis for a taxonomy of social facts. I have given reasons for building a taxonomy of social facts with social power as its central feature: first, power is the central social concept; second, a taxonomy of social facts in virtue of social power is theoretically useful. My taxonomy consists of five main types of social facts: social facts not about social power, social facts about deontic power, social facts about telic power, social facts about spillover power, and social facts about structural power. The development of the power view means that I have built a bridge between the two worlds of contemporary social ontology.

# References

Andersson [now Burman], Åsa. 2007. *Power and Social Ontology*. Lund: Bokbox.

Ásta. 2017. "Social Kinds." In *The Routledge Handbook of Collective Intentionality*, edited by Marija Jankovic and Kirk Ludwig, 290–299. New York: Routledge.

Ásta. 2018. *Categories We Live By: The Construction of Sex, Gender, Race, and Other Social Categories*. New York: Oxford University Press.

Ásta. 2019. "Categorical Injustice." *Journal of Social Philosophy* 50, no. 4: 392–406.

Ásta. 2020. "Response to Critics." *Journal of Social Ontology* 5, no. 2: 273–283.

Austin, J. L. 1955. *How To Do Things with Words*. Oxford: Clarendon Press.

Barnes, Barry. 1983. "Social Life as Bootstrapped Induction." *Sociology* 17, no. 4: 524–545.

Barnes, Barry. 1988. *The Nature of Power*. Champaign: University of Illinois Press.

Brynjarsdóttir, Eyja M. 2018. *The Reality of Money*. Lanham: Rowman & Littlefield.

Brännmark, Johan. 2019a. "Contested Institutional Facts." *Erkenntnis* 84, no. 5: 1047–1064.

Brännmark, Johan. 2019b. "Institutions, Ideology, and Nonideal Social Ontology." *Philosophy of the Social Sciences* 49, no. 2: 137–159.

Burman, Åsa. 2018. "A Critique of the Status Function Account of Human Rights." *Philosophy of the Social Sciences* 48, no. 5: 463–473.

Correia, Fabrice. 2008. "Ontological Dependence." *Philosophy Compass* 3: 1013–1032.

Cudd, Ann E. 2006. *Analyzing Oppression*. Oxford: Oxford University Press.

Dembroff, Robin. 2020. "Beyond Binary: Genderqueer as Critical Gender Kind." *Philosophers' Imprint* 20, no. 9: 1–23.

Epstein, Brian. 2014. "Social Objects Without Intentions." In *Institutions, Emotions, and Group Agents: Contributions to Social Ontology*, edited by Anita Konzelmann Ziv and Hans Bernhard Schmid, 53–60. Dordrecht: Springer.

Epstein, Brian. 2016. "A Framework for a Social Ontology." *Philosophy of the Social Sciences* 46, no. 2: 147–167.

230  REFERENCES

Fine, Kit. 1995. "Ontological Dependence." *Proceedings of the Aristotelian Society* 95: 269–290.

Fricker, Miranda. 2007. *Epistemic Injustice: Power and the Ethics of Knowing.* Oxford: Oxford University Press.

Frye, Marilyn. 1983. "Oppression." In *The Politics of Reality: Essays in Feminist Theory*, 1–16. New York: The Crossing Press.

Gilbert, Margaret. 1990. "Walking Together: A Paradigmatic Social Phenomenon." *Midwest Studies in Philosophy* 15: 1–14.

Gilbert, Margaret. [1989] 1992. *On Social Facts.* Princeton: Princeton University Press.

Gilbert, Margaret. 1996. *Living Together: Rationality, Sociality, and Obligation.* Lanham: Rowman & Littlefield.

Gilbert, Margaret. 2000. *Sociality and Responsibility: New Essays in Plural Subject Theory.* Lanham: Rowman & Littlefield.

Gilbert, Margaret. 2018. *Rights and Demands: A Foundational Inquiry.* Oxford: Oxford University Press.

Guala, Francesco. 2007. "The Philosophy of Social Science: Metaphysical and Empirical." *Philosophy Compass* 2: 954–980.

Hacking, Ian. 1995. "The Looping Effects of Human Kinds." In *Causal Cognition: A Multidisciplinary Debate*, edited by D. Sperber, D. Premack, and A. J. Premack, 351–394. New York: Oxford University Press.

Halldenius, Lena. 2001. *Liberty Revisited.* Lund: Bokbox.

Hampton, Jean. 1992. "Correcting Harms versus Righting Wrongs: The Goal of Retribution." *UCLA Law Review* 39, no. 6: 1659–1702.

Haslanger, Sally. 2000. "Gender and Race: (What) Are They? (What) Do We Want Them To Be?" *Noûs* 34, no. 1: 31–55.

Haslanger, Sally. 2011. "Ideology, Generics and Common Ground." In *Feminist Metaphysics: Explorations in the Ontology of Sex, Gender and the Self*, edited by Charlotte Witt, 179–207. Dordrecht: Springer.

Haslanger, Sally. 2012. "On Being Objective and Being Objectified." In *Resisting Reality: Social Construction and Social Critique*, 35–82. Oxford: Oxford University Press.

Haslanger, Sally. 2016. "What Is a (Social) Structural Explanation?" *Philosophical Studies* 173: 113–130.

Haslanger, Sally. 2018. "What is a Social Practice?" *Royal Institute of Philosophy Supplement* 82: 231–247.

Haslanger, Sally. 2018. "Ideal and Nonideal Social Ontology." Keynote address. *Social Ontology: The 11th Biennial Collective Intentionality Conference.* Boston, Tufts University, August 22–25. https://www.youtube.com/watch?v=6eAFIl5Tbbo.

Heyd, David. 2002. "Supererogation." In *The Stanford Encyclopedia of Philosophy*, Spring 2016 ed., edited by Edward N. Zalta. https://plato.stanf ord.edu/archives/spr2016/entries/supererogation/.

REFERENCES 231

Hill Collins, Patricia. 1990. *Black Feminist Thought: Knowledge, Consciousness, and the Politics of Empowerment*. Boston: Unwin Hyman.

Hindriks, Frank. 2008. "The Status Account of Corporate Agents." In *Concepts of Sharedness: Essays on Collective Intentionality*, edited by Hans Bernhard Schmid, Katinka Schulte-Ostermann, and Nikos Psarros, 119–144. Frankfurt: Ontos Verlag.

Hindriks, Frank. 2017. "Institutions and Collective Intentionality." In *The Routledge Handbook on Collective Intentionality*, edited by Marija Jankovic and Kirk Ludwig, 353–362. New York: Routledge.

Hindriks, Frank, and Francesco Guala. 2021. "The Functions of Institutions: Etiology and Teleology." *Synthese* 198: 2027–2043.

James, Susan. 2003. "Rights as Enforceble Claims." *Proceedings of the Aristotelian Society* 103, no. 2: 133–147.

Jenkins, Katharine. 2016. "Ontic Injustice." PhD diss., University of Sheffield.

Jenkins, Katharine. 2020. "Ontic Injustice." *Journal of the American Philosophical Association* 6, no. 2: 188–205.

Jenkins, Katharine. 2023. *Ontological Oppression*. New York: Oxford University Press.

Khalidi, Muhammad Ali. 2015. "Three Kinds of Social Kinds." *Philosophy and Phenomenological Research* 90, no. 1: 96–112.

Krishna, Daya. 1971. " 'The Self-Fulfilling Prophecy' and the Nature of Society." *American Sociological Review* 36, no. 6: 1104–1107.

Kuhn, Thomas S. 1962. *The Structure of Scientific Revolutions*. Chicago: University of Chicago Press.

Kutz, Christopher. 2000. "Acting Together." *Philosophy and Phenomenological Research* 61, no. 1: 1–31.

Kutz, Christopher. 2000. *Complicity: Ethics and Law for a Collective Age*. Cambridge: Cambridge University Press.

Lagerspetz, Eerik. 1995. *Opposite Mirrors: An Essay on the Conventionalist Theory of Institutions*. Dordrecht: Kluwer Academic Publishers.

Lewis, David. [1969] 2002. *Convention: A Philosophical Study*. London, UK: Blackwell Publishers.

Lukes, Steven. 2005. *Power: A Radical View*. 2nd ed. New York: Palgrave Macmillan.

Malmström, Malin, Jeaneth Johansson, and Joakim Wincent. 2017. "We Recorded VCs' Conversations and Analyzed How Differently They Talk About Female Entrepreneurs." *Harvard Business Review* (May). https://hbr.org/2017/05/we-recorded-vcs-conversations-and-analyzed-how-differen tly-they-talk-about-female-entrepreneurs.

Merton, Robert K. 1948. "The Self-Fulfilling Prophecy." *The Antioch Review* 8, no. 2: 193–210.

## 232 REFERENCES

Mikkola, Mari. 2018. "Feminist Metaphysics as Non-Ideal Metaphysics." In *The Bloomsbury Companion to Analytic Feminism*, edited by Pieranna Garavaso, 80–102. London, UK: Bloomsbury Academic.

Miller, Seumas. 2001. *Social Action: A Teleological Account*. Cambridge: Cambridge University Press.

Mills, Charles W. 2005. "'Ideal Theory' as Ideology." *Hypatia* 20, no. 3: 165–184.

Mills, Charles W. 2017. "Kant's Untermenschen." In *Black Rights/White Wrongs: The Critique of Racial Liberalism*, 91–112. New York: Oxford University Press.

Morriss, Peter. 2002. *Power: A Philosophical Analysis*. 2nd ed. Manchester: Manchester University Press.

Okin, Susan Moller. 1987. "Justice and Gender." *Philosophy & Public Affairs* 16, no. 1: 42–72.

Olsson-Yaouzis, Nicolas, Lisa Furberg, and Åsa Burman. 2018. "Philosophy for All?" (internal working paper). Department of Philosophy, Stockholm University.

Ortner, Sherry B. 1998. "Identities: The Hidden Life of Class." *Journal of Anthropological Research* 54, no. 1: 1–17.

Passinsky, Asya. 2020. "Should Bitcoin Be Classified as Money?" *Journal of Social Ontology* 6, no. 2: 281–292.

Pettit, Philip. 1997. *Republicanism: A Theory of Freedom and Government*. Oxford: Oxford University Press.

Rawls, John. 1971. *A Theory of Justice*. Cambridge: The Belknap Press of Harvard University Press.

Ritchie, Katherine. 2020. "Social Structures and the Ontology of Social Groups." *Philosophy and Phenomenological Research* 100, no. 2: 402–424.

Ross, Alan S. C. 1956. "U and Non-U: An Essay in Sociological Linguistics." In *Noblesse Oblige: An Enquiry into the Identifiable Characteristics of the English Aristocracy*, edited by Nancy Mitford, 11–36. London: Hamish Hamilton.

Rousseau, Jean Jacques. [1755] 1997. "A Discourse on the Origin of Inequality." In *Classics of Modern Political Theory: Machiavelli to Mill*, edited by Steven M. Kahn, 370–419. Oxford: Oxford University Press.

Searle, John R. 1969. *Speech Acts: An Essay in the Philosophy of Language*. New York: Cambridge University Press.

Searle, John R. 1983. *Intentionality: An Essay in the Philosophy of Mind*. New York: Cambridge University Press.

Searle, John R. 1990. "Collective Intentions and Action." In *Intentions in Communication*, edited by Philip. R. Cohen, Jerry Morgan, and Martha E. Pollack, 401–415. Boston: MIT Press.

Searle, John R. 1995. *The Construction of Social Reality*. New York: Free Press.

Searle, John R. 1999. *Mind, Language, and Society: Philosophy in the Real World*. New York: Basic Books.

Searle, John R. 2001. *Rationality in Action*. Oxford: Oxford University Press.

## REFERENCES 233

Searle, John R. 2006. "Social Ontology: Some Basic Principles." *Anthropological Theory* 6, no. 1: 12–29.

Searle, John R. 2010. *Making the Social World: The Structure of Human Civilisation*. Oxford: Oxford University Press.

Skeggs, Beverley. 1997. *Formations of Class and Gender: Becoming Respectable*. London: Sage Publications.

Smith, Barry, and John R. Searle. 2003. "The Construction of Social Reality: An Exchange." *The American Journal of Economics and Sociology* 62, no. 1: 285–309.

Thomasson, Amie. 2003. "Foundations for a Social Ontology." *ProtoSociology* 18–19: 269–290.

Tuomela, Raimo. 2001. "Collective Acceptance and Social Reality." In *On the Nature of Social and Institutional Reality*, edited by Heiki Ikäheimo, Eerik Lagerspetz, and Jussi Kotkavirta, 102–135. Jyväskylä: University of Jyväskylä.

Tuomela, Raimo. 2002. *The Philosophy of Social Practices: A Collective Acceptance View*. Cambridge: Cambridge University Press.

Tuomela, Raimo. 2003. "Collective Acceptance, Social Institutions, and Social Reality." *American Journal of Economics and Sociology* 62: 123–165.

Tuomela, Raimo. 2005. "We-Intentions Revisited." *Philosophical Studies* 125: 327–369.

Tuomela, Raimo. 2007. *The Philosophy of Sociality: The Shared Point of View*. Oxford: Oxford University Press.

Ylikoski, Petri, and Pekka Mäkelä. 2002. "We-Attitudes and Social Institutions." In *Social Facts and Collective Intentionality*, edited by Georg Meggle, 459–474. Frankfurt: Dr. Hänsel-Hohenhausen.

Young, Iris Marion. 1994. "Gender as Seriality: Thinking about Women as a Social Collective." *Signs* 19, no. 3: 713–738.

Valentini, Laura. 2012. "Ideal vs. Nonideal Theory: A Conceptual Map." *Philosophy Compass* 7, no. 9: 654–664.

Wennerås, Christine, and Agnes Wold. 1997. "Nepotism and Sexism in Peer-Review." *Nature* 387: 341–343.

White, Edmund. 1982. *A Boy's Own Story*. Boston: E. P. Dutton.

Witt, Charlotte. 2011. *The Metaphysics of Gender*. New York: Oxford University Press.

Wittgenstein, Ludwig. [1953] 1958. *Philosophical Investigations*, Oxford: Basil Blackwell.

Wollstonecraft, Mary. [1792] 2004. *A Vindication of the Rights of Woman*. New York: Penguin Classics.

# Index

*For the benefit of digital users, indexed terms that span two pages (e.g., 52–53) may, on occasion, appear on only one of those pages.*

Figures are indicated by *f* following the page number

abstraction
  abstract social objects, 1–3, 10–95, 113–15
  nonideal social ontology and, 2–3, 11–12
  standard model of ideal social ontology and, 1–2, 10, 11, 12, 73, 76–77, 113–15, 128–29
  two-worlds metaphor and, 1–2
ameliorative analysis, 145–47
anomaly of economic class being overlooked, 2n.1, 5n.5, 8, 156, 157, 162, 173–74
Ascriptivist Account of Social Normativity (Witt), 185–88
Ásta. *See also* conferralism
  base properties, 124, 130, 162, 163–64
  communal properties, 122–24, 125–28, 130, 165–66, 179
  constraints and enablements and, 125–26
  intersectionality and, 165
  methodological approach of, 22–23, 122–23, 130, 142–43, 158–59, 161, 165
  normative commitments of, 122–23, 129–30, 142–43, 162, 164–65, 167–68
  oppression and, 129, 142–43, 158–59, 164

  paradigmatic social phenomena and, 122–23, 127, 142, 158–59, 162, 166
  social injustice and, 122–23, 162, 163–64, 167–68
  social kinds and, 22–23, 160–61, 168
  social power and, 127–28, 179
  social properties and, 22–23, 122, 124
  social significance and, 167–68
Austin, J. L., 22

Barnes, Barry
  performativity and, 22–23
  reflexivity and, 21n.1, 24
  social power and, 24, 212–13, 214
  standard model of ideal social ontology and, 20, 21n.1, 22, 24
Bourdieu, Pierre, 108
Brännmark, Johan. *See also* Institutions as Distributions
  conditions of adequacy and, 131–32, 133–34, 154, 170
  contested institutional facts and, 79n.13
  deontic power and, 127–28, 131–32
  Hohfeldian incidents and, 137–38
  institutions and, 88, 97n.12, 134, 139–40, 141–42

## 236 INDEX

Brännmark, Johan (*cont.*)
    methodological approach of, 132–34, 140–41, 142–43
    moral and political commitments of, 133–34, 140–41, 142–43
    nonideal social ontology and, 131–32
    opaque social phenomena and, 134
    paradigmatic social phenomena and, 142
    racism and, 134, 140–41, 142
    sexism and, 134, 140–41, 142
    social positions and, 127–28, 169
    social power and, 127–28, 179
Bratman, Michael, 20, 23–24, 74, 77–78, 95, 110, 116

*Categories We Live By* (Ásta), 1, 122–23, 127–30, 158–59, 161, 164, 167–68
class. *See* economic class; social class
collective acceptance, 47–48, 52, 57–58, 88–89, 90–91
Collective Acceptance Account of Sociality (Tuomela)
    aims of, 59–60, 108
    basic building blocks of, 60–61
    bright side of institutions and, 65, 67–68, 70–72, 97, 98–99
    collective commitment and, 63–65, 98
    collective intentionality and, 59, 60–62, 71–72, 87, 98–99
    deontic power and, 64–65, 68, 70, 177
    ethos and, 64–65
    forgroupness and, 63–65, 98
    I-mode in, 62–63, 65, 97–98, 108
    institutions and, 62, 67–70, 97–100, 108–9
    objects of analysis in, 77
    paradigmatic social phenomena and, 70–72, 79

    social power and, 99–101, 108–9
    social practices and, 59–60, 65–70
    standard model of social ontology and, 71, 97
    we-mode in, 59–66, 97–100, 108
collective commitment, 63–65, 98
collective intentionality
    collective agreement and, 47–48
    collective recognition and, 90–91
    common knowledge and, 89, 116
    cooperation and, 90–91
    definition of, 23
    institutional facts and, 43–48, 54, 56–59, 71–72, 84–85, 86–87, 88–89, 94–97, 100
    institutions and, 5–6, 30–31, 62, 83–100, 88n.3, 116
    marriage and, 91–92, 95–96
    nonideal social ontology and, 95
    social power and, 109, 110–11, 205–6
    standard model of ideal social ontology and, 5–6, 20, 23, 72–73, 74–75, 77, 79, 83–100, 107–8, 111–12
    string quartet paradigm and, 70–71, 74, 77, 95
    as unnecessary for institutional facts, 94–97
    as unnecessary for standard institutions, 97–100
    we-attitudes and, 59, 60–61
commitments. *See* joint commitments; moral and political commitments; normative commitment, the
common knowledge
    collective intentionality and, 89, 116
    standard model of ideal social ontology and, 23, 90–93, 94, 95–96

# INDEX 237

conditions of adequacy
  conferralism and, 142–43, 158, 161, 165
  emancipatory social ontology and, 153–54, 155
  Institutions as Distributions and, 133–34, 140–41, 154, 168–69
  nonideal social ontology and, 142–44, 154–55, 156, 173–74
  standard model of ideal social ontology and, 19–20, 81–82, 110–11, 117–18, 142–43, 154–55, 156
conferralism (Ásta)
  aims of, 122–23, 143, 153, 162, 166
  communal properties and, 122–24, 125–28, 179
  conditions of adequacy and, 142–43, 158, 161, 165
  constraints and enablements and, 125–27, 131–32, 156, 162, 163
  definition of, 122–23
  deontic power and, 127–28, 179
  descriptive aim of, 143, 153
  economic class overlooked in, 157, 158–68, 169
  feminist theory and, 122–23, 142–43, 158–59, 165
  gender and, 127, 158–59, 162
  intersectionality and, 165
  nonideal social ontology and, 128–31
  normative commitments of, 122–23, 164–65
  opaque social phenomena and, 158, 162–64
  oppression as central in, 122–23, 129–30, 161–62, 164–65
  paradigmatic social phenomena and, 122–23, 158–62
  race and, 158–59, 162
  social injustice and, 122–23, 162, 164–65

social power and, 125–28, 156, 179
  social properties and, 122–28, 130–31, 165–68
  standard model of ideal social ontology and, 122–23, 129, 130, 156
conflict and contestation, 3, 81, 109, 115, 131–33, 176, 198
consensus-oriented view of social phenomena, 3, 39, 81–82, 115, 176, 198
constitutive rules
  definition of, 46
  institutional facts and, 47–49, 50, 52–53, 57–58
  institutions as system of, 48–49, 88–89
  performativity and, 48–49, 58–59
constraints and enablements
  conferralism and, 125–27, 131–32, 156, 162, 163
  deontic power and, 212
  economic class and, 163–64
  Institutions as Distributions and, 156
  ontic injustice and, 149–51, 156, 172–73
  rights and obligations and, 127
*Construction of Social Reality, The* (Searle), 3n.2, 42, 54, 56, 58–59, 90–91, 206n.4
conventional power, 53–56
cooperation, 39, 90–91
Correia, Fabrice, 205–6n.2

Dembroff, Robin, 144
deontic normativity, 181–82, 183–84, 188
deontic power
  definition of, 30
  deonticity claim, 28–29, 30–31, 41, 54–55, 56, 58–59, 64–65, 70, 73, 75, 131–32, 176, 177

## 238 INDEX

deontic power (*cont.*)
as dispositional, 209–10
formal deontic power, 211–12
Hohfeldian incidents and,
127–28, 131–32, 135–36, 179–
80, 210–13
informal deontic power, 211–12
institutional facts and, 53, 57–58,
194–95, 200, 201, 206–7
negative deontic power, 54, 55,
125–26, 178, 186–87, 207–
9, 216–17
nonideal social ontology
and, 179–80
positive deontic power, 54, 55, 125–
26, 127–28, 136, 181–82, 191,
195, 209–10, 212, 223–24, 226–27
Power View and, 131–32
privilege and, 54
reasons for action and, 54, 57–58,
178, 207–9
spillover power, relation to, 75,
215–19, 226–27
standard model of ideal social
ontology and, 54–55, 73, 75,
114–15, 176, 177, 210–11
status functions and, 54–55, 57–59
structural power, relation to, 223–
24, 226–27
taxonomy of social facts and, 200–
1, 204–13, 225–26, 228
telic power, relation to, 181–82,
188–89, 191–93, 197–98, 207–9,
213, 214
depoliticized examples, 79–81
derived social phenomena, 38, 71,
78, 111–12, 214
descriptive metaphysics, 154, 156, 174–75
descriptive social ontology, 143–44,
145, 153
direct social phenomena. *See* social
phenomena
social kinds and, 48–49

standard model of ideal social
ontology and, 71, 74, 78
*Discourse on Inequality*
(Rousseau), 46–47
Durkheim, Émile, 25, 33, 108

economic class
as analytical tool, 147–48, 174–75
conferralism and, 157, 158–
68, 169
emancipatory social ontology
and, 171–72
gender and, 4–5, 147–48, 169–70,
171–72, 224
Institutions as Distributions and,
141, 168–71
intentionalism and, 103
intersectionality and, 4–5, 147–48
Marxist sense of, 147–48, 163
nonideal social ontology and,
2n.1, 4–6, 8, 156, 157–58, 162,
168–69, 173–75
opaque social phenomena and,
38, 162–64
paradigmatic social phenomena
and, 38, 100–4, 107
Plural Subject Theory and, 100–3
Power View and, 8
race and, 170, 171, 224
social attitudes and, 169,
170, 171–72
social class distinguished
from, 163–64
social groups and, 38, 103
social injustice and, 157, 163–64
social kinds and, 8, 110–11, 162–
64, 171
social structures and, 222
standard model of ideal social
ontology and, 83–84, 100–3,
107, 110–11, 115–16
taxonomy of social facts and, 225
two-worlds metaphor and, 1–2

emancipatory social ontology
  aims of, 143, 155
  conditions of adequacy and, 153–54, 155
  definition of, 26–27
  deontic power and, 179
  economic class overlooked in, 171–72
  gender and, 142, 143, 144–47, 153–54
  moral and political commitments of, 143
  normative commitments of, 26–27
  ontic injustice and, 144, 152–54
  oppression as central in, 144, 153–54, 155
  race and, 142, 143, 144–47
  social change as primary aim of, 2–3, 143–44, 174–75
  social injustice and, 143, 144, 145, 155
  social kinds and, 155
  standard model of ideal social ontology contrasted with, 143–45, 153, 154–55, 174–75
enablements. *See* constraints and enablements
Epstein, Brian, 6n.7, 86
exemplars, 183–84, 189–90, 191, 195, 214, 227

facts. *See* generic stylized facts; institutional facts; taxonomy of social facts
feedback loops, 195, 198, 227
feminist theory, 122–23, 142–43, 147–48, 158–59, 165
first-person point of view, 39, 56–57, 73, 102–3, 110, 113
*Formations of Class and Gender* (Skeggs), 180–81
Foucault, Michel, 75–76, 108
foundation claim
  definition of, 26–27

standard model of ideal social ontology and, 72, 81–82, 109, 110–11
Fricker, Miranda, 196–97
Frye, Marilyn, 196

game theory, 20, 35, 89
gender
  bias concerning, 193–94, 202, 220–21, 222
  conflicting standards and, 195–97
  deontic power and, 210–12
  economic class and, 4–5, 147–48, 169–70, 171–72, 224
  emancipatory social ontology and, 142, 143, 144–47, 153–54
  Hohfeldian incidents and, 137–38, 139–40
  ideals and, 196
  institutional facts and, 132–33
  as mega social role, 185–88
  norms concerning, 180, 182–85, 192, 196
  ontic injustice and, 149–50
  paradigmatic social phenomena and, 77, 102, 113–14, 117–18, 142
  Plural Subject Theory and, 33, 39, 102, 103
  privilege and, 139–40, 146
  sexism and, 132–34, 139–41, 142, 143, 193–94
  social positions and, 136–38, 139–40
  social power and, 205–6
  social roles and, 185–86
  social structures and, 221–22
  standard model of ideal social ontology and, 77, 79, 102, 103, 113–14, 143
  structural power and, 220–23
  subordination and, 146, 147–48
  substandard and, 183–84, 189, 195, 196, 227

240 INDEX

gender (*cont.*)
    taxonomy of social facts and, 202–3, 206–7, 225–27
    teleological normativity and, 180–85
    telic power and, 189, 190, 192, 193–97, 213
    two-worlds metaphor and, 1–3
generic stylized facts, 40, 76–77, 113–15, 117–18, 156
Gilbert, Margaret. *See also* joint commitments; Plural Subject Theory
    aims of, 25–26, 31, 33, 41–42, 76
    cooperation and, 39–41
    deontic power and, 30–31, 54–55
    economic class and, 38, 40–41
    equality and, 39–41
    intentionalism and, 102–3
    methodological approach of, 33, 102–3
    nonideal social ontology contrasted with, 26–27, 130–31
    objects of analysis and, 76, 77
    opaque social phenomena and, 38–39, 57, 132–33
    paradigmatic social phenomena and, 25, 26–27, 36–39, 41, 56–57, 58–59, 79–81
    social conventions and, 25, 35, 39, 77, 80–81, 177
    social groups and, 37, 101–2
    social power and, 33, 109
    standard model of ideal social ontology and, 19, 20, 24–25
    two-worlds metaphor and, 39–40
Guala, Francesco
    collective intentionality and, 4n.4, 23, 30–31, 41, 58–59, 70
    generic stylized facts and, 73n.9
    performativity and, 4n.4, 22, 41, 58–59, 70
    reflexivity and, 4n.4, 20–21, 41, 58–59, 70
    standard model of ideal social ontology and, 4n.4, 20, 21–22, 23–24

Hacking, Ian, 20, 23–24, 79
Hampton, Jean, 150
Haslanger, Sally
    aims of, 145
    background ideology and, 145–48
    conditions of adequacy and, 147–48, 171–72
    emancipatory social ontology and, 144–45
    gender and, 121, 144–47, 171–72, 179, 182–85, 206n.4
    ideal social ontology distinguished from theory of, 145
    intersectionality and, 171–72
    material conditions in social ontology and, 86
    methodological approach of, 145–47
    norms concerning gender and, 182–85
    objects of analysis and, 148
    paradigmatic social phenomena and, 37–38
    privilege and, 146–47, 156
    race and, 121, 144–47, 171–72, 179
    social injustice and, 145, 148, 171–72
    social power and, 145, 146, 147–48, 156
    standard model of ideal social ontology and, 145
    subordination and, 145, 146–47, 156
    teleological normativity and, 180, 182–85
hermeneutical injustice, 196–97
hierarchy, 2–3, 36, 146, 147, 179, 205–6

INDEX 241

Hindriks, Frank, 87–88, 89–90, 135n.6, 180
Hohfeldian incidents
  as basic building blocks, 134–40
  claims and, 135, 136–38
  definition of, 135–36
  deontic power and, 127–28, 131–32, 135–36, 179–80, 210–13
  gender and, 137–38, 139–40
  immunities and, 136–37
  institutional facts and, 136–37, 138
  Institutions as Distributions and, 134–41, 156, 169, 179
  liberties and, 135, 136–37
  nonideal social ontology and, 134–40
  powers and, 136–37
  Power View and, 131–32
  privilege and, 137–38, 139–40
  rights and obligations and, 210–11
  social positions and, 127–28, 136–38, 140–41, 169, 179
human rights, 23n.2, 177

ideals
  deontic power and, 195–96
  gender and, 196
  nonideal social ontology and, 9–10
  standard model of ideal social ontology and, 9–10
  teleological normativity and, 182, 183–85
  telic power and, 188, 192–93, 195–96, 197–98, 214
ideal social ontology. See standard model of ideal social ontology
ideal theory, 9–13
"Ideal Theory as Ideology" (Mills), 10–11
illegitimate power relations, 11–12, 13–14, 77–78, 128–29, 142–43

indirect social phenomena. See social phenomena
injustice. See ontic injustice; social injustice
institutional facts
  collective acceptance and, 47–48, 52, 57–58
  collective intentionality and, 43–48, 54, 56–59, 71–72, 84–85, 86–87, 88–89, 94–97, 100
  contested institutional facts, 131–41
  conventional power and, 53–56
  definition of, 52
  deontic power and, 53, 57–58, 194–95, 200, 201, 206–7
  Hohfeldian incidents and, 136–37, 138
  Institutions as Distributions and, 132–37, 138, 140–41
  standard model of ideal social ontology and, 74, 77, 86–87, 94–97, 113–14, 116, 132–33, 139, 141–42, 154
  status functions and, 45–46, 47, 52
  taxonomy of social facts and, 201–2, 204–5
institutional properties, 122–23, 124–26, 179
institutions
  coercion and, 99–100
  constitutive rules, as system of, 48–49, 88–89
  definition of, 48–49
  deontic power and, 68, 109, 192, 212
  Hohfeldian incidents and, 134, 135
  institutional power relations and, 55, 56
  nonideal social ontology and, 141–42
  norms and, 67–68, 87, 108, 109

242 INDEX

institutions (*cont.*)
  opaque social phenomena
    and, 139–40
  standard model of ideal social
    ontology and, 13–14, 23, 73,
    75–76, 86–100, 141–42
  standard sense of, 97–100
  status functions and, 88n.3
  types of, 68
  we-attitudes and, 62, 67–
    68, 97–100
Institutions as Distributions
  (Brännmark)
  aims of, 133, 140–41, 143
  basic building blocks and, 134–41
  conditions of adequacy and, 133–
    34, 140–41, 154, 168–69
  definition of, 135
  deontic power and, 131–32, 135,
    156, 179, 179n.2
  descriptive aim of, 143, 156
  descriptive contestation
    and, 132–33
  economic class as incompatible
    with, 141, 168–71
  gender and, 132–33, 134, 137–
    38, 139–41
  Hohfeldian incidents and, 134–41,
    156, 169, 179
  normative contestation and, 132–33
  opaque social phenomena and,
    132–33, 134, 138, 140–41
  paradigmatic social phenomena
    and, 132–33, 142
  privilege and, 140–41
  race and, 132–33, 134, 137–
    38, 139–41
  social change and, 143–44
  social positions and, 135–38, 169–
    71, 179
  subordination and, 140–41
intentionalism
  collective awareness and, 102–3

  definition of, 102–3
  economic class and, 103
  opaque social phenomena and, 39
  paradigmatic social phenomena
    and, 103
  social groups and, 103, 113
  standard model of ideal social
    ontology and, 73, 102–3,
    110, 113–15
*Intentionality* (Searle), 41–42
intersectionality
  conditions of adequacy and, 147–
    48, 171–72
  Conferralism and, 165
  economic class and, 4–5, 147–48
  nonideal social ontology and, 4–5
  two-worlds metaphor and, 2–3

James, Susan, 211n.7
Jenkins, Katharine. *See also* ontic
  injustice
  constraints and enablements and, 172
  economic class and, 172–73
  emancipatory social ontology and,
    144, 152–54
  gender and, 149–50, 152–
    53, 210–11
  ideal social ontology distinguished
    from theory of, 152–54
  methodological approach of, 152–53
  moral and political commitments
    of, 152–53
  ontic oppression and, 121, 153–54
  race and, 152–53
joint commitments
  definition of, 27–28
  genesis of, 28, 33–34
  ontological holism and, 28–29, 31–36

Kant, Immanuel, 197n.12
Khalidi, Muhammad Ali, 7–8, 21,
  22–23, 76, 83–84, 139, 159–61,
  168, 201

## INDEX 243

Krishna, Daya, 20–21
Kuhn, Thomas, 6–7
Kutz, Christopher, 36, 74n.11

Lagerspetz, Eerik, 208n.5
Lewis, David, 25, 35
Lukes, Steven, 210n.6

Mäkelä, Pekka, 86–87, 93–94
*Making the Social World* (Searle), 90–91
marriage
  bright side of institutions and, 95
  collective intentionality and, 91–
    92, 95–96
  nonideal social ontology
    and, 95–96
  ontic injustice and, 151
  paradigmatic social phenomena
    and, 85, 116
  standard model of ideal social
    ontology and, 85, 116
Medical Research Council (MRC),
  193–95, 202, 205–6, 207–9, 226
Merton, Robert K., 20–21
metaphysics, descriptive, 154,
  156, 174–75
Miller, Seumas, 180, 188n.7
Mills, Charles
  ideal and nonideal theory
    distinguished by, 9–13, 128–
    29, 155–56
  ideology and, 10–11
  standard model of ideal social
    ontology and, 14–15
moral and political commitments,
  122–23, 129–30, 133–34, 140–
  41, 142–43, 152–53
Morriss, Peter, 210n.6

*Nature of Power, The* (Barnes), 212–13
nonideal social ontology
  agreements with ideal social
    ontology of, 121–22, 156

conditions of adequacy and, 142–
  44, 154–55, 156, 173–74
Conferralism and, 128–31
definition of, 2–3, 13–14
deontic power and, 179–80
descriptive metaphysics and, 156
economic class and, 2n.1, 4–6,
  8, 156, 157–58, 162, 168–
  69, 173–75
ideal social ontology distinguished
  from, 1–3, 13–15, 77–78, 141–
  44, 154–56
ideal theory's relation to, 9–13
intersectionality and, 4–5
moral and political commitments
  and, 122–23, 142–43
normative commitment and, 26–
  27, 164–65
opaque social phenomena and,
  134, 141–42
oppression as central in, 13–14,
  48, 129, 155–56
paradigmatic social phenomena
  and, 3, 26–27, 79–80, 95,
  142, 156
paradigm shift from ideal social
  ontology to, 4–6, 19–20, 83, 85,
  116, 121, 155–56
Power View and, 5–6
privilege and, 131–32
social injustice and, 157
social power and, 5–6, 114–15,
  151, 156, 157–58, 199
two-worlds metaphor and, 2–3
normative commitment, the, 26–27,
  122–23, 129, 142–43, 162, 164–
  65, 167–68
normativity. *See also* deontic
  normativity; rights and
  obligations; social normativity;
  teleological normativity
deontic normativity, 181–82, 183–
  84, 188

244 INDEX

normativity (*cont.*)
  nonideal social ontology
    and, 26–27
norms
  class norms, 180–81
  definition of, 68
  gender norms, 180, 182–85,
    192, 196
  institutions and, 32–68, 87,
    108, 109
  social power and, 68
  social roles and, 186–87
  standard model of ideal social
    ontology and, 75–76
  telic power and, 192, 214

objects of analysis, 73–74, 76, 77,
  78, 153–54
obligations. *See* rights and
  obligations
one-sided diet of examples, 112, 117,
  158–59, 176–77
*On Social Facts* (Gilbert), 25–26, 31,
  33, 177
ontic injustice (Jenkins)
  constraints and enablements and,
    149–51, 156, 172–73
  definition of, 149
  economic class and, 151, 172–
    73, 174–75
  emancipatory social ontology and,
    144, 152–54
  gender and, 149–50
  marriage and, 151
ontic oppression, 121, 144
ontological dependence, 205–6n.2
ontological holism, 28–29, 31–36
ontological oppression, 144
opacity
  conceptual opacity, 164n.2, 220
  epistemic opacity, 220–21, 223–24
  opaque kinds of social facts, 5–6,
    21, 43–44, 48, 84–85, 100–1,

103, 105–6, 113–14, 203, 219,
    223, 226
opaque social phenomena
  intentionalism and, 39
  nonideal social ontology and,
    134, 141–42
  paradigmatic social phenomena
    and, 38–39
  social groups and, 38
  social kinds and, 110–11
  social structures and, 83–84, 110–
    11, 113, 221–22
  standard model of ideal social
    ontology and, 5–6, 21, 39, 71,
    74, 76, 104–7, 113, 134, 139
  structural power and, 219n.9,
    220–21, 222
  taxonomy of social facts and, 104–
    5, 200–1, 202, 219
oppression
  Conferralism and, 122–23, 129–
    30, 161–62, 164–65
  emancipatory social ontology and,
    144, 153–54, 155
  ideal social ontology as silent on,
    13–14, 37–38, 77–78, 129, 153–
    54, 155–56
  nonideal social ontology and, 13–
    14, 48, 129, 155–56
  ontic oppression, 121, 144
  ontological oppression, 144
  privilege and, 156
  social kinds and, 155
  social power and, 156
  subordination and, 156
  two-worlds metaphor and, 2–3
Ortner, Sherry B., 5n.5

paradigmatic social phenomena
  bright side of institutions and, 37–
    38, 41, 56, 74
  economic class and, 38, 100–4,
    107

gender and, 77, 102, 113–14, 117–18, 142
intentionalism and, 103
marriage and, 85, 116
nonideal social ontology and, 3, 26–27, 79–80, 95, 142, 156
one-sided diet of examples and, 112, 117, 158–59, 176–77
opaque social phenomena and, 38–39
paradigmatic examples and, 37–38, 41, 56, 57, 58–59, 73, 77, 95, 113–14
race and, 117–18
social kinds and, 153–54
social structures and, 107
standard model of ideal social ontology and, 3, 74, 77, 79–81, 95, 100–3, 106–7, 111–15, 142, 176, 206–7
taxonomy of social facts and, 206–7, 225
telic power and, 193–97
two-worlds metaphor and, 3, 6–7
paradigm shift from ideal to nonideal social ontology, 4–6, 19–20, 83, 84, 85, 116, 121, 155–56
performativity
Background and, 50
definition of, 22
group membership and, 76
performativity claim, 34–36, 48–50, 62, 73, 76, 106–7, 110, 111–12, 117, 134
social kinds and, 83–84, 107
social reality account and, 48–52, 56, 58–59
speech acts and, 22
standard model of ideal social ontology and, 20, 22–23, 73, 76, 79, 83–84, 106–7, 111–12, 117, 134

Pettit, Philip, 217–18
*Philosophical Investigations* (Wittgenstein), 158–59
*Philosophy of Sociality, The* (Tuomela), 3n.2
*Philosophy of Social Practices, The* (Tuomela), 59
pluralistic account of social power, 176–77, 199, 228
Plural Subject Theory (Gilbert). *See also* joint commitments
aims of, 25–26, 41
basic building blocks of, 27–31
collective intentionality and, 30–31, 41, 71–72, 87
common knowledge and, 28, 33–34
consensus-oriented view and, 39–41
cooperation prioritized in, 109
definition of, 26, 27–28
economic class and, 100–3
equality and, 39–41
foundation claim and, 26–27, 31, 41
gender and, 33, 39, 102, 103
intentionalism of, 102–3
objects of analysis and, 77
opaque social phenomena and, 39
paradigmatic social phenomena and, 36–39, 79–81, 100–3
rights and obligations and, 29–30, 33
social groups and, 101–3, 177
social power and, 33, 41
standard model of ideal social ontology and, 41
political commitments. *See* moral and political commitments
power. *See also* deontic power; social power; spillover power; structural power; telic power
brute power, 53, 205–6

246 INDEX

power (*cont.*)
  conventional power, 53–56
  illegitimate power relations,
    11–12, 13–14, 77–78, 128–
    29, 142–43
  institutional power
    relations, 55, 56
  positive and negative power,
    178, 191, 197–98, 209, 216–
    17, 222–23
  power-to-do distinguished from
    power-over others, 210n.6
  productive aspects of, 33, 71–72,
    75–76, 77
power claim
  Collective Acceptance Account of
    Sociality and, 69–70
  constitutive rules and, 58–59
  definition of, 70
  institutions and, 69–70
  Plural Subject Theory and, 33, 41
  rights and obligations and, 33, 55,
    69–70, 73, 75–76
  social reality account and, 55
  standard model of ideal social
    ontology and, 55, 73, 75–76,
    109–10, 114–15, 131–32
Power View, The (Burman)
  definition of, 3–5
  deontic power and, 131–32
  economic class and, 8
  Hohfeldian incidents and, 131–32
  nonideal social ontology and, 5–6
  purpose and main claims of, 4–8
  social kinds and, 8
  standard model of ideal social
    ontology and, 4–5
  taxonomy of social facts and,
    200, 228
privilege
  deontic power and, 54
  gender and, 139–40,
    146

  Hohfeldian incidents and, 137–
    38, 139–40
  ideal theory and, 10–11, 12
  Institutions as Distributions
    and, 140–41
  nonideal social ontology
    and, 131–32
  oppression and, 156
  race and, 147
  social positions and, 131–32, 137–
    38, 139–40

race
  Conferralism and, 158–59, 162
  economic class and, 170, 171, 224
  emancipatory social ontology and,
    142, 143, 144–47
  Institutions as Distributions and,
    132–33, 134, 137–38, 139–41
  paradigmatic social phenomena
    and, 117–18
  privilege and, 147
  racism and, 134, 140–41, 142, 143
  standard model of ideal social
    ontology and, 77, 113–14, 143
  subordination and, 147
  two-worlds metaphor and, 1–3
*Rationality in Action* (Searle), 54
Rawls, John, 9, 13
reasons for action
  deontic power and, 54, 57–58,
    178, 207–9
  ideals and, 182, 184–85
  norms and, 87
  social normativity and, 87
  telic power and, 75, 207–9, 214
reflexivity
  definition of, 20–21, 104
  reflexivity claim, 33–34, 47–48,
    61–62, 73, 76, 104, 106–7, 112
  self-fulfilling prophecies and, 20–
    21, 33–34, 73, 106
  social kinds and, 21, 106, 107, 110

standard model of ideal social
ontology and, 20–21, 73, 76, 79,
83–84, 104, 106–7, 110, 111–12
taxonomy of social facts
and, 104–5
we-attitudes and, 61
*Rights and Demands* (Gilbert), 3n.2
rights and obligations
constraints and enablements
and, 127
formal forms of, 210–11
Hohfeldian incidents and, 210–11
informal forms of, 127
standard model of ideal social
ontology and, 183–84
telic power and, 192, 194–95, 207–9
Rousseau, Jean-Jacques, 46–47, 48–49

scope claim
conditions of adequacy
and, 110–11
definition of, 25–26
standard model of ideal social
ontology and, 72, 81–82, 110–11
Searle, John. *See also* constitutive
rules; social reality account;
status functions
aims of, 41–42, 56
bright side of institutions and, 56,
58–59, 70–71
brute facts, 44, 47, 201, 204–5
brute power, 53, 205–6
collective acceptance and, 90–91
collective intentionality and, 43–
44, 45, 67, 86–87, 90–92
collective recognition and, 90–91
conventional power and, 54
cooperation and, 90–91
deontic power and, 54, 56, 58–59,
109, 178
institutional facts and, 41–42, 46–
48, 67, 77, 86–87, 88–89, 90–92,
104, 109

methodological choices of, 56–57
opaque social phenomena and,
43–44, 56–57, 105–6, 132–
33, 203
oppression and, 56
paradigmatic social phenomena
and, 56–57, 58–59, 70–71, 79
power relations and, 56
standard model of ideal social
ontology and, 19, 20, 23–25
two-worlds metaphor and, 1
sexism, 132–34, 139–41, 142,
143, 193–94
Simmel, Georg, 25
Skeggs, Beverley, 180–81, 183
SMOSO (standard model of social
ontology), 20, 21–22, 23–24
*Social Action* (Miller), 180
social attitudes
Conferralism and, 156, 157
constraints and enablements
and, 172
economic class and, 169,
170, 171–72
Institutions as Distributions and,
156, 157
nonideal social ontology and,
157, 173–75
social kinds and, 172, 173–74
social change, 2–3, 143–44,
152, 174–75
social class, 2n.1, 146, 147–
48, 163–64
social construction, 88–89, 142, 161,
165, 168
social conventions, 25, 33, 35–36,
40–41, 77, 78, 80–81, 177
social facts. *See* taxonomy of
social facts
social groups
collective awareness and, 101–2
definition of, 101–2
deontic power and, 194–95

248 INDEX

social groups (*cont.*)
economic class and, 38, 103
intentionalism and, 103, 113
opaque social phenomena and, 38
Plural Subject Theory and, 101–3, 177
standard model of ideal social ontology and, 110
structural power and, 222
social injustice
Conferralism and, 122–23, 162, 164–65
economic class and, 157, 163–64
emancipatory social ontology and, 143, 144, 145, 155
nonideal social ontology and, 157
social justice, 152
social kinds
classification of, 7–8, 21, 22–23, 76, 139, 159–61
Conferralism and, 22–23, 161–64, 168
economic class and, 8, 110–11, 162–64, 171
emancipatory social ontology and, 155
first kind of, 8, 21, 76, 78, 83–84, 100–1, 106–7, 110–13, 115, 117–18, 155, 160–61, 162–63, 168, 172–73, 199, 228
opaque social phenomena and, 110–11
oppression and, 155
paradigmatic social phenomena and, 153–54
Power View and, 8
second kind of, 8, 22–23, 107, 112, 130–31, 139, 160–61, 168
standard model of ideal social ontology and, 8, 83–84, 100–1, 110–11, 112
third kind of, 8, 22–23, 107, 112, 130–31, 160–61, 168

social normativity
ascriptivist accounts of, 185–88
ethical normativity distinguished from, 186–87
social roles and, 186–87
telic power and, 188–89, 214
social ontology. *See* descriptive social ontology; emancipatory social ontology; nonideal social ontology; standard model of ideal social ontology
social phenomena. *See also* consensus-oriented view of social phenomena; derived social phenomena;; irreducibility of social phenomena; opaque social phenomena; paradigmatic social phenomena
direct social phenomena, 38, 48–49, 56–57, 58–59, 71, 74, 214, 223
indirect social phenomena, 38, 71, 78, 112, 214
social positions
conditions of adequacy and, 140–41
economic class and, 169–71
gender and, 136–38, 139–40
Hohfeldian incidents and, 127–28, 136–38, 140–41, 169, 179
Institutions as Distributions and, 135–38, 169–71, 179
privilege and, 131–32, 137–38, 139–40
social normativity and, 186
subordination and, 137–38, 139–40
social power. *See also* deontic power; spillover power; structural power; telic power
brute power distinguished from, 205–6

definition of, 3–4
deontic power distinguished
   from, 205–6
direct forms of, 207–14
indirect forms of, 215–25
institutions and, 109
nonideal social ontology and, 5–6,
   151, 156, 157–58, 199
norms and, 68
oppression and, 156
pluralistic account of, 176–77,
   199, 228
standard model of ideal social
   ontology and, 75, 83–84, 100–1,
   107–9, 114–15, 117–18
taxonomy of social facts and, 3–4,
   33, 200–7, 225–26
two-worlds metaphor and, 3–4
as underdeveloped concept, 3–4
underemphasis on, 107–9
social practices
   Collective Acceptance Account of
      Sociality and, 59–60, 65–70
   definition of, 66
   social power and, 108
   standard model of ideal social
      ontology and, 75–76, 78
   we-attitudes and, 59–60, 61, 62, 66
social properties
   communal social properties, 122–
      24, 125–28, 130, 165–66, 179
   Conferralism and, 122–28, 130–
      31, 165–68
   constraints and enablements
      and, 125
   economic class and, 8
social reality account (Searle). See
      also constitutive rules; status
      functions
   basic building blocks of, 42–46
   conventional power and, 53–56
   deontic power and, 54–55, 57–58,
      109, 177–78, 206n.4, 210n.6

institutional facts and, 42, 44,
   46–50, 53–56, 57–58, 86–87,
   104, 109
institutions and, 42, 48–49, 86–87,
   88–89, 109
opaque social phenomena and, 48,
   100–1, 104–6, 203
paradigmatic social phenomena
   and, 56–57, 79
performativity and, 48–52,
   56, 58–59
reasons for action and, 178
social power and, 109
standard model of ideal social
   ontology and, 57–59
taxonomy of social facts and, 44
social reason, 66, 68
social roles
   gender and, 185–86
   intersectionality and, 2–3
   norms and, 186–87
   rights and obligations and, 186–87
   social normativity and, 186–87
   standard model of ideal social
      ontology and, 77
   telic power and, 194–95
social structures
   definition of, 221
   economic class and, 222
   gender and, 221–22
   opaque social structures, 83–84,
      110–11, 113, 221–22
   paradigmatic social phenomena
      and, 107
   standard model of ideal social
      ontology and, 83–84
   structural power and, 220–22, 223
speech acts, 22, 41–42, 200
*Speech Acts* (Searle), 41–42
spillover power
   definition of, 216
   negative spillover power, 216–17
   positive spillover power, 216–17

## 250 INDEX

spillover power (*cont.*)
  standard model of ideal social
    ontology and, 75
  status functions and, 215–17
  taxonomy of social facts and, 219,
    225–26, 228
standard model of ideal social
  ontology
  abstraction's role in, 1–2, 10, 11,
    12, 73, 76–77, 113–15, 128–29
  agreements with nonideal social
    ontology of, 121–22, 156
  aims of, 5–6, 72, 152
  as analytical tool, 111–12, 115–
    16, 117
  basic building blocks of, 72–73,
    79, 81–82, 111–12
  bright side of institutions and, 37–
    38, 74, 77–78, 95, 110, 116
  central features of, 14–15, 81–
    82, 83–84
  central social phenomena
    overlooked in, 83–84, 100–
    11, 116–17
  conceivability critique of, 85, 90–
    92, 95, 116
  concepts and assumptions of ideal
    theory and, 12–13
  conditions of adequacy and,
    19–20, 81–82, 110–11, 117–18,
    142–43, 154–55, 156
  consensus-oriented view and, 3,
    39, 81–82, 115, 176, 198
  culpability of paradigmatic
    features of, 113–15
  definition of, 1–2, 13–14
  deontic normativity and, 183–84
  deontic power and, 54–55, 73, 75,
    114–15, 176, 177, 210–11
  descriptive metaphysics used in,
    154, 156, 173–74
  economic class overlooked in, 83–
    84, 100–3, 107, 110–11, 115–16

emancipatory ontology
  distinguished from, 143–45,
    152, 153, 154–55, 174–75
engagement by nonideal social
  ontologists with, 3
foundation claim and, 72, 81–82,
  109, 110–11
gender and, 77, 79, 102, 103, 113–
  14, 143
generic stylized facts and, 73
group membership and, 76
ideals and, 9–10
ideal theory's relation to, 9–13
Institutions as Distributions and,
  131–33, 136, 141–42
intentionalism and, 73, 102–3,
  110, 113–15
material conditions overlooked
  in, 79, 86
methodological approach of, 73,
  76, 103, 113–15
moral and political commitments
  and, 122–23, 142–43
nonideal ontology distinguished
  from, 1–3, 13–15, 77–78, 141–
  44, 154–56
normative commitment
  and, 26–27
norms and, 75–76
objects of analysis in, 73–74, 77, 78
opaque social phenomena
  overlooked by, 5–6, 21, 39, 71,
  74, 76, 104–7, 113, 134, 139
oppression, as silent on, 13–14,
  37–38, 77–78, 129, 153–
  54, 155–56
paradigmatic social phenomena
  and, 3, 74, 77, 79–81, 95, 100–3,
  106–7, 111–15, 142,
  176, 206–7
paradigm shift toward nonideal
  ontology from, 4–6, 19–20, 83,
  84, 85, 116, 121, 155–56

performativity and, 20, 22–23, 73, 76, 79, 83–84, 106–7, 111–12, 117, 134

power claim and, 55, 73, 75–76, 109–10, 114–15, 131–32

Power View and, 4–5

race and, 77, 113–14, 143

reflexivity and, 20–21, 73, 76, 79, 83–84, 104, 106–7, 110, 111–12

rights and obligations and, 183–84

scope claim and, 72, 81–82, 110–11

social groups and, 110

social kinds overlooked in, 8, 83–84, 100–1, 104–7, 110–11, 112

social power as underemphasized in, 75, 83–84, 100–1, 107–9, 114–15, 117–18

social structures and, 83–84

spillover power overlooked by, 75

status functions and, 183–84

strict compliance and, 14n.9

string quartet paradigm and, 74, 77–78, 95, 97, 110, 116

stylized facts and, 76–77, 114–15, 156

taxonomy of social facts and, 74

teleological normativity and, 180

telic power overlooked by, 75

two-worlds metaphor and, 1–2, 3, 39

standard model of social ontology (SMOSO), 20, 21–22, 23–24

status functions

conventional power and, 53, 54

definition of, 45–46

deontic power and, 54–55, 57–59

institutional facts and, 45–46, 47, 52

institutions and, 88n.3

logical structure of, 48–50

reasons for action and, 178

rights and obligations and, 53, 183–84

standard model of ideal social ontology and, 183–84

string quartet paradigm

Collective Acceptance Account of Sociality and, 70–71

collective intentionality and, 70–71, 74, 77, 95

definition of, 36

institutional facts and, 95

standard model of ideal social ontology and, 74, 77–78, 95, 97, 110, 116

structural power

definition of, 222

deontic power, relation to, 223–24, 226–27

negative structural power, 127–28, 222–24, 226–27

opaque social phenomena and, 219n.9, 220–21, 222

positive structural power, 222–23, 227

social groups and, 222

social structures and, 220–22, 223

taxonomy of social facts and, 219, 223, 225–27, 228

theoretical usefulness of, 219n.9, 223–24

stylized facts, 73, 76–77, 113–15, 117–18, 156

subordination

gender and, 146, 147–48

Institutions as Distributions and, 140–41

oppression and, 156

race and, 147

social positions and, 137–38, 139–40

substandard

gender and, 183–84, 189, 195, 196, 227

teleological normativity and, 183–84, 189

252  INDEX

substandard (*cont.*)
    telic power and, 190, 191, 195,
        196–97, 198, 214, 226

taxonomy of social facts
    as analytical tool, 227
    central distinctions for, 203–4
    class and, 206–7
    definition of, 204–5
    deontic power and, 200–1, 204–
        13, 225–26, 228
    diagram of, 203*f*, 225
    direct social facts, 203–4
    economic class and, 225
    gender and, 202–3, 206–7, 225–27
    indirect social facts and, 203–4, 225
    non-power-related and power-
        related facts distinguished
        in, 204–7
    opaque social phenomena and,
        104–5, 200–1, 202, 219
    Power View and, 200, 228
    spillover power and, 219, 225–
        26, 228
    standard model of ideal social
        ontology and, 74
    structural power and, 219, 223,
        225–27, 228
    telic power and, 200–1, 204–7,
        213–14, 225–27, 228
teleological normativity
    deontic normativity contrasted
        with, 181–82, 184–85
    exemplars and, 183–84
    gender and, 180–85
    ideals and, 182, 183–85
    paradigmatic social phenomena
        and, 180
    standard model of ideal social
        ontology and, 180
    substandard and, 183–84, 189
    telic power and, 181–82, 188,
        192, 213

telic power
    conflicting standards explained
        by, 195–97
    definition of, 188
    deontic power, relation to, 181–82,
        188–89, 191–93, 197–98, 207–9,
        213, 214
    exemplars and, 189–90, 191, 195,
        214, 227
    gender and, 189, 190, 192, 193–
        97, 213
    hermeneutical injustice
        and, 196–97
    ideals and, 188, 192–93, 195–96,
        197–98, 214
    negative telic power, 190, 191, 195,
        214, 226, 227
    normative reasons and, 207–9
    norms and, 192, 214
    paradigmatic social phenomena
        and, 193–97
    positive telic power, 189, 190, 191,
        195, 214, 227
    reasons for action and, 75, 207–
        9, 214
    rights and obligations and, 192,
        194–95, 207–9
    social normativity and, 188–
        89, 214
    social roles and, 194–95
    standard model of ideal social
        ontology and, 75
    substandard and, 190, 191, 195,
        196–97, 198, 214, 226
    taxonomy of social facts and, 200–
        1, 204–7, 213–14, 225–27, 228
    teleological normativity and, 181–
        82, 188, 192, 213
*Theory of Justice, A* (Rawls), 9
Thomasson, Amie
    opaque social phenomena and, 48,
        104–5, 164n.2, 203, 219–20
    reflexivity and, 104–6

INDEX    253

social reality account and, 48, 104–6, 164n.2, 203
standard model of ideal social ontology and, 106
status functions and, 48–49
Tuomela, Raimo. *See also* Collective Acceptance Account of Sociality; we-attitudes
  aims of, 59–60
  collective intentionality and, 61, 96–97
  deontic power and, 64–65, 177
  forgroupness and, 63
  institutions and, 67–70, 87, 93–94, 97, 98, 108–9
  intentionalism and, 103
  methodological approach of, 59–60, 103
  norms and, 109
  opaque social phenomena and, 132–33
  paradigmatic social phenomena and, 70–72, 79
  social practices and, 20, 60, 67, 77, 177
  standard model of ideal social ontology and, 19, 20, 23–25, 76
  string quartet paradigm and, 33–35, 99
two-worlds metaphor
  Collective Acceptance Account of Sociality and, 109
  conditions of adequacy and, 6–7
  conflict and contestation and, 1–3
  consensus-oriented view and, 1–2

economic class and, 1–2
formal and informal roles in, 1–3
gender and, 1–3
hierarchy and, 2–3
intersectionality and, 2–3
methodological disagreements and, 6–7
nonideal social ontology and, 2–3
oppression and, 2–3
paradigmatic social phenomena and, 3, 6–7
race and, 1–3
social change and, 2–3
social power and, 3–4
standard model of ideal social ontology and, 1–2, 3, 39

"Walking Together" (Gilbert), 34–35
we-attitudes
  definition of, 62–63, 64
  irreducibility and, 60–62
  social practices and, 59–60, 61, 62, 66
Weber, Max, 25
Wenar, Leif, 135n.7
Wennerås, Christine, 193–94, 202, 221–22
Witt, Charlotte, 180, 185–88, 196n.11
Wittgenstein, Ludwig, 158–59
Wold, Agnes, 193–94, 202, 221–22
Wollstonecraft, Mary, 75–76

Ylikoski, Petri, 86–87, 93–94
Young, Iris Marion, 102n.13